FACILITATOR'S AND TRAINER'S TOOLKIT

Engage and Energize Participants for Success in Meetings, Classes, and Workshops

first edition

Artie Mahal

Published by:
Technics Publications, LLC
2 Lindsley Road
Basking Ridge, NJ 07920 USA

http://www.TechnicsPub.com

Cover design by Mark Brye
Charts by Mike Foresman
Illustrations by Michele Fulmer
Edited by Peggy Peterson

DISCLAIMER:
The material in this book is intended for informational and educational purposes only. No expressed or implied guarantee as to the effects of the use of the recommendations or practices can be given nor liability taken.

ISBN, print ed.   978-1-935504-89-4
ISBN, Kindle ed.   978-1-935504-90-0
ISBN, ePub ed.   978-1-935504-91-7

First Printing 2014

Library of Congress Control Number: 2014947977

Praise For
Facilitator's and Trainer's Toolkit

Good facilitation is often the difference between a meeting that delivers outputs and actions, and one that delivers breakthrough solutions and results. Artie Mahal, who is a master facilitator and trainer, has delivered an easy to read book that describes the science and art of effective facilitation. He offers insights, techniques, tools, and knowledge that anyone can use to improve their facilitation and training skills.

Paul Marabella
Vice President and Chief Information Office
K. Hovnanian Companies, LLC
USA

I must congratulate Mr. Arjit "Artie" Mahal for coming out with such a significant contribution for Facilitators and Trainers. The book justifies the saying "Practice is the hardest part of learning, and training is the essence of transformation." The chapters are logically sequenced in order to bring all the concepts to the mind of the reader in an appropriate manner. The context of Facilitation and Training is taken by Artie in right spirit by referring it to trainers engaged in cooperation and collaboration in work teams, developing strategies and solutions, executing programs/projects and process and learning and development of their skills and competencies. Most importantly, this toolkit is useful to all practitioners, educators, young trainers, students, and managers, irrespective of their industry or nature of organization. I find that the frameworks mentioned in the book are original; the techniques are practical, understandable and effective.

Dr. Sandhir Sharma
Dean, Chitkara Business School
Chitkara University
India

In this book Artie has brought together a great collection of tools, techniques and advice that provide a sound basis for anyone looking to become a more engaging and effective facilitator. In his first book he explains 'how work gets done.' In this book he helps explains 'how to get work done'! People are complex and groups of people even more so. Artie provides proven ways to engage a group and to get the maximum from them through the use of tools and techniques but also through the softer side of building rapport and trust.

Phil Short
IT Director, Speaker, Business Process Practitioner
Canada

Facilitator's and Trainer's Toolkit *is a book that we've been waiting for. Artie Mahal used his wealth of experience in process management to present logical and easy to use knowledge for facilitators and trainers. The book contains valuable tools, templates, checklists, methodologies, and frameworks. He created a great framework structure for any facilitated session to deal with various business issues such as strategies, processes, projects, and team cooperation and collaboration.*

Bassam A. AlKharashi
Director of Business Innovation Services, ES Consulting
Saudi Arabia

If facilitation is the process of making something easier, this book should be called "The Facilitator's Facilitation." Artie Mahal has taken a difficult and often misunderstood skill and made it easy to learn for the professional and novice alike. As a skilled facilitator for the past twenty-five years, this book has helped me "sharpen the saw" with new tools and concepts to help tackle any business challenge. For the novice facilitator, this book is an excellent guide as Mr. Mahal provides in-depth background and context for each facilitation concept before diving in with tools, tips, and techniques to master that concept. An easy yet must read for anyone who needs to facilitate meetings, gain collaboration and alignment amongst individuals or groups with differing points of view, or for any educator or trainer.

Jeffrey Diton
Business Process Center of Excellence Director
USA

For any of you that are responsible for facilitating training sessions or leading group meetings or workshops then this is a must read because it is your Bible! Artie Mahal has kindly given the blueprint on how to "wow" your audience every time they attend a session. In essence, the book lays out practical processes facilitators can follow to ensure learning is happening, collaboration is taking place and learners are engaged! After reading this book, you will never facilitate a workshop, training session or meeting the same again.

Faisal Usta
Senior Account Executive in Learning and Development
USA

This book is full of useful and tested ideas and full of wisdom. Some books are made of ideas: fresh, old, useful or not so useful. Some books are made of wisdom: hints and pieces of advice coming from real experience. As an "Alchemist" would, Artie, in this book has provided the best mixture of both: tested ideas and useful wisdom. Sooner or later you will have to facilitate. You have two options to get or improve facilitation competence: a) the long and painful trial and error way, or b) the short and smart way, namely, using other experiences to prevent the errors, learn the shortcuts, and avoid the pitfalls. This is a book for novice and even experienced facilitators. Read it. Use it. Learn from it. Take the short and smart way!

Alexandre Magno Vazquez Mello
BPM Experts, Partner and CEO
Brazil

People working together provide the foundation of human achievement. As we continue to move toward work that is more intellectual than physical, unlocking, compiling and harmonizing divergent views toward some common understanding is best accomplished through competent facilitation. This is not easy. In this groundbreaking book, Arjit Mahal moves far beyond a description of tools and techniques by providing a framework for the development of a career and, if desired, a successful business in the growing area of facilitation. This book is a must read for anyone considering entering the field.

Dr. Edward Peters
Chief Executive Officer, OpenConnect Systems Incorporated
USA

To Millie Mahal

My wife and best friend, for motivating my professional journey.

Contents at a Glance

Table of Contents

Acknowledgements

In your career you meet people who educate and inspire you in a way that instills not only new ways of thinking but also the confidence to take on the road to success. In addition to my gratitude to Mars, Incorporated for giving me numerous opportunities to learn and grow, I am deeply indebted to Gary Rush and Eric Jensen—two *Gurus of Facilitation*. I take this opportunity to thank them for their contribution to my professional destiny.

Just as the saying goes, "It takes a village to raise a child," it takes "many to write a book." The author is instrumental in conceiving a vision and writing a book, but there are many people who contribute to this effort in different ways. They deserve my thanks.

Three chapters in this book are contributed by my colleagues who are Gurus in their own right: Angela Gallogly for Virtual Facilitation, Catherine Mercer Bing for Cross-Cultural Facilitation, and Kevin Woodson and Michael Stark for assistance in Visual Facilitation.

I'm grateful for the contributions of Carlos Valdes-Dapena for High Performance Collaboration Framework, Anne Pauker Kreitzberg for Strategy Definition, and Carol Weiss Riches for Voice Care Techniques.

My thanks also go to Mike Foresman, a colleague and friend, for creating the slides on various frameworks.

As you go through the book, you will notice numerous hand drawn illustrations. I am very thankful to Michele Fulmer, a young artist and teacher who has made the concepts and their messages in the book come alive in ink and paper.

My editor, Peggy Peterson, has been instrumental in not only correcting my grammar and sentence structures, but also suggesting ideas to make the flow of this professional "story" better. I am grateful to her for her contribution.

My special thanks to many other colleagues and friends who contributed their ideas by allowing me to bounce off my concepts and for providing valuable opinions: Vincent Arecchi, Ernest Baker, Mary Barnett, Debra Batista, Gene Fucetola, Dr. Sandy Goldstein, Brian Kupersmit, Jagjot Singh Nagra, and Nancy Settle-Murphy.

Last, but not least, my gratitude goes to all of my students and workshop participants who over the years offered me the opportunity to serve them; their engagement and feedback taught me to be a better facilitator.

My publisher and friend Steve Hoberman and his staff have been once again a pleasure to work with and deserve my heartfelt thanks.

Foreword
By Gary Rush

Facilitation has been a passion of mine for over 30 years. I believe that facilitation skills are essential skills in everything we do—they are truly people skills and leadership skills. In the seventies and eighties we thought that Facilitators provided added value so organizations needed to develop a cadre of facilitators housed in a facilitation department. This cadre would facilitate workshops throughout the organization. What we found was that facilitation grew to be a required skill set for many *other* jobs. Few companies have job descriptions for "Facilitators." What they do have are many other jobs—project managers, business analysts, trainers, and leaders—that require facilitation skills. The original idea of creating cadres of facilitators is now viewed as giving all employees the skills to effectively facilitate, no matter what their roles are within an organization. Who knew that facilitation skills would turn out to be *the* skill set of the twenty-first century?

If you have not developed facilitation skills in your work, you need to do that now. Technology grows at a rapid rate but having People Skills ties it to your job and life—i.e., Facilitator Skills. More than half of all projects fail due to poor people skills of the project manager. Since every job requires working with people, you need to learn facilitation skills.

Artie Mahal has taken this very large topic and condensed it into a comprehensive overview of facilitation, its use, and its importance in any position or job. His book is easily read due to his use of graphics and clear language. He covers when and how facilitation helps as a group facilitator, learning facilitator, and as a facilitative leader. Artie provides practical advice for anyone who wants to delve further into the field and develop his or her abilities. He provides tools and templates that are clear and easy to use in developing your workshop and your career. His anecdotes are helpful in grasping concepts and seeing how facilitation has worked.

Chapters 6 (Tools) and 12 (Tools Library), describe a plethora of tools and their uses in easy to follow directions. Chapter 11 (Self-Development) provides sound advice regarding developing your career. Chapter 9 (Cross Cultural Facilitation) provides an effective understanding of the effect of cultures on workshops and work, and provides effective insights into how to understand culture and how to avoid common blunders.

If you are new to facilitation, wanting to understand how facilitation fits into your work life, or looking for guidance on how to grow your facilitation practice, this book will help you. If you want to enhance your career, this book will help you—I have never met anyone with effective facilitator skills who didn't do better in his or her career than someone without facilitator skills, regardless of the career. Enjoy the reading.

Gary Rush, IAF CPF
Chicago, IL, USA

Introduction

Organizations are made up of people, processes and technology. Collectively these capabilities produce products and services for customers and consumers—fulfilling Missions and achieving Visions shaped by the Principals and Values of organizations. This basic concept applies to all organizations whether they are for-profit, not-for-profit, or any Governmental agency, regardless of the nature of the industry.

Typically all organizations are constantly improving their ways of working, developing strategic and tactical solutions, innovating for viability and competitiveness, and solving problems to meet shifting challenges and competing priorities. Organizations also address their *Human Capital* needs. "Human capital' refers to the skills, education, health, and training of an organization's employees because these skills and capabilities make organizations successful. To enhance human capital, organizations provide learning opportunities to their employees through transfer of knowledge and training in relevant skills and competencies required for their work assignments. To successfully achieve work outcomes, people—employees and other stakeholders—need to have productive meetings, dialogue, and debate on differing points of view. They must challenge assumptions and priorities to establish an effective direction for action. Employees also need to learn optimal ways of cooperation and collaboration across functional and business unit boundaries to ensure their organizations have the best possible capability to shape strategies and then execute them through programs and processes.

The larger the organization, the more complex are the decision making processes—particularly in today's hyper-competitive and global work environment. It is imperative that effective strategies, solutions, programs, processes, learning needs and teams are aligned to the strategic intent of organizations before valuable resources are committed to action. This alignment is achieved through a process of *Facilitation*.

The art and craft of enabling individuals and groups to discuss issues and opportunities around a shared objective and develop agreed strategies for a common direction is generally referred to as *Facilitation*. In addition to meetings, Facilitation also includes enabling people to learn through transfer of knowledge and training in specific skills by a subject matter expert. The person or persons skilled in facilitation are called *Facilitators*. The method for creating agendas, conducting research, and facilitating sessions to deliver planned outputs and outcomes is referred to as the *Facilitation Process*.

The Facilitation Process uses a variety of frameworks, methods, techniques, and tools. Skilled facilitators use a combination of these tools along with several other methods that include managing group dynamics, managing the time and process, and leading the sessions to successful conclusions. Some of these tools are general in nature and may be used around any topic such as Icebreakers used for meetings. There are also techniques and tools specific to professional practices such as Stakeholder Analysis used for improving products and services in an organization. Facilitators possess a set of specific training tools for their subject matter to ensure the knowledge transfer is effective.

In some large organizations, facilitators are provided by Human Resource functions, Learning and Development Departments, and other functional areas around specialized Centers of Excellence. In some organizations, however, all line and senior managers are expected to have facilitation skills. *Facilitating is a Role*, and typically not a job title. Organizations that define and nurture facilitation as one of the core competencies for their managers have both improved and sustainable outcomes in their initiatives and solutions, and developed employees' leadership attributes. To run and win a race, the horse needs a skilled jockey. Facilitators are the organizational "jockeys" that lead the "race horses"—the work groups—to optimize their success.

Individuals who, whether by accident or design, learn about the facilitation discipline and develop a taste and passion for this unique competency by learning and application, broaden their capabilities beyond their normal functional roles. Good facilitators become more visible and are in demand. This opens up many opportunities for professional and personal advancement in addition to self-fulfillment because of the satisfaction of leading groups to their desired outcomes. Organizations employ facilitators either as internal consultants or from the outside as free agents or consultants. Their skills are similar and complementary. In today's dynamically changing market and business environment, a skilled facilitator enjoys great flexibility, whether working within organizations or working outside organizations as true free agents.

In the art of facilitation, 50 percent of success is preparation, preparation, preparation and the other 50 percent is "theatrics" (keeping work groups engaged, energized and focused on the topic at hand while "entertaining" them with relevant stories, metaphors, exercises, and good humor). Good facilitators are in the "entertainment business." The more they practice the more they enjoy this very rewarding discipline, which opens up many windows of opportunities outside of their routine roles that they would have not imagined. The role of a facilitator is truly transferable, regardless of the industry and the nature of the organization. While most organizations do not define facilitation as a core competency for their employees, they use this practice extensively but informally at varying levels of the organization.

The role of facilitation in workplaces has existed since humans began collaborating on their tribal and village resources to provide for their families and protect their interests for survival. As villages formed chiefdoms, then states, and then countries, the role of "facilitation" continued to mature in politics and commerce and the wellbeing of people. Embassies play such a role on behalf of their countries in foreign lands and the United Nations organization plays that role among its member nations. Thus, the role of facilitation can have numerous forms and dimensions. In this book, the focus is on workplace facilitation, which includes all three types of facilitator roles performed by knowledge workers, managers, and executives: *Group Facilitator, Learning Facilitator*, and *Facilitative Leader. Knowledge worker* refers to an employee whose job involves use of information and knowledge rather than manually producing goods and services. While there are some unique aspects of the use of the techniques and tools in the above mentioned three role types, the overarching principles, practices and tools used by these roles are very similar. The scope of this book covers all three types in an amalgamated way—as a unified, complete Facilitator Role—rather than segmenting each one separately.

Gary Rush, one of the gurus in facilitation, provides a historic perspective: In the context of organizational workplace, the role of Facilitator is referred to as "Session Leader," "Group Leader," "Process Leader," and so on. As late as the 1990s, facilitation was not even considered a formal competency by organizations. In the 1980s, with the increased demand for information technology training, the need for facilitation began to take shape in the form of "facilitated workshops." This concept started to take hold in various other aspects of the organization such as strategic planning, problem solving and innovation. Some organizations created the role of facilitator as part of human resource functions. Since 2000, the role of the facilitator has become main stream due the realization that good facilitation provides exceptional value for businesses to expedite their projects to gain competitive advantage and productivity that significantly contributes to their bottom lines.

It is hoped that through awareness of the value of facilitation, organizations will incorporate the role of a facilitator as one of the core competencies required of knowledge workers, including individual contributors and managers at all levels. Furthermore, it is my hope that universities and learning institutions will offer facilitation courses to students as a practical skill to better prepare them for their development and success in the workplace.

This book is based on my personal experience of learning about facilitation and then embarking on a passionate journey to become a dynamic and accomplished facilitator, both inside an organization and later as a consultant/free agent. I have outlined practical and proven techniques and ready-to-use templates and checklists for immediate use. The facilitation know-how in the book is described in an easy to understand format and is guaranteed to enhance the capability of any manager or professional in any industry and at any level of the organization. This book provides the building blocks for effective facilitation practice to enable individuals to be successful in delivering superior results and advancing in their careers while adding unique value to organizational initiatives and decision making.

Enjoy your facilitation journey!

Best wishes,
"Artie" Arjit Singh Mahal

My Personal Facilitation Journey

Until I began working for Mars, Incorporated in the eighties as a computer programmer analyst, I had never even heard of the term *Facilitator,* let alone knew what it meant. Facilitator as a skill or competency was not mentioned in my job description and nor was it included in the corporate core competencies—at that time.

My manager and I were in charge of gathering requirements for a new data dictionary for the organization, which required having cross-functional meetings with various departmental analysts. My boss suggested that since we were to be neutral in our opinions regarding the requirements gathering, it would be best to get an external facilitator to conduct a workshop for us. What was a facilitator? What did a facilitator do? How did one locate a facilitator?

Having experienced a successful workshop facilitated by an external consultant, I was intrigued by that role and decided to explore learning this skill for myself.

I learned that Gary Rush in Chicago had a six-day highly rated "boot camp" on facilitation training and I signed up for it. On the first day of the class on a Sunday morning, Gary Rush greeted his eight students and stated, "I promise you that by Tuesday you will not know what day of the week it is." And he was right. After an eight hour interactive class room session, he gave homework assignments that consumed three to four hours each evening.

When I flew back to New Jersey, certificate of graduation in hand from this intensive and comprehensive workshop, I couldn't stop thinking about the possibilities I envisioned for myself if I became a facilitator and applied all the things I had learned and even went beyond the limits of my current role at that time. The workshop had opened a window where not only the fresh air of amazement started to flow in my mind, but also the possibilities of views I could imagine. This was a turning point in my facilitation skills journey, which led me to develop expertise in Business Process Management and later motivated me in my role of the formation of the Mars University managerial training programs in North America.

In that role there were many courses to be designed or refreshed for roll out. I learned of a course design concept based on Brain Based Learning or Brain Compatible Learning that helps maximize the effectiveness of course material design and its delivery. I signed up for Eric Jensen's five-day course at the Eric Jenson Learning Institute in San Diego. The concepts of effective learning transfer and facilitation that I learned there elevated my thinking and skills to an even higher level of competence.

After a twenty-year successful career at Mars, I took an early retirement and founded my own consulting firm and partnered with others to facilitate and train in my specialty areas. In over ten years as a free agent, I have been committed to teaching facilitation and knowledge transfer to a variety of managers and executives around the world, including delivery of corporate workshops through Boston University Corporate Education Group and Duke University Business School.

Book Overview

The term "Toolkit" in the title of the book describes the purpose of this book: to provide frameworks, methods, techniques and tools for all who conduct meetings, lead group sessions and workshops, and transfer knowledge through education and training.

The various aspects of a facilitator's role may be classified as *Group Facilitator, Learning Facilitator*, and *Facilitative Leader*. This book covers the scope of all three as one whole rather than segmenting them separately. The reason for this is that facilitators play these roles in unison in most of their facilitation work—with some exceptions. For example, a Group Facilitator transfers knowledge on a specific topic while leading the session—all three aspects in one engagement—while a Learning Facilitator may not use facilitation tools that are necessary to develop solutions to a process or problem. The book chapters are created to transfer knowledge on all three aspects—without pointing out which one is specific to which type.

This book is meant for a broad audience that includes executives, managers, workers, subject matter experts, educators, trainers, and free agents—regardless of the industry or type of organizations and their professional practices. Even college students preparing to enter the workforce will benefit from this book by being aware of the underlying concepts and principles of effective engagement and participation as employees and leaders in organizations.

The broad definition of "Facilitation and Training" is in the context of adults engaged in cooperation and collaboration in work teams, developing strategies and solutions, executing programs/projects and processes, and learning and development of their skills and competencies.

This book has been written using simple, succinct content, with numerous visuals designed for greater understanding of the concepts and for immediate application by the readers. The examples are primarily for group sessions of up to 20 to 25 people, but the concepts equally apply to larger groups as well. This is a practical toolkit for success and excellence in all work engagements. There is something in it for everyone and it is meant to be a reference for ongoing use, both by beginners and experienced facilitators.

The chapters are logically written to build upon the concepts first and then introduce the tools step-by-step. In addition to industry-proven frameworks shared in the book, there are three unique frameworks introduced here for the first time and developed through three decades of the author's experience: *Mahal Facilitation Framework, Career Steps Framework,* and *Facilitation Leadership Framework.* Another new framework *Virtual Facilitation Framework* and the chapter on this approach have been developed for this book by Angela Gallogly.

Considering the changing need for state-of-the-art facilitation methods, Catherine Mercer Bing has written the chapter on Cross-Cultural Facilitation along with a framework on the latest thinking on this concept.

Kevin Woodson and Michael Stark of Visual Ink Creative have provided insights and methodology on Visual Facilitation.

While "tools of the trade" are spread throughout the book in support of the unique frameworks, there are 35 methods, techniques and tools provided in the Tools Library Chapter that every facilitator will have a use for at one time or another, and many of these can be easily mastered with some practice.

If you are an individual who believes in developing your facilitation skills and competencies for excellence and want to enjoy the journey of a professional facilitator in leading sessions, then this book is for you. You are not just purchasing this book; you are making an investment in your self-development.

Chapter 1, **Facilitation Framework**, introduces a unique framework called the *Mahal Facilitation Framework.* This framework classifies all facilitation types in organizations into four generic categories: Strategies and Solutions, Programs and Processes, Learning and Development, and Cooperation and Collaboration. It will be a guide for all executives, managers, and workers, including professional subject matter experts, facilitators and trainers, and so on, to understand the scope and possibilities of facilitation necessary to build their skills and competencies for success and career advancement. The chapter begins by describing the value of facilitation and a generic structure of an organization which provides the context for the use of the facilitation framework.

Chapter 2, **Value Proposition**, establishes the value proposition of facilitation skills and competency through a unique concept: *Career Steps Framework*. Typically the competencies in the industry fall into two categories: Functional/Technical and Behavioral/Effectiveness. Very little attention is paid to *Facilitation* being the underlying competency that enables these two competency types. I have created this framework to propose a new competency type: *Enabling Competency*. When you examine your own professional growth or of those you see being successful in their careers, you will observe that facilitation skills play a critical role in enabling success. Facilitation includes demonstrating leadership in leading groups to develop strategies, delivering training, promoting team collaboration, and more. Don't wait for Human Resources to include facilitation in their core competency models. Understand yourself the value proposition defined in this chapter. If it inspires you, then embark on this journey to develop your own professional self.

Chapter 3, **Facilitation Process**, covers these phases: *Contract, Prepare, During Session, Conclude,* and *Evaluate*. Each of these phases is defined in detail along with relevant templates and examples. Whether it is leading a meeting, training session, or group workshop, there is an underlying process that lays out from beginning to end, the execution of how that work is done. Intuitively we may continue to go through the informal steps, but understanding the formal process makes us more competent and professional in our work. You will learn how to engage in an assignment effectively, how to calculate the value of your time, how to create two types of agendas, how to conduct the workshop as a leader, and how to conclude successfully. With the understanding of this process you will become more professional and conduct effective workshops in all engagements.

Chapter 4, **Facilitation Leadership**, embraces the theme of bringing who you are to what you do. This theme is presented in a unique *Facilitation Leadership Framework* which constitutes Leadership, Values and Ethics as the core of the framework supported by two major enablers—Self-Awareness &

Style, and Skills & Competencies—that are critical to the success of facilitators in how they behave and perform as professionals. Among the many roles (trainer, educator, speaker, and coach etc.) a facilitator plays, leadership is of paramount importance. Napoleon Hills' eleven factors of leadership are outlined in the context of facilitation and are complemented by the statement of values and ethics and competencies established by the International Association of Facilitators. Understanding and internalizing the attributes identified both for the personal and professional realm of facilitation provides a roadmap to becoming a competent and successful facilitator.

Chapter 5, **Engagers and Energizers**, explores how adults learn. Adults learn and engage in learning events differently than children do. *Pedagogy* is referred to as the art and science of teaching children and *Andragogy* is referred to as the art and science of educating and transferring learning to adults. An understanding of the underlying principles helps facilitators/trainers design more effective workshop agendas and content. This chapter also introduces Dr. Howard Gardner's Multiple Intelligences, which, when used in workshops, optimizes the engagement and energizes the participating adults. The *Engagers* are physical activity, mental activity, or concepts, which enhance the involvement of participants in the purpose of their activity. The *Energizers* are physical activity, mental activity, or a conceptual exercise that holds the attention of the participants during a session. These are integrated in meetings, workshops, and group sessions to enhance the experience and alertness of the participants. The *Engagers* enhance the involvement and *Energizers* hold the attention of people when intentionally incorporated in the agendas. The main segments in the chapter are the integration points in agenda activities, including icebreakers and context setting. Principles and phrases referred to as "Artie-Facts" are the author's own experiences in optimizing facilitation. The chapter concludes with the Facilitator's Mantra—a wise and practical behavior to be adopted for success in facilitation practice.

Chapter 6, **Tools**, sets the foundation of the "Tools" (described in Chapter 12) by first describing the most commonly used and proven tool: Brainstorming. A structure around how brainstorming may be sequenced is shown as: Brainstorming, Affinity Diagram, and Analysis and Actions. A brief introduction of basic tools that support brainstorming such as sticky notes, clustering of themes, and sticky dots for prioritization are exemplified with diagrams. A Tools Catalogue, is the highlight of this chapter. It lists 35 tools in that can be used in a variety of facilitation assignments/activities. Some of these may have multiple uses in workshops. The catalogue has a purpose statement, tool title and a unique identifier, followed by a brief description of the tool and its usage. The detailed instructions for each of the tools are in Chapter: 12: Tools Library, which is placed at the end to serve as a future reference library. This is a foundation toolkit for any facilitator, whether experienced or still on the developmental journey.

Chapter 7, **Workshop Environment**, focuses on the facility, the seating arrangement, the food, and the ambiance to increase success of a meeting, group workshop, or a training session. It is the responsibility of the facilitator to identify the requirements for the workshop environment to the client during the preparation phase of the facilitation process. It is also wise for the facilitator to check out the facility ahead of time if possible and to set up the room ahead of the workshop start time. The aspects of a workshop environment are a facilitation-friendly room, seating set up, equipment, supplies, and safety and security. This chapter outlines the success factors necessary to the workshop environment by starting with facilitation-friendly principles followed by guidance on room set up, various seating patterns, equipment, food, supplies, and effective workshop guidelines. A checklist of room set up requirements and a supplies list is provided.

Chapter 8, **Virtual Facilitation**, provides practical techniques using a Virtual Facilitation Framework with four key areas that are critical for producing optimal outcomes. These are *Engagement, Relationship, Communication* and *Technology*. With the globalization of many organizations and an increasing prevalence of remote and virtual teaming, virtual facilitation has become more of a norm than an exception. Many facilitators confess to initial skepticism when an opportunity to facilitate virtually appears. How can the engagement, energy and collaboration essential to an effective facilitated event be replicated in the sterile confines of an online meeting? Fortunately, experience and technology are demonstrating that not only is virtual facilitation a suitable alternative to traditional face-to-face facilitation, it can be a more advantageous option in some cases. Virtual facilitation overcomes the boundaries of geography, physical space, and budgetary constraints. It allows different facets of an organization the opportunity to come together in a virtual forum to achieve session goals efficiently and economically. Virtual facilitation can be successfully applied to all elements of the Mahal Facilitation Framework to promote engagement.

Chapter 9, **Cross-Cultural Facilitation**, focuses on the considerations of design and delivery of materials specifically around the cultural aspects to support cross-cultural dialogue and communication. With the globalization of organizations, employees around the world are interacting more often with each other, both virtually and in face-to-face work sessions. It is imperative that multiculturalism in the workplace be understood and managed well. These cross cultural considerations either directly or indirectly include geography, language, history, ethnicity, ways of working, handling business dealings, and more. All four aspects of the Mahal Facilitation Framework are impacted by cross-cultural considerations. A unique Cross-Cultural Framework, Cultural Metacognition (knowing about knowing), is introduced in this chapter that is the basis for all cultural assumptions. It is worth noting that these concepts and principles also apply to facilitation of workshops.

Chapter 10, **Visual Facilitation**, explains the process of gathering information in a group setting to create a compelling picture that communicates the business objective of the group. Incorporating visuals elicits participation, ownership, and creativity from all group members. The use of graphics is collaborative and ensures an outcome that participants are more likely to support. The use of visual aids includes computer-generated graphics such as animation, story boarding, and others, but in this chapter, *Visual Facilitation* is described as an effective craft of capturing the stories and ideas from the participants through hand-drawn images, drawings, icons, symbols, and more. Five approaches are outlined for the use of visuals for facilitation. Some approaches can be used by anyone in the organization, and the others are to be conducted by a trained artist familiar with organizational workings. These are: *Personal Graphics Kit, Group Graphics Exercises, Reusable Graphic Templates,* and *Graphic Recording and Visual Facilitation.* The supporting techniques are described giving examples of their usage and benefits.

Chapter 11, **Self-Development**, builds on the 70/20/10 learning framework from Chapter 1, and provides guidelines as to how to experience and develop your facilitation competency and how to track your progress. It also introduces the Self-Development Mantra, a strategy for positioning yourself for success: How to *write, speak, learn, think, present,* and *network.* This chapter concludes with the author's own journey to becoming an accomplished facilitator. As stated in the Introduction of this book, while more and more organizations are formally recognizing facilitation to be a skill in their core competency models, a majority have still to grasp the concept that facilitation is a critical enabling competency. Therefore, many of you are on your own to take charge of your professional destiny in building facilitation competency. By doing this you will develop and grow in your organization while preparing for a day when you become a free agent/consultant. No matter what your professional track might be, facilitation skills and competencies will expand your horizon to new possibilities you may have not even thought of.

Chapter 12, **Tools Library**, builds upon Chapter 6: Tools, where the foundational concepts are described along with a catalogue of tools that can be used in a variety of workshop opportunities. Each of the tools outlines a step-by-step approach along with templates and examples where appropriate. This library is intended to be an ongoing reference chapter for any facilitator, whether experienced or on the developmental journey. In this chapter there is something (and more) for everyone.

Resources includes books, suppliers of materials needed by the facilitators; and useful websites and user forums, that are relevant to facilitation and training and are those that the author has either used over time or is familiar with. **Notes** references sources of material used in this book. The sources used or referenced are in sequence to the chapters of the book. The book concludes with a comprehensive **Index**.

Chapter 1
Facilitation Framework

A Framework facilitates the understanding of complexity through context and its constructs.
~ Arjit Mahal, Author, Educator and Facilitator

UNDERSTANDING THE VALUE OF FACILITATION

To facilitate is to "to make easier." So it follows that facilitation is the process of "making something easier." Teachers facilitate knowledge; physicians facilitate healing; politicians facilitate legislation; the United Nations facilitates programs for countries (in the broader context of the definition). The scope of this book is facilitation in organizations, including for profit or not-for-profit organizations, educational institutions, and governmental entities, regardless of the profession or industry.

The audience for this book, therefore, is every knowledge worker, professional, manager, and executive engaged in four broad areas of any organization: improving performance, optimizing execution of operations, enhancing human capital, and people collaboration. To understand the context of these concepts, it is imperative that the reader is familiar with the basic structure of an organization. The outline below describes a generic and common structure of an organization.

WHAT IS AN ORGANIZATION?
In the broadest context, organizations are people, processes, technologies, and infrastructure assembled to accomplish a mission through an agreed vision and its supporting strategies. Most organizations have a similar structure regardless of their purposes, product offerings, and services. See the conceptual view of a generic organization structure depicted in Figure 1.1.

Figure 1.1 – Organizational Structure

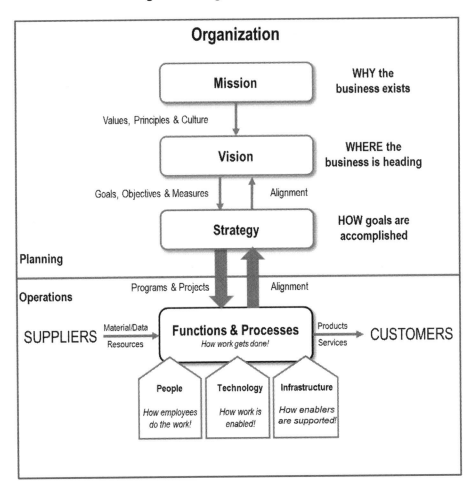

Organizations generally consist of two broad areas: Planning and Operations. Planning constitutes the Mission, Vision, Strategies, Programs, and Projects. The mission defines the purpose for why the organization exists. Based on their mission, organizations define the values and principles by which all employees are expected to conduct themselves in all aspects of organizational work, including their brands, goods and services, and all stakeholder interactions. The manifestation of these values and principles is known as the *Culture* of the organization.

Organizations and their organizational units (including business units, divisions, departments, and so on) create a vision for their future state of being. This vision includes goals and objectives to be achieved along with measures by which the accomplishment of the vision is tracked and adjusted for changing conditions.

To realize the vision, strategies are created. These strategies define the ways and means by which the goals and objectives of the vision will be achieved. The strategy is always aligned with the vision and may also be adjusted from time to time due to changing business environments.

To make the strategy actionable, programs and projects are created and then headed by program managers and project managers, respectively. These constitute a professional practice that identifies ways of achieving the desired strategic results and allocates needed resources such as money, people, technology, and equipment. Programs are first created and then within each program, projects are defined for unique actions and their deliverables. Programs are always aligned with strategies and are adjusted as changing needs require. Programs directly impact and influence the operations of the organization.

Within operations are the functional areas and processes directly involved in fulfilling the mission of the organization, namely, producing goods and services. Functions such as manufacturing, sales, finance, human resources, and others, are a legacy of the Industrial Age whereby employees are organized in the area of their skills and the cost of their labor. Work performed in all organizations is done through processes (or business processes).

A process is defined as "how work gets done" and end-to-end processes deliver goods and service to all stakeholders including internal and external customers. Examples of business processes are: Order-to-Cash Process, Procure-to-Pay Process, the Process to Acquire Capable Talent, and the Process to Provide Services, to name just a few.

For organizations that struggle with the established concept of function-centric to process-centric operations, a hybrid approach can be applied. Operations may be viewed as a giant process where the inputs come from suppliers and are transformed through functional skills and process manipulation into outputs for customers. The inputs may be materials, resources and data that are transformed into goods and services and information. (Data becomes information.)

Functions and processes are enabled by three types of resources: people—how employees perform their work, technology—how work is enabled, and infrastructure—how employees and technology are supported. Management of organizations is delegated to professionals ranging from general leadership to line managers to professionals in specific disciplines required to deliver goods and services. I have just summarized an organization with a generic structure that is also conceptually similar to all types of enterprises.

HOW TO USE THIS KNOWLEDGE

All employees and particularly those in the roles of internal or external consultants, facilitators and trainers, must have the basic knowledge of the organizational structure in which they are working or doing business with in order to make well informed decisions for the success of their roles, their organizations, and for their own development and career advancement. Knowledge is power; leverage it!

MAHAL FACILITATION FRAMEWORK

The art and craft of enabling individuals and groups to discuss issues and opportunities around a shared objective and develop agreed strategies for a common direction is generally referred to as *Facilitation*. Facilitation also allows people to learn through transfer of knowledge—learning and training in specific skills by subject matter experts. The person or persons skilled in facilitation are called *Facilitators*. The approach for creating agendas, conducting research, and facilitating sessions to deliver planned outputs is referred to as the *Facilitation Process*.

As we have seen earlier, every organization has two major aspects: *Planning* and *Operations*. Driven by the mission and vision, planning shapes the strategies to achieve agreed upon goals and objectives, and the resulting programs and processes are executed to run the operations. Both planning and operations must be optimized to ensure that organizations deliver performance, optimize the execution of programs and processes, increase the competency of employees to enhance human capital, and enable the work force to be more effective through cooperation and collaborative intentions.

At the center of this organizational view lies the art and craft of facilitation. Facilitation is necessary to assure that there is learning transfer among the members of the group being trained. When used effectively, facilitation is a critical activity and competency that enables the success of an organization.

Opportunities to understand and manage the deployment of facilitation competency in organizations can be divided into four groups. Each of these groups contributes to the success of the organizational objectives as shown in Figure 1.2.

Figure 1.2 – Mahal Facilitation Framework

Facilitation Groupings	Objective
1. Strategies and Solutions	Improve Performance
2. Programs and Processes	Optimize Execution
3. Learning and Development	Enhance Human Capital
4. Cooperation and Collaboration	Enhance Effectiveness

These four facilitation groupings are interrelated and codependent on one another. While individually they contribute to the organization in their unique way, collectively they enhance organizational performance. We will examine each of these four groups to understand the scope of the facilitation opportunities and who might facilitate these groupings.

For thousands of problems of various types in various professions, there are an equal number of methods, techniques and tools that can be used. (See the definition of Frameworks, Methods, Techniques and Tools in this chapter in Figure 1.3.) To define every possible method, technique or tool would be a volume by itself that is outside the scope of this book. This book teaches the underlying process of facilitation and use of some of the commonly used methods, techniques and tools.

While some of the methods are unique to specific vocations and professional practices and require subject matter experts for facilitation, others can be learned and applied by a competent facilitator with a relatively shorter learning curve in most cases. In many instances the terms framework, method, technique, and tool are used interchangeably and are also referred to as simply "tools" for the sake of convenience. Facilitators, however, must be aware of the proper structure of these "tools."

DEFINITIONS: FRAMEWORK, METHOD, TECHNIQUE AND TOOL

"Tools" have a hierarchy, as shown in Figure 1.3. Conceptually you may think of this as a "parent-child" relationship where one concept contains one or more of the subordinate parts.

Figure 1.3 – Framework Structure

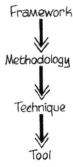

Framework: In the context of a generic organization, a framework is a strategic frame-of-reference that provides a structure of a specific concept, entity or subject matter, including organized ideas, assumptions, theories, practices, and an approach to viewing reality. A framework constitutes one or more relevant methodologies. For example, in an organization, a Change Management Framework may include methodologies such as program management, organization design, technology development, and human change approach.

Methodology: A methodology is an overall plan for a profession or vocation that shapes a strategic intent and provides solutions for a particular area of consideration. A methodology may use one or more techniques and/or tools. Examples:

- A Business Process Improvement Methodology is used for the improvement of organizational performance.

- In dentistry, Maxillofacial Surgery Methodology relates to maxilla and the face.

- A Systems Development Life Cycle Methodology is used for developing information technology applications.

Technique: A technique is an approach or physical movement used to accomplish a desired objective. A technique may be a part of an overall methodology and may use one or more tools. For example: the use of breathing exercises to demonstrate stress management, team-building exercises for optimizing collaboration, or a technique for implanting an artificial tooth to replace a missing tooth.

Tool: A tool is an instrument, apparatus, or template used in a practice, vocation, or profession to achieve desired results. In some professional practices, these may be known as "templates." A tool may be used by one or more techniques. For example, an instrument used by a dentist to extract a tooth or cement an implant, a beaker used in a chemical laboratory, or a template used for project planning.

1st Facilitation Grouping: Strategies and Solutions

The concept of strategy originated from military strategy, which is a collective name for planning the conduct of warfare. Derived from the Greek *strategos*, strategy was seen as the "art of the general." Military strategy and tactics are essential to conducting warfare. Broadly stated, military strategy is the planning, coordination, and direction of military operations to meet overall political and military objectives. Tactics implement strategy by the use of short-term decisions on the movement of troops and employment of weapons on the field of battle. The great military theorist Carl von Clausewitz put it another way: "Tactics is the art of using troops in battle; strategy is the art of using battles to win the war."

Organizations use strategies to fulfill their missions and value propositions. The mission statement clarifies the purpose of the organization, the vision statement describe the organizations future state aspirations. Goals lay out the targets to be achieved. Strategies articulate the overall approach. Tactics outline the ways and solutions to achieve the strategies. Action plans are the road maps of implementation.

All organizations, regardless of the industry, are engaged in acquiring, developing, creating, delivering, and servicing their value propositions. These value propositions can be goods and services, legislation, and wellbeing in all aspects of life. To accomplish this, organizations and their employees continually identify opportunities, conduct feasibility studies, perform tests, solve problems, and roll out improved solutions.

Strategies are created to provide an overall context and deliver the desired results. Strategies are schemes or action plans for achieving the outcomes by deploying necessary resources. In an organizational context, strategies provide direction for programs and processes. The employees working on these strategies and solutions may need facilitators to arrive at collective and comprehensive solutions that can be strategic, tactical, operational, ad hoc, or even temporary in some cases.

The pyramid in Figure 1.4 shows a general concept of how organizational objects are related in a hierarchy in order to produce the value proposition. The Mission is at the top of the pyramid which drives all other aspects of the governance and operations of the organization.

Figure 1.4 – Hierarchy of Organizational Objects

In an organizational context, strategic thinking is the process of constructing and communicating a cohesive, actionable vision of the future based on an integrated, holistic understanding of the external and internal environment, currently and into the foreseeable future. The goal is to honestly assess the organization's options, readiness, core competencies, and value proposition in light of dynamic external pressures to position the organization for sustainability and growth while keeping true to its mission and values. (Source: Anne Pauker Kreitzberg, Co-Founder and Principal, Cognetics Interactive and the Center for Agile Thinking.)

Examples include:

- A manufacturer of coffee machines is solving the problem of water leakage in the machine when consumers dispense a single-serve cup of coffee. Technical experts from several countries meet to discuss root causes and determine solutions. A facilitator is hired to optimize the process of trouble shooting and recommending the solution.

- A hospital system has a high rate of patients catching infections in their out-patient surgery area. The hospital management conducts a facilitated session with physicians, nurses, and other medical staff to brainstorm and determine potential causes and their solutions.

- A county college has decreased enrollment of students from the surrounding community. High school students feel intimated by the uncoordinated enrollment process since the facility's administrative staff is located on two separate sites. The college cabinet conducts focus group sessions with the faculty and administration staff to determine the root cause of the problem and find solutions. A facilitator is engaged to conduct the focus groups and synthesize the findings for management to take corrective action.

WHO FACILITATES STRATEGIES AND SOLUTIONS?

Depending on the complexity of the problems to be solved or strategies to be conceived, any one of the following may facilitate—assuming they have knowledge, skills and ability for effective facilitation using relevant methods, techniques and tools.

Internal to the organization:

- Executives, senior managers, line managers or other knowledge workers related to the subject matter

- Subject matter experts (SMEs) and other professionals from practices such as organization development, performance management, change management, program management, process management, and Business and Technology Analysts

- Trained facilitators from other areas such as human resource, organization development, and relevant centers of excellence.

External to the organization:

- Professional consultants and facilitators in a specific profession

- General professional consultants and facilitators.

2ND FACILITATION GROUPING: PROGRAMS AND PROCESSES

PROGRAMS

Strategies and solutions provide a *direction* for operations teams to execute strategies and implement solutions. This direction may be in the form of initiatives that provide the vision and goals to be achieved. The initiatives are organized as Programs and Projects to bring about change. The change includes developing and delivering new products and services through the optimal execution of business processes. The end objective of any change is to improve organizational performance.

Programs may be defined as a structured approach to planning and controlling the execution of strategies to ensure that the defined benefits are realized and the planned outcomes are achieved. A program is headed by a program manager. Each program constitutes one or more projects. See Figure 1.5.

Projects may be defined as a set of unique activities initiated to deliver a specific output or a deliverable of value to one or more stakeholders. A project is headed by a project manager.

Programs are more strategic in nature, while projects may be tactical with a defined beginning and an end.

Figure 1.5 – Programs and Projects

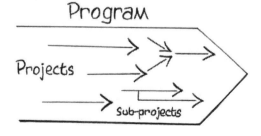

One definition of programs and projects is (Source: Ernest Baker, Start to Finish PM, Inc.):

- *Program*: A group of related projects, subprograms, and program activities managed in a coordinated way to obtain benefits not available by managing them individually.
- *Project*: A temporary endeavor undertaken to produce a unique product, service, or result.
- *Project Management*: The application of knowledge, skills, tools and techniques to meet the project's requirements (Source: PMBOK® Guide, 5th Edition Glossary).

In other words, projects produce outcomes (deliverables) or work products. Programs produce benefits and control that would not be available at the project level. Things like reallocating resources or funds from one project in the program to another, more critical or higher priority project in the same program. The program manager has that "big picture" view of all the projects in his/her program, whereas the project manager is focused down and inside their particular project.

The employees working on programs and projects need facilitators who can assist in various aspects of planning, execution and monitoring to ensure success. For example:

1. Program: A food manufacturing organization plans to launch a function-food snack which contains vitamins and other nutrients for health conscious consumers. This organization would have a strategy for launching function-food products. One of the first programs might be the development and launch of snacks for teenagers. This program would be headed by a program manager.

2. Projects: In our example, the program of function-food snacks may contain projects:
   a. Conduct ideation, develop the snack, and test snack's feasibility
   b. Design and implement the production line and technology to make the snack
   c. Test the snack in the east coast market and assess results.

The strategy would have identified some ROI (Return on Investment) which must be realized through the program and its projects. The program and project managers create plans, deploy and manage resources, mitigate risk, and ensure that the desired deliverables are produced within the budget and timeframe promised.

A concept known as *Triple Constraint* is commonly used by project managers to ensure all critical aspects of a project are executed for success. The scope, quality, time, and resources must be balanced among each other for effective delivery of the desired result. Resources include people, money and equipment. If the scope increases then more time or resources or both are needed. If the time is shrunk the scope/quality has to be decreased or resources have to be expanded. And if resources are limited then the scope and time must be adjusted accordingly.

Figure 1.6 – Triple Constraint

WHO FACILITATES PROGRAMS AND PROJECTS?

Typically program managers and project managers are expected to act as facilitators for various aspects of the life cycle of programs/projects with the basic management of the Triple Constraint (maintaining the balance among the scope, time and resources). Facilitation needs can include: program development/project charter, program/project kickoff, stakeholder and communication management, risk assessment and mitigation, status reporting, and decision making.

Internal to the organization:

- Program and project managers
- Subject matter experts (SMEs) from the professional practices being utilized
- Trained facilitators from other areas such as human resources, organization development, and relevant centers of excellence.

External to the organization:

- Professional consultants and facilitators in program/project management
- General professional consultants and facilitators.

PROCESSES

Programs and projects bring about changes in an organization's products and services and how they work—the processes. A process or a business process is defined as "how work gets done"—a series of steps undertaken to produce a specific output or outcome to meet stakeholder needs.

While programs and projects have a defined beginning and end, processes are perpetual in nature. They are always there even if not properly defined and documented. Processes are managed collectively by process owners, process managers, and process performers. Process owners are typically senior managers who are accountable for ensuring that the processes perform as desired and are continually improved. Under the direction of the process owners, the process managers are responsible for the day-to-day execution of the processes, and the process performers are employees who are assigned to work in the relevant process areas.

In the context of the *Mahal Facilitation Framework*, processes include technology (including Information Technology), mechanisms, and infrastructure. The reason for this is simple: Processes are enabled by technology and infrastructure and therefore may be considered an integral part of their existence. One working definition of a business process is:

An organization's business processes clearly describe the work performed by all resources involved in creating outcomes of value for its customers and other stakeholders. (Source: *Business Process Manifesto,* by Roger Burlton. www.bptrends.com).

Processes may be classified in several ways. One view may include business processes and operational processes. Business processes are how an organization works at the planning level and operational processes are at the work level.

Another more prevalent view of managing processes is through what is called a "Process Architecture" or, simply, a Process Blueprint that defines how work gets done in an organization at the macro or enterprise level (see Figure 1.7).

Figure 1.7 – Business Process Architecture (Blueprint)

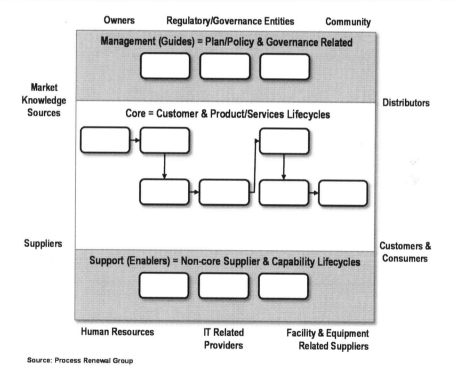

Source: Process Renewal Group

In this case, processes are classified in the following three areas:

1. *Management Processes*, which are most often executed by senior management. Example: Planning and monitoring the business.

2. *Core Processes*, which are the operational processes directly responsible for creating and delivering products and services to stakeholders. Example: Converting Raw Material into finished goods.

3. *Support Processes*, which enable the execution of the Core processes. Example: Providing human resources and information technology services.

WHO FACILITATES PROCESSES?

Processes or business processes are impacted by business and organizational changes. Typically process owners and process managers act as program/project managers for specific process areas. They collaborate with other managers of professional practices impacted by process change. When a process changes, it may influences changes to organization, technology and infrastructure. Therefore, subject matter experts or managers of these professional practices are engaged by the process owners/managers to facilitate change.

Internal to the organization:

- Process owners, process managers, and process performers

- Subject matter experts (SMEs) from relevant professional practices being utilized

- Trained facilitators from process centers of excellence, who are familiar with process change methodology.

External to the organization:

- Professional consultants and facilitators in Business Process Management

- Professional consultants and facilitators in organizational change, technology implementation, and Infrastructure development.

3RD FACILITATION GROUPING: LEARNING AND DEVELOPMENT

When programs/projects are initiated to improve an organization's products, services, or a specific value proposition—as directed by the strategies and the processes—both business and operations would be involved either for leveraging them or changing them. The employees and managers assigned to these initiatives are likely to be educated and trained to bring about the changes and also to learn the new ways of working. This triggers the need to up-skill people in competencies that include functional/technical skills or effectiveness/behavioral skills in relevant industries and professional practices.

In addition to the project-driven need, employees are generally developed for their career paths on an ongoing basis to enhance the *Human Capital* of the organization. The objective of Learning and Development facilitation is to transfer knowledge and skills in a way that the employees become competent and are effective in their roles, which include cooperation and collaboration with others. Learning and development constitutes several frameworks, methods, techniques, and tools. Two proven and complementary frameworks that define how competency is achieved by an individual—are described in this chapter:

- *Competency Framework* (Inspired by Peter Honey's A way to enhance learning from experience). See Figure 1.8.
- *70/20/10 Learning Framework* (inspired by the Center of Creative Leadership).

Figure 1.8 – Competency Framework

Competency:

Knowledge + Skills + Attitude / Motivation = Behavior

"Who and what you are!"

Drives Experience

COMPETENCY FRAMEWORK

Knowledge   Learning happens when people can demonstrate that they know something they didn't know before. This includes facts as well as insights or realizations.

Skills   Skills have been learned when people demonstrate that they can do something they couldn't do before, or can do something better than they could previously.

Experience   With experience, people have the attitude of applying knowledge learned, skills gained, and motivating themselves to seek more opportunities. This is also known as experiential learning. An experience is anything that happens to you, good or bad, planned or unplanned, expected or unexpected, dramatic or mundane, including lessons from ups and downs of life.

70/20/10 LEARNING FRAMEWORK

Research at the Center of Creative Leadership has shown that four kinds of experience contribute to an individual's development: 70 percent comes from on-the-job experience; 20 percent from others (managers, professionals, coaches, peers, mentors, and feedback); 10 percent from formal training, reading, and seminars. Learning from bad bounces of life—is pervasive throughout the learning process.

An individual's one-to-one learning contributes to group learning, which in turn contributes to the organization's learning—a pyramid concept, if you will. When learning programs are planned and executed, organizations become what is known as "learning organizations." Thus, enhancing their Human Capital results in improving the performance of the organization overall. Alan Mumford, in his book *Effective Learning*, defines the learning organization as: Creating an environment where the behaviors and practices involved in continuous development are actively encouraged. See Figure 1.9.

Figure 1.9 – A Learning Organization

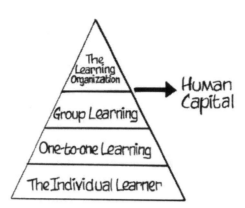

WHO FACILITATES LEARNING AND DEVELOPMENT?

Basically, two entities are responsible for this learning and development: the individuals who are responsible for developing their own competencies and the organization that provides opportunities and resources for the employees—both for the benefit of the organization and for the employees' own career aspirations. I believe that for an individual, "self-development is self-accountability."

There are numerous frameworks and methods used to facilitate learning and development. For example: coaching, mentoring, performance development processes, experiential learning, action learning, blended learning, brain-based or brain-compatible learning, flipped class room learning, eLearning, and more. A facilitator must become familiar with these and other emerging trends.

Internal to the organization:

- Executives, managers and mentors (their roles include providing coaching to employees)
- Subject matter experts (SMEs) from relevant professional practices
- Trained facilitators from learning and development centers of excellence
- Human resources groups and management. They establish the strategy and allocate resources, thereby facilitating an overall learning organization.

External to the organization:

- Professional consultants, facilitators and trainers in relevant subject matters
- Professional and trade organizations that provide seminars and industry expertise
- Mentors (from outside of an organization).

4TH FACILITATION GROUPING: COOPERATION AND COLLABORATION

In organizations, strategies and solutions are created to provide direction for their initiatives. The initiatives are organized into programs and projects that use relevant processes to bring about changes and improvements. Programs, projects and processes that are impacted need skilled staff in professional practices to implement these changes and improvements effectively. Employees need to be trained and developed to ensure they gain the necessary skills and competencies to be able to perform as effective teams. Good team cooperation and collaboration results in the productive engagement of workers in relevant strategies and solutions; thus enhancing their effectiveness to deliver desired organizational performance. In this manner, the cycle of the four facilitation groupings is connected and complete.

Webster's' Ninth New Collegiate Dictionary defines cooperation and collaboration as:

- *Cooperation*: The action of cooperating—common effort; association of persons for common benefit.

- *Collaborate*: To work jointly with others or together; to cooperate with or willingly assist in common entities, etc.

Cooperation and collaboration are almost two sides of the same coin. These complementary concepts have existed from the beginning of human history—when all peoples were hunter-gatherers. They must have realized that for survival and security they would be better off cooperating to obtain sustenance and collaborating with others to face common enemies.

As societies evolved, these hunter-gatherers became farmers and engaged in food production, thereby having the need to store, protect and share food. For these activities more sophisticated organization or cooperation and collaboration was needed, which transformed tribes into chiefdoms and later into states. Various elders within the societies then played the role of "facilitating" the management of people, resources and strategies.

Human transformation carried on into the Industrial Age and beyond where cooperation and collaboration began to be recognized as a formal discipline—giving rise to concepts such a formal work groups, project teams, and so on. In recent times, this discipline has become part of organization development and design, including human change professional practice. All through history, cooperation and collaboration has been shown to improve the performance of individuals, organizations, and communities.

In this grouping, our focus is on facilitating people to promote their cooperation and collaboration for enhancing organizational performance. Typically, all organizations continuously seek to improve their ways of working, developing strategic and tactical solutions, innovating for viability and competitiveness, and solving problems to meet shifting challenges and competing priorities.

To achieve this, employees must be shown optimal methods of cooperation and collaboration that result in creating collective team contributions to effectiveness and performance. When individuals are committed to this belief, they realize their intrinsic worth, which means both the team members and their organizations benefit—a win-win for all. In India there is proverb: *One and one is not two, it is 11.*

HIGH PERFORMANCE COLLABORATION FRAMEWORK (HPC)

The optimal cooperation and collaboration concept is defined as High Performance Collaboration in pioneering work done by Carlos Valdes-Dapena, a Consultant at Mars University, Mars, Incorporated. In his words: "Most people think of their teams as a collection of individuals who work for the same person, or work on related things or both. Most team members working in this kind of a mindset see their greatest value as doing their job well: *If I do my job well, and you do your job well, and they do their jobs well, it all adds up to a successful team.* Maybe. But, what it won't add up to is high performance collaboration or a high performing team!"

Figure 1.10 – High Performance Collaboration Framework (HPC)

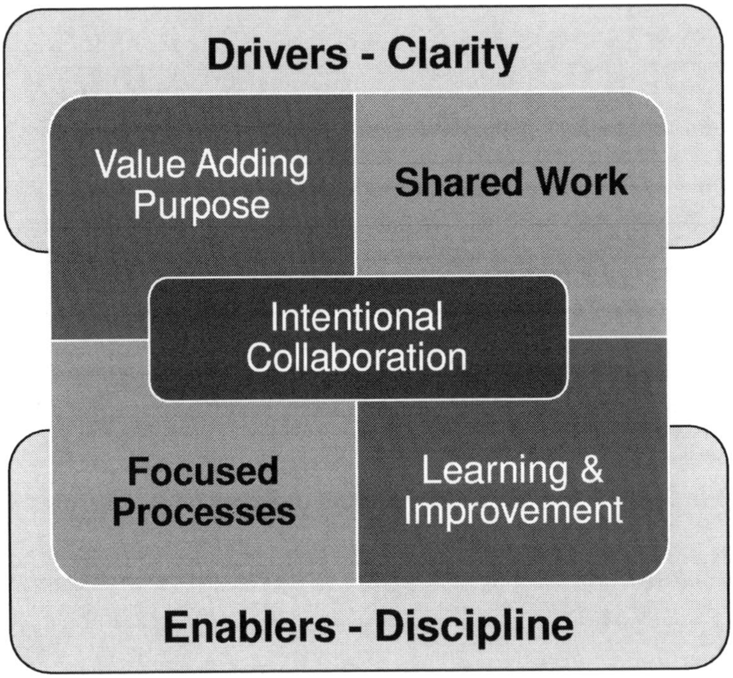

High performing teams are dedicated to figuring out how they can unlock new value for the business through the ways in which they work together. What's more, truly high performing teams create value at three levels: for the business, for the team, and for individual team members. What are the keys to high performance collaboration?

    a. High performing teams know why their teamwork, their collaboration, is essential to creating value and accelerating business results.

    b. High performing teams know what is most important. They establish crystal clear priorities within their strategy.

c. High performing team members identify and commit to areas of mutual accountability and support. They expect to be held just as accountable by their leader for effective collaboration as for their individual performance.

d. High performing teams establish and follow ways of working in key areas like decision making and conflict management.

e. Teams who practice high performance collaboration continuously adapt to new realities and foster continuous learning, development and improvement.

Drivers and Enablers of Intentional Collaboration

- The aim of HPC model is to increase the levels of intentional collaboration.
- To allow this to happen, we need to be clear on the Why and the What—the purpose and intent. These are the Drivers of increased collaboration.
- Once we are clear on the Why and the What we may be clear on the need to collaborate, but not on the How or the How To Do It Better. These are the Enablers of increased collaboration.

Examples of initiatives needing high performance collaboration:

- Merger and Acquisition. A food manufacturing organization wanted to expand their market in South East Asia. They acquired a business which had complementary products and an extensive network of sales and distribution in that region. Many functions had to be combined, thus creating redundancy of roles. Organization design and human change practices had to be deployed through hundreds of employees to unify them in collaborative teams.

- Process Integration. A county college had separate physical locations for admissions and enrollment services. There were inefficiencies in the enrollment process that were compounded by the "them and us" view among the employees. A focus group initiative identified issues around mistrust, non-cooperation and non-collaboration. External facilitators were engaged to promote team building.

- Systems Integration. An insurance company initiated a large information technology systems project that is going to be developed by employees spread over several geographic areas, inside and outside the country. With several managers in IT and business departments being responsible for various activities, their teams needed to work collaboratively to ensure success. It was agreed to have an external facilitator design an approach for virtual team building and then implement the plan.

WHO FACILITATES COOPERATION AND COLLABORATION?

It is the responsibility of all managers to coach and mentor their subordinates and to inspire and motivate them to be good team players. As leaders, managers are expected to assess their teams and ensure that they are cooperating and collaborating not only with internal stakeholders, but the external stakeholders as well.

To create high performing teams, in addition to the latest addition of Carlos Valdes-Dapena's HPC Framework, there are several methodologies that have been around for some years which include: High Performing Teams (HPT), the Drexler-Sibbet Team Performance Model, and Tuckman's Stages of Group Development. Managers must be aware of these various methods and use them as appropriate. As the managers are themselves part of the team, they typically engage facilitators who have expertise in team building methodologies. The following professionals may be called upon to facilitate team building exercises.

Internal to the organization:

- All managers
- Trained facilitators from functional areas such as human resources, organization development centers of excellence, and learning and development groups.

External to the organization:

- Professional consultants and facilitators in team building and organizational development and human change management practices.

Chapter 2
Value Proposition

Do not go where the path may lead, go instead where there is no path and leave a trail.
~ Ralph Waldo Emerson, American writer

Value Proposition is a term used by organizations to define the benefits delivered to their customers and stakeholders through their product and service offerings. In this chapter, the value proposition is your offering of your skills and competencies as an individual professional, to your employer, clients and other stakeholders. While the focus of the value proposition is in the context of an employee's career steps in an organization, the principles are equally applicable to independent contractors providing services to their clients. Your value proposition is your own "brand." You are responsible for creating, nurturing and enhancing it throughout your career.

The concept of career steps is applicable in all professions and industries and must be cultivated for self-development and career advancement. Educated and skilled people who are first hired at entry-level positions by organizations are given employment contracts that are based on their knowledge, skills and abilities to perform specific jobs that may include multiple roles or activities. At the entry-level stage, these employees are individual contributors and would be considered as the "managers of self" as shown in Figure 2.1. The value proposition of these individuals is measured on their competency in delivering desired performance to their organizations.

The competencies are defined in two main categories: Functional Competencies and Effectiveness Competencies. The functional competencies include technical skills, while the effectiveness competencies include behavioral skills. The definition below describes what constitutes a competency. Reference Figure 1.8 (Competency Framework), in Chapter 1.

Figure 2.1 – Career Steps Framework

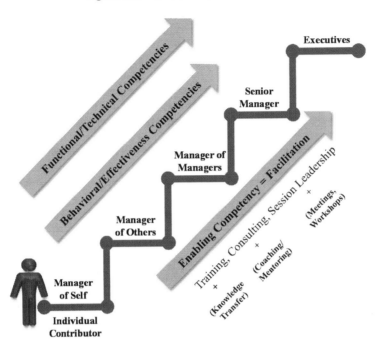

KNOWLEDGE + SKILLS + ATTITUDE / MOTIVATION = BEHAVIOR

For any topic or professional practice, one needs to acquire the knowledge and skills for "how to do it," including learning through trial and error, in order to possess the abilities, motivation, and attitude for "doing it" (putting these attributes in practice).

The functional and effectiveness competencies are two sides of the same coin. The individual contributor, or *manager of self*, must demonstrate performance through the interplay of these two sets of competencies in all aspects of the role in order to be considered successful in delivering the value proposition to the organization.

For example, when a college graduate is hired to be a sales representative, she is expected to perform well in her functional role of knowing how to sell a product—to take and execute orders (functional competency). At the same time, she is expected to be effective in dealing with customers and to have the interpersonal skills to manage business relationships (effectiveness competency). The value proposition of the *manager of self* then is the performance she delivers for her organization in achieving the expected outcomes of her role.

Over time, this entry-level individual develops more business acumen and moves up one step to become the *manager of others*. Now, this manager must develop managerial competencies, both functional and effectiveness, which include managing other employees and coaching and mentoring them for delivering performance. This higher position calls for greater leadership competencies, and the execution of the responsibility is her value proposition. As with other career steps, the *manager of others* is recognized, rewarded and compensated according to the established compensation and benefit plans for that level in the organization.

Upon demonstrating leadership capabilities and competencies, the next logical career advancement is to become a *manager of managers*, a higher career step in the organization. The value proposition at this level is to create a vision for the organizational entities they are responsible for, and to develop and execute strategies to advance the mission of the organization. In a general sense these managers may have responsibilities equivalent to a director or vice president.

At this level, the paths of functional and effectiveness competencies may diverge. Some individuals may follow a functional/technical career path and others may choose to follow the executive role in an organization, thus becoming *senior managers*, a yet higher career step. Now, executives may be heads of business units and managers of global responsibilities and may have titles such as general manager, president, chief executive officer, and others. Their value proposition is the overall success of the organization for the owners, employees, and shareholders. In the case of government, these roles would include the head of governmental agencies.

The career steps described above are generic, yet they represent a profound way of describing how one enhances one's own value proposition in every professional practice, a step at a time. However, there are many other factors such as opportunity, organizational culture and politics, and self-development that contribute to career advancement. Depending on the nature of the organizational line of business and the organizational culture of developing their employees, people may have a variety of experiences along the career steps of their chosen professions.

ENABLING COMPETENCY: FACILITATION

My purpose in this chapter is not to get into a deeper discussion of organizational employee development processes, but rather to introduce you to yet another type of competency that I call *Enabling Competency*. This is in addition to the functional/technical and effectiveness/behavioral competencies already discussed here.

The enabling competency is a set of knowledge, skills and abilities (KSAs) that directly *enable* employees to leverage their functional and effectiveness competencies more effectively. This enabling competency is *Facilitation*. Reference Figure 1.2 (Mahal Facilitation Framework), in Chapter 1. To be successful at each of the career steps of organizational advancement, one has to *facilitate* various aspects of functional and effectiveness competencies in their realm of responsibility.

Facilitation includes developing strategies and solutions, executing programs and processes, providing learning and development, and promoting cooperation and collaboration to deliver enhanced value proposition. Thus, facilitation is a catalyst for advancement along the organizational career steps.

For example an industrial engineer has functional/technical competency in engineering obtained through a degree from a university. She is also expected to possess the necessary interpersonal and communication skills (behavioral/effectiveness competencies) for her position. In order to develop strategies and solutions for a given area of responsibility, she will need to gather requirements from various stakeholders, and with the help of variety of employees, design, test and implement a solution. All this requires facilitation of various aspects as discussed in Chapter 1, thus, is a key enabler to all her other abilities.

While many large organizations define their "competency models" for employees to adapt to and strive for, they seldom include facilitation as one of the core competencies in those models. It is almost by accident that some employees discover the importance of facilitation along their career journey. I believe that college students preparing to enter the work force must be educated and trained in facilitation. And organizations must recognize and incorporate facilitation as a core competency for all workers—particularly line managers and managers at all levels. This critical capability enhances the value proposition of employees and makes them more effective in their respective functional competencies—a win-win for the employees and for the organizations.

FACILITATOR'S ROLES: WHAT'S WHAT

Employees at various levels of their organizations act as internal consultants and facilitators. This enabling competency is part of their role. Of course, external consultants and contractors are also facilitators in their chosen professional practices. Notwithstanding the facilitation competency that is discussed in Chapter 4 in the context of career steps, the following aspects constitute the enabling competency of facilitation:

- **Education.** The process of acquiring and imparting knowledge and skills through formal instruction especially in a skill, trade or a profession may be defined as education. The deliverer is known as an *Educator*.
- **Training.** The act of providing knowledge and skills on a unique topic using hands-on practice. In the case of adults, training is known as "learning transfer." The deliverer is known as a *Trainer*.
- **Consulting.** The act of providing professional or expert advice and related services in a recognized discipline. The deliverer is known as a *Consultant*. The consultant may be internal to the organization, or external as a free-agent.
- **Facilitation.** The process of making "something easier." In the context of organizations, it is the activity performed by a neutral individual who acts a catalyst for groups to solve problems and develop solutions. The deliverer is known as a *Facilitator*. The practice of facilitation includes consulting, education and training.

- **Session/Workshop Leader.** While delivering their services to any group, educators, trainers, consultants, and facilitators may be referred to as *Session* or *Workshop Leaders*. Part of the session leader's role is to inspire and motivate the group being facilitated.

STRATEGY FOR YOUR CAREER STEPS

In Chapter 4 there is a detailed description of facilitation skills and how to go about building this competency. To start with, however, you can assess where you are on the career steps of your chosen line of work and initiate your own developmental steps toward facilitation expertise:

1. Understand the career steps concepts outlined in this chapter along with the three types of competencies—with particular focus on facilitation as the enabler to other competencies.
2. Review your organization's competency model and determine how you can align and leverage your self-development in facilitation skills. If you are in a leadership position then influence your human capital management group, such as human resources, to include facilitation in the organization's core competency model.
3. Understand the facilitation framework in Chapter 1 and incorporate desired aspects of specialization in your own development plan. In organizations where there are no formal competency models, define your own set with the knowledge you now have of the career steps outlined in this chapter and the competency model to be defined in Chapter 4.

FACILITATION VALUE PROPOSITION FOR ORGANIZATIONS

The Facilitation Value Proposition is a two-sided coin: On one side of the coin are the individuals who learn and then use facilitation skills for success in their work and profession, and on the other side of the coin are the organizations who are the beneficiaries of the facilitation competency offered by the employees. Organizations make investments in any professional practice based, generally, on the ROI (Return on Investment). The ROI includes several aspects such as business growth, performance, market share, and more, providing tangible and intangible benefits. As the facilitation practice matures, organizations pay more attention to the benefits of facilitation. The International Association of Facilitators (IAF) has initiated the Facilitation Impact Awards (FIA) program to demonstrate the value of facilitation at the organization level.

The IAF Facilitation Impact Awards are the most prestigious international awards honoring excellence in facilitation and its positive, measurable impact on organizations around the world. The award recipients come from the business, non-profit and government sectors. Each recipient demonstrates evidence of achievement through significant tangible and intangible results by the descriptions of their processes. Additional information about the application process, submission guidelines, evaluation methodology, governance policy, and project charter can be found at www.iaf-fia.org (http://www.iaf-world.org/FacilitationImpactAwards.aspx).

FACILITATION IMPACT AWARDS (FIA) PURPOSE

The overall purpose of the International Association of Facilitators (IAF) Facilitation Impact Awards initiative is to provide a vehicle for:

- Promoting the awareness of the role of facilitation in achieving positive, impactful results
- Rewarding the use of facilitation within organizations and communities
- Recognizing excellence in facilitation practices
- Acknowledging outstanding contributions by IAF members
- Promoting IAF and its conferences as vehicles for advancing the profession of facilitation.

The FIA website outlines examples of results achieved by various types of organizations:

- Two hundred and thirty employee-facilitated events exploring workplace issues generating a savings of nearly $500,000 (Defense, Human Resources)

- Management commitment to develop a core of full time, trained facilitators; 117 issues addressed with 300 employees directly involved; heavy equipment utilization increased from 28 percent to 92 percent, resulting in increased productivity due to a drop in wait times (Hydro/Energy)

- Estimated to achieve 40 percent to 45 percent reduction in time and effort spent on initiating projects, netting a significant savings in 2013; shortened project lead time enabling businesses to start realizing benefits earlier (Insurance)

- Employee grievances down 50 percent; 13 internal staff promoted or advanced in their career paths; 79 new recognition awards given to staff for showing initiative (Property Group)

- "Uncontentious structural change" in a major institution; shift from top-down decision making and silos toward a collaborative culture (University)

- Reduced turnaround times from a highly variable five hours to a consistent three hours; several million pounds of additional product sales, reduced per unit costs of production (Agriculture/Farm)

- Nineteen innovative ideas generated and shared; computing design improvements resulting in greater than 25 percent increase in performance (Semiconductors)

- Accelerated the pace of growth on all fronts including revenue, number of customers and development of intellectual capital; built buy-in and commitment of team toward a common vision (Consultant Services)

- A workforce focused on outcomes for citizens and working together to make that happen; more than 20 different previously autonomous change initiatives aligned; a new definition of success for staff; more efficient and effective delivery of 500 different lines of business (City Management).

Facilitators in organizations and free agent facilitators in general are encouraged to measure and document the value of the facilitation service and participate in the International Association of Facilitators (IAF) Facilitation Impact Awards initiative outlined here. This will help promote the awareness and value of facilitation practices, thus resulting in a win-win for both individuals and organizations.

Chapter 3
Facilitation Process

If you can't describe what you are doing as a process,
you don't know what you're doing.
~ William Edwards Deming
(American statistician, professor, author, lecturer, and consultant)

Facilitation of all aspects as defined in the *Mahal Facilitation Framework* is a process. A process, as defined in my book, *How Work Gets Done,* is: "How work gets done. It is a series of activities or tasks that are performed together to produce desired results. Typically a process has inputs that are transformed into outputs and outcomes. In simple terms, a process is triggered by an event, governed by business rules using relevant knowledge, and executed through people using enabling technology and supporting infrastructure such as facilities."

Figure 3.1 shows the context of the facilitation process having three major process areas: Engagement, During Session, and Follow-up. The process of marketing and selling services to clients, which happens prior to the facilitation process, is not within the scope of this book as it is a separate professional practice.

Engagement includes the process of contracting with the client and preparing for the workshop. **During Session** is the process of managing the purpose of the workshop as contracted and ensuring the agreed outcome is achieved. **Follow-Up** concludes the process and the workshop outputs are documented and communicated to the relevant stakeholders. Follow-up also includes the evaluate process whereby feedback is solicited from the client on the overall facilitation process and its outcomes. The purpose of follow-up is to understand what went well and what can be improved in the future. Based on the feedback received, the facilitator makes necessary improvements to the process and its methods, techniques and tools as needed to ensure continuous improvement in his services. As it is said: "The biggest room in this world is room for improvement."

Figure 3.1 – Facilitation Process

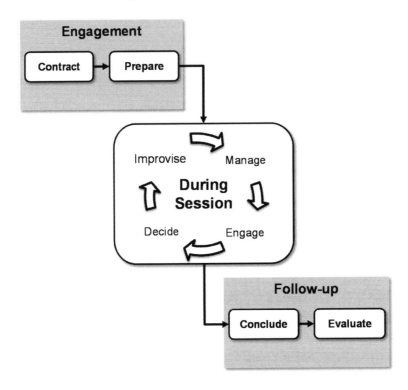

This chapter explains the purpose of each of the process steps and how to execute them, along with expected deliverables. Relevant "tools" and ready-to-use templates for immediate use are provided.

ENGAGEMENT

CONTRACT

The client identifies an opportunity for facilitation through a Statement of Work (SOW). Sometimes the SOW is merely a paragraph or two and in other cases it is more detailed, should the organization seek an external supplier. In some cases, the client may issue a Request for Proposal (RFP) for external suppliers to bid on the opportunity, such as in the case of Governmental Agencies.

The facilitator submits a bid and may be interviewed by the manager in charge, and also the buying office in the case of external suppliers, to demonstrate the capability for successful facilitation. The client requests an initial cost structure that includes an hourly or daily rate as well as other costs involved such as travel, meals and lodging. In the case of training, or transfer of knowledge in a specific subject, this could include the cost of training materials and the use of the organization's proprietary intellectual property.

The facilitator meets with the manager and sponsor of the workshop to understand the purpose and scope of the workshop and the expected outcomes and outputs. This discussion includes who the participants will be and the various roles that will be played during the entire process of facilitating the workshop.

A typical workshop is sponsored by a senior executive or organizational unit within an enterprise and overseen by a manager assigned for this purpose. Sometimes the sponsor and the manager roles are played by the same individual. When the roles are separate, the sponsor is defined as the person in charge of receiving the results of the workshop; has familiarity with the organization and sees that organizational resources are utilized properly; and ensures that the desired outcomes are achieved. My rule of thumb is: The sponsor is the one who writes the check (commits to pay the money) to the facilitator.

Once the purpose and scope of the workshop is understood, a more detailed discussion ensues that includes the frameworks, methodologies, techniques, and tools to be used for the workshop, and a general sense of the agenda including the time frames of various activities. Potential risk and success factors are discussed including political considerations due to the business drivers, stakeholder intents and other factors that the facilitator must be aware of.

At this stage, the facilitator creates a proposal document that includes client's SOW; describes the purpose of the workshop; lays out the logistics, timeframe, and cost throughout the facilitation process; and a high-level agenda of the proposed workshop. In most organizations, the initial discussion of engagement and rates is first discussed with the Purchasing Department, in conjunction with the manager.

When the proposal is submitted by the facilitator, the purchaser may ask for clarification and may negotiate rates and cost and other terms of the contract, for example payments terms of Net 30 Days, in US Dollars. Most organizations also ask the facilitator to agree to and sign a Non-Disclosure Agreement (NDA) that ensures that the proprietary information of the organization will be kept confidential and not be disclosed to another party.

Another requirement organizations may have is for the facilitator to get a certificate of liability insurance of some specified amount to protect the organization from unintended risk caused by the facilitator. When all these requirements are satisfied, the purchaser issues a Purchase Order (PO). This document becomes a binding contract between the organization and the contracting facilitator. Internal consultants and facilitators will probably not need a PO; they follow organizational policies and procedures in this regard.

Roles and responsibilities and communication guidelines are critical elements for a professional facilitation engagement. These are defined in the following two sections.

Facilitation Roles and Responsibilities

The roles outlined below are for a general group workshop; adjustments can be made for meetings and training sessions as applicable and appropriate.

Requester	The person who initiates the request for an engagement.
	• Provides background information on the purpose and expected outputs and outcomes
	• Identifies the sponsor, relevant stakeholders and participants for the workshop
	• Identifies organizational culture and related considerations such as political landscape
	• Initiates and assists in obtaining the purchase order and other needed approvals in a timely manner
	• Helps develop the agenda and ensures agendas and other communications are sent in a timely manner applying organizational policies and procedures
	• Receives and accepts the workshop outputs
	• Provides feedback on the facilitation process.

Sponsor	The person who is the conscious of the organization's interests and provides support, commitment and funding. • Provides perspective on the expected outputs and outcomes • Approves participants for the workshop • Approves the agenda design • Resolves issues before and after the workshop • Kicks off the workshop and motivates the participants toward the purpose and focus. Receives and accepts outcome of the workshop.
Manager	The person in charge of initiating the facilitator's engagement in coordination with the requestor and sponsor. (The Requestor and Manager can be the same individual). • Provides input in participants identification • Assists in agenda design • Ensures compliance with organizational culture, policies, and procedures • Coordinates venue setting, and logistics • Ensures administrative support for items such as facility, food, and equipment arrangements • Receives feedback from the requester, sponsor, and participants and conveys to the facilitator.
Participants	Employees or stakeholders who have a vested interest in the topic being facilitated and have stake in the outputs and outcomes of the workshop. • Provide input to the requestor for agenda design • Conduct relevant research to bring as input to the workshop • Are empowered to make decisions and take on assignments for action.
Expert	Subject matter experts (SMEs) who have a vested interest in the topic of facilitation and have a stake in the outcomes. • Conduct research and bring relevant input for discussion and consideration • Provide perspective on issues and their resolutions • Are empowered to make decisions and take on assignments for action.
Observer	People who may have direct or indirect interest in the topic of the workshop and may be impacted by the outcomes. • Play a passive role • Provide perspective when asked • Do not take direct part in decision making • May take assignments for follow-up actions.

Facilitator	The person who is well versed in the skill of facilitating meetings, workshops, and knowledge transfer, including the methodology of the specific practice of the topic at hand. • Engages with the requestor, manager and sponsor to understand the needs and provide perspective on approach for solutions • Learns about needs and seeks information on other organizational considerations • Proposes the agenda design and delivery of the services including labor, material, travel, and lodging • Assists in the agenda design and creates a Running Order Agenda (ROA) for facilitation • Prepares for the workshop, acquires the necessary supplies, and facilitates the workshop • Ensures the outputs/outcomes are achieved • Conducts After Action Review • Receives feedback and makes recommendations • Invoices/Settles account with the client.
Documenter	The person who is in charge of documenting the workshop proceeding in an agreed and professional format. • Is familiar with the agenda design and coordinates approach with facilitator • Learns about the topic at hand, approach and methodology being deployed • Comes prepared with necessary tools such as camera for taking pictures of the output • Takes action for post-workshop documentation delivery in the agreed timeframe • Delivers documented output to the requestor, manager and the facilitator. Note: In cases where the workshop is interactive and the outputs are being created on flip charts or wall charts, it is often more practical and cost effective for the facilitator to take pictures and create documentation after the workshop concludes.

Good Communication Practice Checklist

There are two aspects to good communication practice which every facilitator must be aware of:

a. General practices and norms of good business communication.

b. Organization-specific policies, procedures and practices to ensure compliance and protect assets such as trademarks and brands. For convenience, these are categorized in the checklist below.

☐ **Approach**
  - o What is the business objective? What should this communication accomplish?
  - o What is the communication goal? To inform, educate, get buy-in, or motivate to action?
  - o What is the key message or messages this communication should convey?
  - o What deadlines are involved in this communication?
  - o Is this part of any larger communication efforts that should be considered?

☐ **Audience**
  - o Who are the audience and the stakeholders for this communication?
  - o Will you need to communicate separately to any of the stakeholders?
  - o What is your audience's preferred method of communication?
  - o What action should this communication prompt the audience to take?

☐ **Application**
  - o Are there any legal or regulatory considerations to this communication?
  - o Is the length of this communication appropriate? Will it fit in an e-mail? Will it require attachments?
  - o Will all members of your audience have access to the vehicles you're using (e.g., e-mail, the internet)?
  - o Will you need face-to-face communications for meetings or training?
  - o If you're planning on net conferences or teleconferences (remote facilitation) do you need to consider employees in other time zones?
  - o Who is responsible for creating the communication?
  - o Who is responsible for disseminating communications to various stakeholders?
  - o What's your internal approval process?

Useful Templates for the Contract Process

- Work Engagement Intake for Information Gathering by the facilitator
- Calculating the Value of Your Billable Time
- Work Proposal for the Engagement.

Work Engagement Intake Example

Case example: NewAge Foods Organization wants to improve their Recruit and Hire Business Process. The potential facilitator meets with the client project requester/manager to understand the requirements.

Table 3.1: Work Engagement Intake Example

General Information	
Name of Client	NewAge Foods
Type of Organization: Work, Products/Services	Manufacturer of healthy snacks
Date	DD Month YYYY
Location of Client	Location address
Client Contact Info	Contact's name, telephone number and e-mail address
Client Website	NewAge.XXX
Type of Work Engagement	Conduct process analysis and improvement workshop for recruit and hire employees process
Name/Title of Sponsor	Name 1, VP of human resources
Name/Title of Manager	Name 2, HR manager – shared services
Name/Title of Coordinator	Name 3, HR support coordinator
Engagement Information	
Purpose	To understand the problems in the recruitment process, document the "As-Is" process, analyze the process for improvement opportunities and make recommendation for changes.
Why is it important and why now?	The external talent acquired in last couple of years is not at the required level of competence. The engagement level of employees is not adequate; and as a result the work teams are not operating at peak performance.
Expected outcomes and deliverables?	A common understanding of the current state of the process issues and challenges by the HR hiring team members; document existing process; analyze process for improvements; recommend changes.
What is the decision making process?	The HR project team will build consensus on understanding issues and making recommendation for solutions; the VP of human resources has the authority to approve/reject recommendations.

What would be considered success?	A clear understanding of the causes of the problems and identification of specific improvement needs for both short-term and long-term changes.
What is the scope and what is included?	Recruitment process for East Coast business unit.
What documentation is available?	Current SOPs (Standard Operating Procedures) for hiring (these have not been updated in several years).
Who are the key stakeholders and what are their roles?	Management team, VP of human resources, HR managers of East Coast, HR staff, hiring managers and third party recruiters.
Type of session (meeting, training, work session, workshop)?	Group workshop, face-to-face (there may be a couple of managers participating remotely through video conference).
Venue (Location, Date(s), Timeframe)?	TBD.
Roles	
Sponsor	Name 1. V P Human Resources.
Workshop Manager	Name 2. HR Manager – East Coast.
Workshop Coordinator	Name 3. HR Support Admin.
Number of participants and their roles? Do they know each other? Any particular styles / behaviors to be aware of?	12 participants. Primarily they are HR staff along with three hiring managers. One of the hiring managers is very vocal and takes over the conversation (needs to be managed). Most of the employees know each other.
Observers (if any)	One HR Manager from the West Coast wants to see the methodology for possible use in their HR function.
Facilitators	Facilitator 1.
Scribe/Documenter	All the work will be done on wall charts and sticky notes. Pictures will be taken and sent to the documenter off site.
Facility / Site	
Room setup (facilitation friendly?)	U-shaped room setup with sufficient room for sub-team exercises. Wall space for large charts. Natural lighting if possible.
Equipment needs (overhead projector, speakers, etc.)	Overhead projector. Video/Audio connection for remote participants.
Room access (time, security, clearance, etc.)	Room needs to be available 1.5 hours before start time.
Terms of Engagement	
Rates (daily/hourly, currency)	Lead facilitator $300/hour ($2,400/day). Documentation would be at $100/hour.
Cost (facilitation supplies and print material)	TBD—will be at cost.
Cost (travel, lodging, and meals)	TBD—will be at cost (travel will be in economy class).

Contract / Next Steps	
SOW (Statement of Work): Client provides this. Agree on a timeframe.	Received.
NDA (Non-Disclosure Agreement). Client provides this. Both parties agree and sign.	Signed by both parties and formalized.
Work Proposal: Facilitator provides this. Agree on a timeframe.	Provide date by which the proposal will be submitted to the client.
Purchase Order: Client provides this. Before work can begin.	Get an estimated timeframe for the issue of PO.
Specific Notes	
Inform and give advance notice to engage the associate who would document the output of the workshop.	

Work Proposal for an Engagement

A facilitator plays the role of a session leader, trainer and a consultant. Facilitators conduct and lead work sessions, trainers facilitate the transfer of knowledge and learning, and consultants provide and "facilitate" solutions in a particular area of expertise. The first question a client needs answered is the cost of hiring you for the facilitation service. Facilitators should expect and prepare for this discussion.

Facilitators must be aware of the value of their time, their minimum billable rate, and the going rate in the market for similar work utilizing similar skills and experience. You must be aware of the cost of overhead, facilitation supplies, travel, lodging and meals, and any other related expenses. Your rate structure depends on your level of experience, the value of your offering, and other factors such as who owns the Intellectual Property (IP) rights to the materials (for example, training materials). Also, the fee for calculating your billable rate varies by the type of work you are hired to do (workshop, training, or consulting on project-based work, fixed-cost work, performance-based work, or some other objective). **Section I** describes the *Workshop* per diem rate structure, followed by examples of *Training* rates in **Section II**.

Consulting

Consulting has a broad range of work options that varies from a low level of expertise to a higher level of expertise in subject matters of lower levels of complexity to higher levels of complexity. The practice of consulting is not in the scope of this book. There are numerous resources in the marketplace dedicated to the Consulting Practice. (See the Resources Chapter for one example: Consultant Journal blog: consultantjournal.com.) In many ways, facilitators also play the role of consultants, and once you understand how to calculate the value of your time and competency in Section I, you can use that as the basis for consulting work as well.

Section I: Workshop Billable Rate

This analysis is always essential for an external facilitator. Internal facilitators may have to be accountable for the internal cross-charging policies of their organizations.

First, understand and be aware of the "value of your brain" in general. In the information and knowledge based economy, workers are compensated for work by their "worth" and value proposition offering (reference Chapter 2). Worth is determined by skills, competencies, experience, abilities, qualifications, and other capabilities that include being productive, effective, and delivering desired results at the appropriate level of responsibly. While there is no absolute method for measuring this value, conceptually this is ascertained by understanding what an organization is willing to pay for your services and your value proposition.

Next, calculate the value of your time in general and your potential billable rate in particular as shown in Section (A). This gives you a baseline or the "lowest possible rate." Then conduct market research and learn what rate is billed by others doing similar work and what organizations are willing to pay as identified in Section (B). Also, consider other factors such geography, country, and type of organization. For example, private corporations are likely to pay more than not-for-profit organizations.

(A) Calculating Value of Your Time and Billable Rate
Assumptions used in the example scenarios in this section are:

- Cash compensation includes salary, bonus and incentives. (The bonus is estimated at 15 percent of only the salary.)

- Benefits are approximately 40 percent to 50 percent of the annual salary—before bonus. (Benefits include health coverage and pension/savings plans, etc.)
- On assignment travel, lodging and meals are over and above the rate and are billed as separate line items to the clients.
- Out of 365 days in a year, there are 261 possible working days and 104 weekend days, totaling 52 weeks.
- Non-billable time consumption is estimated for free agents, and not for facilitators that are internal to organizations.
- The calculations have been rounded to approximate figures.

Instruction: Determine what your cash compensation and benefits would be if you were working in an organization, as a facilitator or in a comparable position, then adjust and calculate the numbers accordingly. The example in Table 3.2 is based on the total compensation being $165,000 (US Dollars).

Calculate your own value of time and billable rate, using your specific assumptions and data in the template in Table 3.3.

Table 3.2 – Example of How to Calculate the Value of Your Time and Your Billable Rate

Calculation of Expected Billable Days Per Year		
Days in a Year		365
Weekend Days		(104)
Total Possible Workdays		261
Estimated Non-Billable Time		
Vacation	15	
Holidays	10	
Marketing 15% (4 to 5 days/month)	48	
Administration 10% (2 to 3 days/month)	25	
Downtime 10% (2 to 3 days/month)	25	
Total	123	(123)
Minimum Billable Days Note: 138 days is about 50% of 261 days. This indicates that one must have a target of earning all income in about half of the possible workdays. This mitigates the risk of higher downtime and non-billable activities.		138 days (1,104 hours)
Example: Total Compensation in US Dollars: *(Salary + Bonus) + Benefits ($100,000 + $15,000) +$50,000 = $165,000 Total Compensation		
Minimum Daily Rate: $165,000 ÷ 138 days = $1,200 rounded		
Minimum Hourly Rate: $165,000 ÷ 1104 hours = $150 rounded		
*Note: You may add incentives/equity in this calculation as appropriate		

(B) Market Research for Similar Work

Determine what rates are being charged for services that are similar to those you offer. Your research should include discussions with peers, calling industry trade organizations, and, of course, looking up relevant websites. Once you have this information you are ready to establish your billable rate. This rate needs to be in a range of minimum to maximum. After some experience, you will be able to further adjust your range of rates.

Table 3.3 – Template for Calculating the Value of Your Time and Your Billable Rate

Calculation of Expected Billable Days Per Year		
Days in a Year		365
Weekend Days		(104)
Total Possible Workdays		261
Estimated Non-Billable Time		
Vacation		
Holidays		
Marketing		
Administration		
Downtime		
Total		( )
Minimum Billable Days		days (hours)
Example: Total Compensation in US Dollars: *(Salary + Bonus) + Benefits ($_____ + $_____) +$_____ = $_____ Total Compensation		
Minimum Daily Rate: $_____ ÷ ___days = $_____ rounded		
Minimum Hourly Rate: $_____ ÷ _____hours = $____ rounded		
*Note: You may add incentives/equity in this calculation as appropriate		

Establish Your Billable Rate: Example using $165,000 total Compensation

There can be numerous rate scenarios for this example, use it as a scalable guide only. Your individual price points will vary based on your qualifications, experience, line of business, geographic area, and other factors. You may want to use your own numbers to get a better idea of billable rate possibilities.

Minimum Rate: For someone with $165,000 in annual compensation, the billable per diem rate would be $1,200. (Per diem is Latin for "per day" or "for each day." A "day" is considered to be a *professional day* of eight working hours, which includes reasonable time for lunch and two breaks.) It is logical to up this number to about $1,300 per day (an increase of $100 per day) to cover basic overhead costs incurred in the course of your doing business, as outlined in the next paragraph.

Cost of Overhead: The reason for adding $100 per diem for basic overhead costs is to cover unforeseen contingencies and numerous intangible expenses, including such costs as business licenses/permits, insurance, car usage, advertising, professional associations and seminars, utilities, internet and telephones, office supplies, paper, ink cartridges, computer equipment, bookkeeping, accounting services, and liability insurance, to name several. Overhead may also include the liability insurance required by many organizations to cover risk caused by the contractor.

Here is the rational: In our example of $165,000 in total compensation, the salary is $100,000. Let's assume the overhead costs to be 15 percent of the salary, or $15,000. Divide this amount by 138 days (minimum billable days in a year). This calculates to about $108, or $100 rounded down. This is only one approach of justifying basic overhead cost. Calculate your own cost of doing business to get an approximate number for assessing your total minimum billable rate.

Market Research Data: Your market research may show that the facilitators in your areas of expertise charge anywhere from $800 to $2,400 per day, depending on variables such as the level of expertise on a specific topic or a methodology, years of experience, or other factors. The average of this range is $1,600 for eight hours of professional work.

Estimated Billable Rate

Based on a minimum of 138 billable days in a year, your minimum rate is $1,300 per day ($160 per hour). The market average is $1,600 per day ($200 per hour). You can command possibly $2,400 ($300 per hour) and up—based on your capabilities and value proposition. These numbers give you the confidence to be flexible and prepare you for rate discussions.

Occasionally facilitators are engaged for work that does not require their highest level of capability, and facilitators lower their rates accordingly. Generally your quote should be above the higher market rate number, because the client may negotiate it down. You may consider starting at $2,800 ($350 per hour) and allow room for negotiation. This assumes a direct engagement relationship with you (the facilitator/contractor) and the client.

If the contract is through a third party, the third party's possible markup can range from 15 percent to 30 percent. If you start your quote at $2,800 ($350 per hour) and settle with the client for $2,400 ($300 per hour), always show on the work proposal that you have given a discount of about $400 per day—a discount of 15 percent. In other words, you just don't arbitrarily bring the value of your worth down—you give a discount on your regular billable rate. If you don't do this, in future possible assignments with the same organization, you may not be able to quote above $2,400 per day.

Documentation Rate

Post-workshop documentation needs to be professionally documented and given to the client on a timely basis. This type of work is based on a lower rate and you will need to determine the going rate.

I am a strong believer in hiring a professional documenter to do this work. A typical professional documenter is one who provides workshop documentation services, both in workshop settings and remotely, and has expertise in basic software tools such Microsoft Word, PowerPoint, Visio, and Excel, and knows how to manipulate data using these tools. The typical hourly rate can range from $50 to $75 per hour. As the facilitator, you may want add a markup of $25 to $35 per hour to cover your time spent in communicating with the documenter and reviewing the final documentation before giving it to the client.

The reason for this smart outsourcing of documentation is simple: the "value of your brain and time" is likely to be higher than that of the "documenter" and it is more cost effective for you to use your time for more strategic activities such as networking and marketing your services.

Supplies Cost

Your supplies are charged at cost in most cases. Make a checklist of supplies you'll use and have an estimate ready. Refer to the Supplies Checklist in Chapter 7.

Travel, Lodging and Meals Cost

Typically clients pay for your travel, lodging, and meals at cost and based on their specified policies. If you spend a full day of travel each way for one day of facilitation, it "costs" you two days of non-billable time. You may want to negotiate with the client to pay for one day of travel (one half day of each day traveled). Additionally, you can justify billing for a day of travel if you are doing work on the client's behalf while flying or at the airport for example.

Work Proposal Example

NewAge Foods Organization has requested an external facilitator to design and conduct a strategic planning workshop for their Customer Solutions Group. The facilitator, after understanding the requirements and establishing the approach and billable rate, creates a work proposal for the client's review and approval. The example in Table 3.4 is based on $2,400 per day ($300 per hour) rate.

Table 3.4 – Example: Work Proposal for a Workshop

Work Proposal for a Workshop	
Client Name	NewAge Foods
Work Proposed	Customer Solutions Workshop
Prepared By	Your Name
Date Prepared	DD, Month, YYYY
Proposal Request	This proposal for a Workshop is submitted at the request of NewAge Foods. It includes the scope, schedule, proposed agenda and expected cost for the effort.
Scope of Work	Conduct a workshop for Customer Solutions to define the value proposition, mission, vision and strategies for action.
Deliverables for Workshop	The deliverables include: Stakeholders Analysis, Value Proposition, Mission, Vision, Strategies and Programs for transformation; and Next Steps. Professionally documented material in PowerPoint will be provided within 72 hours of the workshop completion.
Date and Time of Workshop	November 1-2, YYYY. 8:00 AM – 5:00 PM
Logistics and Roles	Client: Facilitation-friendly room will be provided and organized by the client. This to include equipment and arrangement of food etc. The client will send all communications to the stakeholders. Facilitator: Will bring all supplies for facilitation activities.
Estimated Cost – Initial Draft	
Client engagement, agenda design and preparation*	4 days/32 Hours @ $300/hour = $9,600

Facilitate the Workshop	2 days/16 Hours @ $300/hour = $4,800
Documentation of the Workshop Output	Estimate: 12 Hours @ $100 per Hour = $1,200
Travel, Lodging and Meals	At cost (Estimate TBD)
Participant Material and Facilitation Supply	Estimate: $250.00
Total Estimated Cost (Not to exceed number)	TBD (Add all estimated numbers). *Note: Initially create the proposal as a DRAFT and review with the client; make agreed changes before finalizing the proposal.*

*Note: The rule of thumb for estimating the preparation time is 2:1, or two days of preparation time for each day of actual facilitation. This number varies in cases where the client's business is very familiar to you and the learning curve of the engagement is shorter or where the training has been delivered repeatedly and the material is already packaged. Use your judgment on a case-by-case basis and discuss this with the client *verbally* before formalizing the proposal.

Often, clients don't understand why so much time is needed for preparation. In the Prepare step of the Facilitation Process, agenda design, stakeholder interviews, supplies acquisition, logistics, and other supporting tasks can be very time consuming and easily underestimated even by facilitators. Clients need to understand your time consumption for these activities.

Section II: Training Billable Rate

Training facilitation rates can be classified in several ways depending on the business model of the training and its delivery. The three most common are:

a. ***Delivering training workshops when you have your own proprietary training material and Intellectual Property (IP).*** For the per diem rate, use the same calculation as in Section I: Workshop Rates. The only difference is that you need to charge for your proprietary material/IP because it is an asset that you have developed and maintained. Training organizations charge anywhere from $100 to $150 per student over and above the per diem already discussed. I typically charge $100 using this rational: I estimate the cost of printing the participant workbooks and the cost of the facilitation supplies such as markers, name tents, and other supplies to be less than $40 per student. This gives me $60 to cover the cost of my IP asset per student. Therefore for a one day class with 16 participants using a workshop rate of $2,400 per day plus $1,600 ($100 for IP per participant), I estimate $4,000 in revenue. Of course the expense of travel/lodging, supplies, and other expenses are an additional cost to the client. This scenario assumes the training material already exists. If the training material has to be developed or customized, you must estimate that effort based on course material development rates. Training design and development is not in the scope of this book.

b. **Delivering training workshops with someone else's proprietary material and IP:**

- Scenario 1 - Delivering someone else's training material to your own client, where you have sold the class: In this scenario, you might be delivering a training workshop with another organization's proprietary/IP material. The third party (the owner of the material) allows you to deliver the material under their terms for royalty payment, which can range from 15 percent to 30 percent of total class delivery charges per day. Using the first example in this Section II, where the total daily revenue is estimated to be $4,000, you would pay the material owner a royalty of $800 and keep $3,200 as your own revenue. This is an example based on 20 percent markup.

- Scenario 2 - Delivering someone else's training material to their client, where the third party has sold the class: In this case you are only delivering on a per diem basis. Therefore you would negotiate your rate from the minimum rate discussed in Section I.

c. *Delivering mass market training modules that are generally a one-day delivery program.* Mass market refers to training programs such as One-Day Project Management training that is scheduled throughout the country. This approach varies from organization to organization depending on the demand of their subject matter and the value of their topic to the mass market. In this business model, you are an expert delivering the workshop and all expenses, including selling, logistics and supplies are covered for you. In this case, the per diem rate will be lower than the two other options discussed above.

Contract Process Checklist

Inputs to the Contract Process

☐ Opportunity for facilitation assignment

☐ Non-Disclosure Agreement (NDA) signed by both parties

☐ Statement of Work (SOW) provided by the client

☐ Request for Proposal (RFP) submitted by the facilitator/contractor

☐ Initial understanding of cost structure, logistics, availability, and terms, sometimes referred to as the Terms of Reference (ToR)

☐ Work Proposal for the session/workshop (developed by the facilitator)

☐ Certificate of Liability Insurance (provided by the facilitator for the client-specified terms).

Outputs of the Contract Process

☐ A Purchase Order (PO) issued by the client

☐ An agreed schedule of the work from start to finish.

Helpful Hints

• Do not take an assignment you are not qualified for. If there are any constraints of schedule, or capability, or any other constraint, state them upfront. Be transparent. This will ensure your credibility and the integrity of your work with the client.

• While overcharging is counterproductive, so is undercharging. If you charge a rate that is way under the market rate for similar services, you may not get the contract because the client may perceive that you must not be good enough to command the market rate.

• Don't begin working on an assignment until an approved and signed Purchase Order is in hand. Yogi Berra, the former American Major League Baseball Catcher once observed: "It's not over till it's over."

PREPARE

Prepare

Information Gathering

The preparation process begins as soon as you have a contract in hand. Don't begin working on a facilitation project thinking that the contract is surely on the way. Nothing is sure until you have the signed PO in your hand with an agreed schedule to being work. Generally, most well governed organizations have a policy of not letting any contractor work without a PO.

First step in this process is gathering information regarding the specific project to be facilitated. Research the information provided by the client to gain insights and understand the scope of the project. In addition, gather information about the organization—its line of business, organizational culture, the key stakeholders perspectives, and personalities of the participants in the workshop. For training workshops, it is important to know the intent of the participants, their background and why they are attending the workshop.

Agenda Design

The next step is to draft a first-cut agenda design that includes the methodology, techniques, and tools to be used from your own knowledge and expertise and your library of resources as well as external sources relevant to the topic. This agenda should list the activities in the order of the methodology in mind along with initial thoughts on how long each activity would take. It should lay out the Why, What, How, When, Who, and Where of the workshop flow. In the case of training workshops, a lesson plan may already be developed with relevant activities and timeframes. The agenda design has four stages of development as shown in Figure 3.2.

There are two types of agendas: one for the participants and one for the session leader/facilitator. The facilitator's agenda is the Running Order Agenda (ROA). Develop the participant draft agenda first, followed by the ROA. After receiving approval from the workshop manager, finalize the participant agenda and hand it over to the manager for dissemination. The structure known as OARRs (Objectives, Agenda, Roles and Rules) is a standard practice for conducting meetings; this is included in the ROA for the workshops.

From the client intake—the overall understanding of the purpose, context and scope of the facilitation assignment—the facilitator begins the design of the workshop. This is a collaborative effort where the client (sponsor/manager) and the facilitator brainstorm ideas for the best possible approach for leading and engaging the group to achieve desired outputs and outcomes. This includes discussing workshop roles, the logistics of the venue (including the location, a facilitation-friendly room, timing, food arrangements, and other needed equipment and supplies), any pre-workshop assignment required of the participants, and the stakeholders' communication plan (the communication to the stakeholders must always be done by the workshop manager/sponsor).

Figure 3.2 – Agenda Design Framework

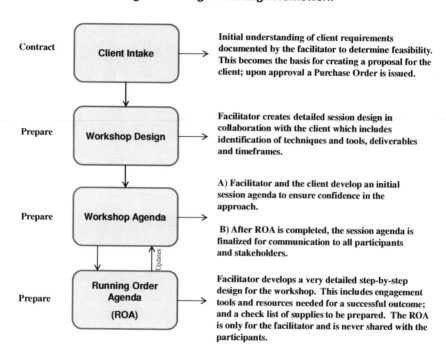

A draft agenda is created for the participants. This sets the confidence level of both the client and the facilitator in the planning of the workshop. Using the draft agenda as input, the facilitator designs a detailed Running Order Agenda (ROA), also known as an Annotated Agenda. The ROA is like a play script for the facilitator to lead the session with confidence, step-by-step. It details the timing, the room setup requirements, and the specific use of all tools and supplies necessary for success. The ROA is then reviewed with the client to gain final agreement on the overall approach. Based on the ROA, the facilitator updates the participants' agenda and hands it over to the client for validation, completion, and communication to the participants and other relevant stakeholders. The final ROA is sometimes shared with the client but never shared with the participants.

Running Order Agenda (ROA)

For designing a learning session or for facilitating a topic, this agenda is a step-by-step detail of every aspect of the session to be conducted, for any type of session to be facilitated. It is a script for the session leader of how the workshop will flow. It is a design for the overall workshop, but put together on an individual topic basis. Although it is time consuming to think and document every little detail of how the topics will flow, it is a critical tool for the facilitator to gain confidence in envisioning success.

The ROA should include principles and techniques of experiential learning and engagement which include (Reference Chapter 5):

- Adult Learning Theory
- Multiple Intelligences Framework
- Engagers and Energizers.

The ROA will incorporate the relevant frameworks, methodology, techniques, and tools based on the subject matter.

ROA Template

Table 3.5 is for developing the play script of every activity and task a facilitator plans to conduct, step-by-step. This is called the Agenda Design. It is developed in collaboration with the workshop sponsor and/or manager, but not shared with them when finalized. And it is never shared with the participants.

Notes:

- The left column is alphabetized only for reference and does not imply any priority
- For each day of a workshop, allow two days for preparation including agenda design, among the other activities identified in the Prepare step of the facilitation process.

Table 3.5 – ROA (Running Order Agenda) Template

#	Item	Description/Steps	Time	Clock Time	Resources
A	Topic Name	Topic name (and any methodology reference as appropriate)			
B	Objective	Precise objective and expected outcome and deliverables			

#	Item	Description/Steps	Time	Clock Time	Resources
C	Total Time	Estimated time based on the design of the ROA	Lapse time	Start and end time	
D	Venue	Date, day, location description			
E	Roles	Program sponsor, manager, coordinator, participants, observers, scribe, session leader(s), etc. Note: While describing the role of the facilitator to be neutral and non-judgmental, it is prudent to state that confidentiality will be maintained for everything that happens inside the work session (heard, seen and documented).			
F	Guidelines	Guidelines for the session participants to optimize the workshop (sometimes referred to as "Rules").			
G	Context	Context of the topic at hand and its organizational purpose (why). Story, motivational talk/video/external speaker to inspire the group. Introductions. Kick off by the sponsor to set the tone of the workshop. Plan transitions from one activity to the next.	15 minutes	8:30am to 8:45am	Sponsor Presentation Material e.g., PowerPoint Deck
H	Framing	Introduce the topic to be initiated using appropriate metaphors or examples so that the participants are clear about what is to happen next.	Lapse time	Start and end time	Material needed (e.g., a PowerPoint slide)
I	Activity	Steps to be covered for training or steps of facilitating an activity in a workshop: Steps: 1. Topic/Description… 2. Topic/Description… 3. Topic/Description…	Lapse time (for each topic) 1. 2. 3.	Start/end time (for each topic) 1. 2. 3.	Identify Resources needed for each of the topics
J	Debrief	Summarize the activity and check for participant engagement and level of comfort	Lapse time	Start and end time	

#	Item	Description/Steps	Time	Clock Time	Resources
K	Actions	Identify actions for any open items. Conduct After Action Review for session learning and continuous improvement.	Lapse time	Start and end time	After Action Review Template
L	Breaks	Include breakfast, breaks and lunch. (Breaks would be inserted at the appropriate time slots throughout the agenda activities.)	Lapse time	Start and end time	

	Supporting Enablers	
	(These are miscellaneous items essential for conducting a successful workshop)	

#	Item	Description/Steps
M	Logistics	Determine room setup requirements, food arrangements, travel arrangements, transportation of supplies, etc. Plan to take team pictures or of the charts for documentation.
N	Techniques and Templates	Identify and prepare methods and tools needed to deliver/facilitate the topic.
O	Presentation Slides/Charts	Identify and prepare slides, charts, etc.
P	Equipment	Identify equipment such as PC, audio visual, music playing needs.
Q	Engagers/ Energizers	Identify and prepare/gather appropriate items.
R	Supplies	Identify, gather and prepare all supplies such as markers, sticky notes (prepare a supplies checklist).
S	Participant notebook/handouts	Develop/print any handouts or notebooks for the participants.
T	Post Workshop Actions	Identify any anticipated actions such as who will document the proceeding or deliverables, etc.
U	Communications	Determine who will send communications to the participants and when. Remember good communication practices and organizational culture compliance.

Participants Agenda – Template

The final participant agenda is derived from the ROA design. This is developed in collaboration with the workshop sponsor/manager and typically distributed to the stakeholders by the sponsor or the manager.

Table 3.6 – Participant Agenda Template

Item	Description	Time	Clock Time
Topic Name	Topic name (and any methodology phase as appropriate)		
Objective	Precise objective and expected outcome and deliverables		
Total Time	Estimated time based on the design of the ROA	Lapse time	Start and end time
Venue	Day, date, location description		
Roles	Program sponsor, manager, coordinator, participants, observers, scribe, session leader(s)		
Guidelines	Guidelines for the session (You may choose not to have this on the agenda, but cover verbally)		
Context	Kick Off Introductions	15 minutes	8:30am
Activity	Steps: Description/Deliverable Description/Deliverable Description/Deliverable	15 min 20 min 15 min	Not to write clock time for each step
Breaks	*Include breaks and lunch (include where applicable)*	*Start time*	*End time*

Table 3.7 – ROA Example

SWOT Analysis Training for Human Resources Group (Strengths, Weaknesses, Opportunities and Threats)	
Date and Time	DD Month, YYYY 10:00 AM to 11:30 AM (1.5 hours)
Location	XYZ, NJ Conference Room: ABC
Objective	To provide training to Human Resource employees in the use of SWOT Analysis.
Roles	Workshop Sponsor: VP Human Resources, Manager ABC, Coordinator DEF, Participants, HR Staff, and Facilitator *Name 1*
Guidelines	Use of PCs at breaks only. Put mobile phones on mute. Respect time (return from breaks on time). Ask if the participants would like to add any additional guidelines. Note: I prefer to use the term "Guidelines" instead of "Rules" because the session is for adults and the term "Rule" implies a class room instruction.
Room Setup	Have a welcome chart, parking lot chart (I call it the "Ice Box" chart for keeping open items fresh), overhead projector, PC with presentation deck. Have workshop agenda hand-outs.
Preparation	Research history of SWOT. Prepare a PowerPoint deck on SWOT.

#	Item	Description/Steps	Time	Clock Time	Resources
1	Kick-off	Purpose of the workshop and expected outcomes by VP of HR (Engager).	7 Min	10:00 – 10:07	Presentation Slides
2	Introductions	(Engager/Energizer) Facilitator: Use the Thumball™ with values. Ask the team to stand in a circle and throw ball. All persons give their name, role and their view on the value where the thumb is placed. By Facilitator.	10 Min	10:10 – 10:20	Thumball
3	Review SWOT Definition	SWOT definition and purpose. By Facilitator. (Frame) Phrase: Do you know what the largest room in the world is? (Pause.) "Room for improvement." SWOT is a proven tool that helps identify strengths, weaknesses, opportunities, threats. Give examples.	10 Min	10:20 – 10:30	SWOT Template Slide
	Comfort Break	Energizer on return?	10 Min	10:30 – 10:40	
State Change					
4	SWOT Instructions	(Activity) By Facilitator: The origin/history of SWOT as a tool commonly used. Variation of SWOT is SPOT (P stands for Problems). When to use which is important. (Ask group when to use one versus the other.) Show how S is to be leveraged, W is to be converted to S, O is to be leveraged and T to be minimized. SWOT can be used to create improvement actions with time frames.	30 Min	10:40 – 11:10	Show SWOT Explanation Slides with examples. After Action Review Template.
5	Summarize / Q&A	(Engager) By Facilitator. Ask team if they can think of one area in HR where they may be able to use SWOT for continuous improvement. (Energizer) Have them write on a large sticky note and place on the Flip Chart across the room.	10 Min	11:10 – 11:20	Large sticky notes and markers
6	Wrap-up and Next Steps	Identify any next steps and thank the participants for their time.	10 Min	11:20 – 11:30	Next steps chart

#	Item	Description/Steps
	ROA Supporting Enablers	
A	Techniques and Templates	SWOT Template
B	Presentation Slides/Charts	PowerPoint Deck, Wall chart/banner
C	Equipment	PC, Overhead Projector, Flip Chart/Easel
D	Engagers/Energizers	Thumball™ for Introductions, Story Library
E	Supplies	Markers, Sticky Notes 6in x 8in, Name Tents
F	Participant notebook/ handouts	Handout with SWOT template
G	Post Workshop Actions	TBD in the workshop
H	Communications	HR project manager will send out the agenda to all participants and arrange for HR VP to kick off the workshop.
I	Logistics	Room is facilitation-friendly. Food/Breakfast is being arranged by the HR coordinator.

Table 3.8 – Participant Agenda Example

	SWOT Analysis Training
	(Strengths, Weaknesses, Opportunities and Threats)
Date and Time	DD Month, YYYY 10:00 AM to 11:30 AM – US EST (1.5 hours)
Location	XYZ, NJ Conference Room: ABC
Objective	To provide training to Human Resource employees in the use SWOT Analysis.
Roles	Workshop Sponsor: VP Human Resources, Manager ABC, Coordinator DEF, Participants, HR Staff, and Facilitator *Name 1.*
Guidelines	Use of PCs at breaks only. Put mobile phones on mute. Respect time (return from breaks on time). Any others?
Pre-Work	Participants are to search for SWOT on the internet; read up on general information.

#	Topic	Description	Time
1	Kick-off	Purpose of the workshop and expected outcomes by VP of HR	Start: 10:00am
2	Introductions	Getting to know cross-functional associates	
3	Review SWOT	SWOT definition and purpose	

#	Topic	Description	Time
	Definition		
	Break		10 minutes 10:30- 10:40am
4	SWOT Overview	• The origin/history of SWOT as a tool and its benefits • Variation of SWOT usage (e.g., SPOT and when to use which) • Uses of SWOT for organizational improvement	
5	Usage in HR	Ideas on use of SWOT in HR	
6	Wrap-Up	Next Steps	Close 11:30am

Logistics and Supplies

Facilitators make preparations for their travel and assemble all supplies needed for the entire workshop. This sometimes entails getting charts enlarged, preparing a PowerPoint presentation, and having handouts printed for the participants. The list of supplies and required resources is generated from the Running Order Agenda. A checklist of supplies is critical to ensure nothing is forgotten when you facilitate the workshop. Any crucial missing item can adversely impact your conducting the workshop activities. Now you are prepared to facilitate the workshop.

Prepare Process Checklist

Inputs to the Prepare Process:

☐ Detailed information about the workshop context and scope
☐ Supporting project documents and organizational information
☐ Understanding of stakeholders and political landscape
☐ Identification of methodology, techniques, tools and templates to be used.

Outputs of the Prepare Process:

☐ Agreed Venue and Logistics
☐ Running Order Agenda (ROA) – Facilitator's Agenda
☐ Workshop Agenda – Participants Agenda

□ Pre-Work Instructions and Material

□ Presentation Material and Handouts

□ Supplies (acquisition and preparation).

Helpful Hints

- The success of the facilitation activity workshop depends on the quality of the design of the detailed agenda—the Running Order Agenda. Maximize the use of adult engagement methods such a Multiple Intelligences (which will be covered in Chapter 5)—to ensure optimal outcomes.

- Be professional in preparing presentation materials and participant handouts.

- To be compliant with sustainability aspirations of the organizations (and your own), use recycled paper—to the extent possible.

- Pay very close attention to every little detail. Leave no stone unturned, as the saying goes, to ensure that every aspect of the workshop design is addressed. Mitigate any possible risk. Pay attention to your intuition as well. Along with your own integrity and professionalism, the client's success and reputation is at stake.

DURING SESSION PROCESS (FACILITATE WORKSHOP)

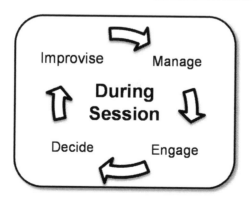

Whether a session is a meeting, a workshop for developing solutions or strategies, or a training and knowledge transfer activity, and whether it's a two hour, four hour, one day or three day event, there are four steps which occur cyclically: *Manage, Engage, Decide,* and *Improvise.* While the Manage step is overarching and pervasive throughout the session, the other steps may occur once or several times depending on the situation and type of session. Let's examine each of these steps. (*During Session* is courtesy of circleindigo: Gary Austin and Justine Marchant.)

MANAGE

There are two aspects to Manage: The workshop manager is responsible for managing the session end-to-end and the facilitator is responsible for managing the agreed process outlined in the workshop agenda. The workshop manager is responsible for the content of what is being addressed, whereas the facilitator manages the context ensuring that the manager and the participants meet expected objectives and have the desired outputs and outcome. In this section we will focus on the role of the facilitator.

Setup

The facilitator ensures that the room or facility is facilitation-friendly, and will have already arranged this in the Prepare Process of the Engagement phase. Facilitation-friendly has many aspects, which are discussed in detail in Chapter 7. Depending on the agenda design, an appropriate room seating arrangement has to be made. The equipment, such as the computer and projector, must be available and functioning. Flip charts and markers must be available along with other relevant supplies. Food and beverages must be pre-arranged for breaks and lunch. It is wise for the facilitator to be at the site about one to two hours in advance of the starting time to ensure all arrangements are in place prior to the arrival of the participants. If possible, a review of the facility on the evening before is advisable.

Process

The facilitator greets all participants, creates a welcoming environment by playing appropriate music and displaying a welcome poster, ensures that the agenda items begin on time, and controls the timeframe allocated. The facilitator uses planned methodology, techniques and tools for the agenda items—as designed earlier in the ROA. In training workshops, the time frames are generally established and tried, whereas in solutions/strategies workshops, the agenda items can overflow in terms of time.

The facilitator monitors and adjusts the overall time frame and calls out for a change in agenda items should the participants desire more time in some areas than the others. This is called "going where the energy of the group wants to go." When this occurs, the facilitator must *re-contract* for a change in agenda items and the timeframe. Re-contracting means having a discussion with the workshop manager to explain why the agenda items should be changed, and with his/her consent, gaining an agreement from the participants to introduce change. This ensures that the workshop expectations and the process of activities are adjusted. The facilitator ensures that appropriate methods are used to capture the key points of discussions, generate outputs and address open items.

ENGAGE

The facilitator has the obligation to involve all participants fully in each step of the process and throughout the workshop. This includes drawing the participants into the agenda topic at hand and holding their attention through the use of the appropriate methodology, techniques and tools being used. The tools described in Chapter 5 must be incorporated in the design of the agenda to maximize engagement.

One way to ensure engagement is the use of energizers. To ensure that the energy level of the participants, both physical and mental, is maintained at all times, the facilitator designs activities in the ROA and uses a multitude of techniques such as icebreakers, exercises, team builders, and challengers, in addition to incorporating stories, quotations, and metaphors to make the topics relevant and interesting.

As a facilitator you are in the "entertainment business." You manage workshop activities to achieve desired objectives through proactive participation of all participants in a variety of ways so that they are not just participating but are *experiencing* the workshop. Good facilitators create this experience as a good memory in the minds of the attendees. It is what I refer to as creating the "wow."

DECIDE

With the exception of the majority of training workshops, decision-making activity is an integral part of a workshop, whether it's a meeting, a workshop, or any other type of session where people are gathered for some common cause. In meeting sessions, the decision making is typically autocratic, where the manager in charge is also the facilitator. While the manager may ask for the opinions of the participants, the final decision on agenda topics will be made by the manager. In sessions where the agreement of the participants is needed, the decision may be made on consensus basis and be more democratic in nature.

Yet there are other situations where decisions are made on weighted criteria, such as in buying technical products or services where an agreed criterion is used to evaluate the decision to be made. The question of "who decides" is generally agreed upon with the workshop manager and the sponsor during the Prepare Process and is incorporated by the facilitator in the ROA process. There are times when a consensus has to be developed on the spot in the workshop regarding how the decision should be made.

For various options around decision making, facilitators have several techniques available. Some are visual, such as a show of hands to determine majority or the use of sticky dots on charts or flip charts. Some are more mathematical, such as weighted criteria based on specific considerations relevant to the topic at hand. Facilitator should design this approach in the ROA and always be prepared to change the approach depending on the dynamics of the discussion and the group. When discussion is called for, a reasonable amount of time is allowed for debate and then the facilitator makes a judgment call to intervene and call for a decision.

IMPROVISE

General George Patton once observed, "All plans fail when you meet the enemy." Even though during work sessions participants are not the enemy, a similar concept is true. A facilitator has to think through every step of the agenda item designed in the ROA, and based on numerous dynamics and situations improvise as required.

For example, a facilitator may be using a technique to solve a problem, and find that the technique is not agreeable to the participants. At that moment the facilitator must quickly propose another option from her library of techniques to ensure the integrity of the process. Good facilitators always have backup techniques to switch to on short notice. One of the competencies of a facilitator is "Standing Alone." That means, making a quick decision to keep the process going while gaining the confidence of the group in the approach or technique being proposed.

Thus the cycle of the four factors, *Manage, Engage, Decide,* and *Improvise* is executed in the session by the facilitator, as a symphony conductor blends the harmony, while leading the ensemble and keeping ears and eyes to every instrument.

DURING SESSION CHECKLIST

Inputs to the During Session:

- ☐ Workshop agenda (participants)
- ☐ Running Order Agenda (ROA)
- ☐ Stakeholders/participants communication
- ☐ Venue logistics including facility, equipment and supplies, food, etc.

Outputs of During Session:

- ☐ Agreed workshop objectives, outputs, and outcomes
- ☐ Satisfied stakeholders which includes workshop manager, sponsor, participants, and the facilitator herself.

HELPFUL HINTS

- Who you are and what you do is played out in the workshop delivery. As a leader of the session, all eyes are focused on you and therefore utmost professionalism is critical, both in the subject matter and personal behavior.

- Be always equipped with your library of facilitation tools so that you can change and adapt on the fly, as and when needed. The participants are the key stakeholders of the session and to meet their expectations, be prepared for the agenda design to be adjusted at any time. *The flow of the agenda items is as good as the energy flow of the participants.*

- Whether at a meeting, a group workshop, or training session, as a facilitator you are a leader, a speaker, presenter, a subject matter expert, a trainer, an educator, a coach, a mentor, a diplomat—all in one. Therefore govern yourself accordingly. It is a privilege to be in this role. Be proud of it and enjoy it.

FOLLOW-UP

CONCLUDE

Conclude

The old English adage is applicable here: All is well that ends well. The conclude step happens partially in the workshop itself and partially after the workshop. As the session comes to an end, the agreed upon next steps are complied with. This includes professional documentation and prompt answers to any unaddressed questions from the participants. It is my belief that professionals should document the workshop outcomes and deliver them to the clients in 72 hours or less; 48 hours is even better.

After Action Review Template

This template is for the facilitator to conduct an After Action Review in the workshop with the participants present. Generally this is done at the end of a topic, a session or a workshop. The facilitator can use a flip chart to gather information or provide sticky notes to the participants and have them generate their feedback. There are two types of After Action Reviews: informal and formal. Table 3.9 is example of an informal review. Refer to Tool #2 in Chapter 12 for detailed instructions on how to use this template and how to facilitate a formal review.

Table 3.9 – After Action Review Template

I Liked	I Wish
Example of a training workshop: *The content of the topic*	Example of a training workshop: *There were more visuals in the material*
Example of a group session: *The agenda design*	Example of a group session: *The facilitator had allowed more time for exercises*

Training Workshop Evaluation Template

This template is designed for participants to provide feedback to the organization. Some organizations don't let the facilitator see this input until after their training manager has reviewed and evaluated the result.

Table 3.10 – Training Workshop Evaluation Template

Date: Workshop Name: Organization:	Facilitator: Participant Name: Site/City:					
	Strongly Agree (6)	Agree (5)	Somewhat Agree (4)	Somewhat Disagree (3)	Disagree (2)	Strongly Disagree (1)
This course was relevant to my needs.						
I will be able to apply what I learned to my work.						
I would recommend this course to others.						
The learning material was of high quality.						
5(a). The facilitator was well prepared, knowledgeable and delivered the course effectively.						
5(b). The facilitator was able to listen effectively, respond to questions and encourage participation.						
The venue and facilities were acceptable for the learning event.						
7. What sections were of the greatest value to you and why?						
8. Were there any sections you felt were not useful and why?						
9. Were there any parts of the course you would like to spend more time on? If so please specify.						
10. What else would you like this course to cover?						
11. How can we improve on this course to make it more effective?						
12. Are there any other areas you would like to receive training in?						

Conclude Process Checklist

Inputs to Conclude Process:

- ☐ Workshop output
- ☐ Next steps items and schedule
- ☐ Workshop feedback (participants/stakeholders input: See Table 3.9).

Outputs of Conclude Process:

- ☐ Participant's feedback: After Action Review (See Table 3.9 and Tool #2 in Chapter 12)
- ☐ Training participants feedback (See Table 3.10)
- ☐ Workshop deliverables: professional documentation
- ☐ Completion of assigned tasks, if any
- ☐ Note of thanks to the client, relevant stakeholders and any enablers who helped make the workshop successful.

Helpful Hints

- Say what you mean and do what you say. This builds credibility and trust. If you promise an action, you must complete it as stated or agreed.

- The documentation deliverables must look professional and be turned around in a timely and agreed manner. Documenting outputs is not my forte. I outsource that task to a colleague for three reasons:
  1. The output will be a professional showcase
  2. I can free up my time for continuous improvement and other actions
  3. It is cost effective, as my billable rate is higher than that of my colleague.

- The word "Thanks" goes a long way in human relationships. Those who will make your workshop successful are clients, participants, stakeholders, suppliers, enablers, colleagues, and others. Take the time to send a note of thanks. It is an honorable thing to do.

EVALUATE

> **Evaluate**

It has been said that, "The biggest room in this world is room for improvement." No matter how well you may have managed the entire facilitation process, you will likely find room for improvement, whether given as feedback or from self-realization. From every negative comes some positive. List the areas that need improvement, which may include tools and their usage, handling of certain situations, agenda design, or other areas. Schedule and complete those improvements fairly soon after the workshop while they are fresh in your mind and you are motivated. Update your ongoing list of accomplishments and list of contacts as appropriate.

Workshop Evaluation Template

This template is for facilitators to gather information from clients and participants wherein they evaluate the workshop and the effectiveness of the facilitator. It is also a platform for facilitators to provide their feedback on the workshop and their performance as professional facilitators.

Table 3.11 – Workshop Evaluation Template

Template for Facilitator	
Client	
Topic	
Sponsor / Manager	
Date	
Location	
Participants	
Facilitator(s)	
Did anything unusual occur? What is the lesson learned?	
Are there any follow-up actions?	
Feedback	
Client Feedback	
Facilitator's Own Feedback	
Things That Went Well (I Liked)	
Room for Improvement (I Wish)	
Follow-Up	
☐ Update client database (names, email addresses, contact information for future marketing)	
☐ Send a note of thanks to the client / stakeholders	
☐ Tools and supplies (tools to be improved and supplies to be replenished)	

Evaluate Process Checklist

Inputs to the Evaluate Process:

- ☐ After Action Review (generated in the workshop)
- ☐ Workshop feedback (client/participants/stakeholders).

Outputs of the Evaluate Process:

- ☐ Opportunity for continues improvement in all aspects of facilitation process including process, tools, and your own style
- ☐ Update your database of contacts you may have made through the workshop.

Helpful Hints

- It is not easy to be critical of your own self. But in every engagement and workshop, there will be positive or negative events that teach us something—all the time. Think of these as a gift to better yourself and improve your craft.

- Every person you meet through any work engagement is a potential contact for future networking and is a valuable resource. Gather contact information from those you meet. It may come handy for marketing and seeking other connections. Use this information responsibly.

- The completion of every engagement is a finished project, so celebrate. Celebrate with your colleagues, your staff, and even family members and give them the opportunity to appreciate and learn more about what you do.

Chapter 4
Facilitation Leadership

He who knows others is learned; he who knows himself is wise.
~ Lao Tsu

As the name implies, the facilitator is the leader of the session when facilitating workshops, meetings, training or teams. He or she has the obligation to possess good leadership attributes and use them effectively. A leadership role in facilitating work groups is different from leadership roles in organizations or in politics. Session leader attributes are broken down into three areas as depicted in Figure 4.1.

Figure 4.1 – Facilitation Leadership Framework: *"Bringing who you are, to what you do"*

This framework has been developed by me based on my practical experience in facilitation and training for three decades. This chapter provides an introduction and insights into the dimensions of these attributes and why a facilitator must inculcate them to be successful:

- Leadership, Values and Ethics (core of the framework)
- Self-Awareness and Style
- Skills and Competencies.

Author Geoff Bellman in his book *The Consultant's Calling* wisely uses the phrase "Bringing who you are to what you do." Who you are as a person and what you do in terms of your services as a consultant/facilitator defines your "Brand," or your hallmark.

LEADERSHIP

Napoleon Hill was an American author in the area of the new thought movement who was one of the earliest producers of the modern genre of personal success literature. He is widely considered to be one of the great writers on success. His most famous work, *Think and Grow Rich* (1937), is one of the best-selling books of all time (at the time of Hill's death in 1970, *Think and Grow Rich* had sold 20 million copies).

Hill's works examine the power of personal beliefs, and the role they play in personal success. He was an advisor to President Franklin D. Roosevelt from 1933 to 1936. "What the mind of man can conceive and believe, it can achieve." is one of Hill's hallmark expressions. How achievement actually occurs, and a formula for it that puts success in reach of the average person, were the focal points of Hill's books. (Source: Wikipedia)

A facilitator plays several roles in the facilitation process, including those of mediator, diplomat, consultant, educator, trainer, coach, speaker, and more. But above all, the facilitator is the leader of the session and is responsible for ensuring that the all participants are fully engaged and participative in all aspects of the session. See Figure 4.2. Leadership does not happen by accident; it is mostly a learned behavior based on personal values and sound principles.

Figure 4.2 – Facilitator's Many Roles

I have found that the following eleven factors of leadership outlined by Napoleon Hill are critical for a facilitator to conduct workshops and deliver successful results. While these eleven factors are written in the context of leadership in general, I have found these to be equally applicable to the role of a facilitator. I have used current manners of expression as they apply to facilitation, without changing the spirit of his message.

Leadership:

1. **Unwavering courage based upon knowledge of self, and of one's occupation**. No participant wishes to be dominated by a leader who lacks self-confidence and courage. No intelligent follower will be dominated by such a leader for very long.

2. **Self-control.** The person who cannot control himself or herself can never guide others. Self-control sets a mighty example for work groups, which the more intelligent will emulate.

3. **A keen sense of justice.** Without a sense of fairness and justice, no leader can command and retain the respect of his work groups.

4. **Definiteness of decision.** The person who wavers when making decisions, shows uncertainty in those decisions and cannot lead others successfully.

5. **Definiteness of plans.** Successful leaders plan their work, and work their plan. A leader who moves by guesswork, without practical, definite plans, is comparable to a ship without a rudder. Sooner or later the ship will land on the rocks. In the facilitation process this translates into taking steps to engage and prepare, where every detail is thought through for success.

6. **The habit of doing more than paid for.** One of the challenges of leadership is the necessity for leaders to be willing to do more than they require of their work groups. Facilitators should "go the extra mile" and strive to create customer delight and not just customer satisfaction.

7. **A pleasing personality.** No slovenly, careless person can become a successful leader. Leadership calls for respect. Work groups will not respect leaders who do not grade high on all of the factors of a pleasing personality.

8. **Sympathy and understanding.** Successful leaders must be in sympathy with their session participants. Moreover, they must understand them and their problems and challenges.

9. **Mastery of detail.** Successful leadership calls for mastery of the details of the leader's position. Facilitators must pay a close attention to all aspects of the facilitation process, including agenda design, conducting the session, and delivering the agreed outputs. This also includes paying a close attention to the energy of the group and making adjustments promptly.

10. **Willingness to assume full responsibility.** Successful leaders must be willing to assume responsibility for any shortcomings in workshop design and usage of tools—should they not be effective. Leaders who try to shift this responsibility will find it difficult to be accepted as leaders by the groups they lead. Leaders should explain why some aspect of the session is not working and make changes immediately to try another

tool or technique that is acceptable to the group and offers greater chances of success.

11. **Cooperation.** Successful leaders understand and apply the principle of cooperative effort and induce their session participants to do the same. In facilitation, the participants and their management put their trust in the facilitator to inculcate cooperation and collaboration to achieve the desired objectives.

These eleven factors are governed by the other two dimensions of session leaders shown Figure 4.1: values and ethics.

VALUES AND ETHICS

This is the Statement of Values and Code of Ethics of the International Association of Facilitators (IAF). The development of this Code has involved extensive dialogue and a wide diversity of views from IAF members from around the world. A consensus has been achieved across regional and cultural boundaries.

The Statement of Values and Code of Ethics (the Code) was adopted by the IAF Association Coordinating Team (ACT) in June 2004. The Ethics and Values Think Tank (EVTT) continue to provide a forum for discussion of pertinent issues and potential revisions of this Code.

PREAMBLE (IN THE WORDS OF IAF)

Facilitators are called upon to fill an impartial role in helping groups become more effective. We act as process guides to create a balance between participation and results.

We, the members of the International Association of Facilitators (IAF), believe that our profession gives us a unique opportunity to make a positive contribution to individuals, organizations, and society. Our effectiveness is based on our personal integrity and the trust developed between ourselves and those with whom we work. Therefore, we recognize the importance of defining and making known the values and ethical principles that guide our actions.

This Statement of Values and Code of Ethics recognizes the complexity of our roles, including the full spectrum of personal, professional and cultural diversity in the IAF membership and in the field of facilitation. Members of the International Association of Facilitators are committed to using these values and ethics to guide their professional practice. These principles are expressed in broad statements to guide ethical practice; they provide a framework and are not intended to dictate conduct for particular situations. Questions or advice about the application of these values and ethics may be addressed to the International Association of Facilitators.

STATEMENT OF VALUES

As group facilitators, we believe in the inherent value of the individual and the collective wisdom of the group. We strive to help the group make the best use of the contributions of each of its members. We set aside our personal opinions and support the group's right to make its own choices. We believe that collaborative and cooperative interaction builds consensus and produces meaningful outcomes. We value professional collaboration to improve our profession.

CODE OF ETHICS

1. **Client Service:** We are in service to our clients, using our group facilitation competencies to add value to their work. Our clients include the groups we facilitate and those who contract with us on their behalf. We work closely with our clients to understand their expectations so that we provide the appropriate service, and that the group produces the desired outcomes. It is our responsibility to ensure that we are competent to handle the intervention. If the group decides it needs to go in a direction other than that originally intended by either the group or its representatives, our role is to help the group move forward, reconciling the original intent with the emergent direction.

2. **Conflict of Interest:** We openly acknowledge any potential conflict of interest. Prior to agreeing to work with our clients, we discuss openly and honestly any possible conflict of interest, personal bias, prior knowledge of the organization or any other matter which may be perceived as preventing us from working effectively with the interests of all group members. We do this so that, together, we may make an

informed decision about proceeding and to prevent misunderstanding that could detract from the success or credibility of the clients or ourselves. We refrain from using our position to secure unfair or inappropriate privilege, gain, or benefit.

3. **Group Autonomy:** We respect the culture, rights, and autonomy of the group. We seek the group's conscious agreement to the process and their commitment to participate. We do not impose anything that risks the welfare and dignity of the participants, the freedom of choice of the group, or the credibility of its work.

4. **Processes, Methods, and Tools:** We use processes, methods, and tools responsibly. In dialogue with the group or its representatives we design processes that will achieve the group's goals, and select and adapt the most appropriate methods and tools. We avoid using processes, methods or tools with which we are insufficiently skilled, or which are poorly matched to the needs of the group.

5. **Respect, Safety, Equity, and Trust:** We strive to engender an environment of respect and safety where all participants trust that they can speak freely and where individual boundaries are honored. We use our skills, knowledge, tools, and wisdom to elicit and honor the perspectives of all. We seek to have all relevant stakeholders represented and involved. We promote equitable relationships among the participants and facilitator and ensure that all participants have an opportunity to examine and share their thoughts and feelings. We use a variety of methods to enable the group to access the natural gifts, talents and life experiences of each member. We work in ways that honor the wholeness and self-expression of others, designing sessions that respect different styles of interaction. We understand that any action we take is an intervention that may affect the process.

6. **Stewardship of Process:** We practice stewardship of process and impartiality toward content. While participants bring knowledge and expertise concerning the substance of their situation, we bring knowledge and expertise concerning the group interaction process. We are vigilant to minimize our influence on group outcomes. When we

have content knowledge not otherwise available to the group, and that the group must have to be effective, we offer it after explaining our change in role.

7. **Confidentiality:** We maintain confidentiality of information. We observe confidentiality of all client information. Therefore, we do not share information about a client within or outside of the client's organization, nor do we report on group content, or the individual opinions or behavior of members of the group without consent.

8. **Professional Development:** We are responsible for continuous improvement of our facilitation skills and knowledge. We continuously learn and grow. We seek opportunities to improve our knowledge and facilitation skills to better assist groups in their work. We remain current in the field of facilitation through our practical group experiences and ongoing personal development. We offer our skills within a spirit of collaboration to develop our professional work practices.

SELF-AWARENESS AND STYLE

Being aware of one's strengths and shortcomings in the role of a session leader helps better manage the facilitation process and creates opportunities to continuously improve upon them with every engagement. One's personal beliefs, values and qualities result in the "style" of a facilitators conduct. Style is the mode of expressions of the self. The style influences the participants and stakeholders in a way that nurtures trust and generates confidence in the leadership of the facilitator. Of course in training workshops, the style permeates in the subject matter of knowledge transfer. Here are some considerations that facilitators must be aware of and have strategies regarding style of conduct and expression:

Dress: Dress for success is an old axiom. Success for a facilitator means being presentable and professional appropriate to that role. The growing scientific field called *embodied cognition* suggests that we think not just with our brains but with our bodies, reports Sandra Blakeslee in the New York Times (April 3,

2012). If you wear a white coat that you believe belongs to a doctor, your ability to pay attention increases sharply. In the article, Dr. Adam D. Galinsky, a professor at the Kellogg School of Management at Northwestern University, is quoted as saying, "Our thought processes are based on physical experiences that set off associated abstract concepts. Now it appears that those experiences include the clothes we wear." If our behavior is influenced by what we wear, a facilitator must consider a scientific approach to dress.

Two views are commonly prevalent regarding a facilitator's dress code. Some believe that a facilitator should dress just as the audience would. For example if the audience, or participants, dress in casual clothing because their organization rules allow that dress code then the facilitator should dress casual as well. Others believe that the facilitator, being a session leader must dress one notch above the audience.

Unless a manager of a given organization is leading the session, I believe the second point of view is the correct one—that the facilitator should dress one notch above. For example, if the audience is dressed in business casual then the facilitator should wear a business suit or jacket and tie for men and a jacket for women. This style of dress sends a message to the participants that you are in charge and are ready for your role as their session leader. After the initial introductions and kick off, it's okay to take the jacket off and put it away for conducting the rest of the business. Of course the dress code mentioned here is for Western cultures; for different geographies and cultures, facilitators may use their own preferred dress practices.

Eye Contact and Glasses: Direct eye contact is a powerful communicator. It is imperative that facilitators who wear eyeglasses have non-glare glasses that don't reflect light. Regular glasses reflect light and the audience cannot see the eyes of the facilitator through the glasses and, therefore, cannot establish the connection that is so important for human interaction.

Connection with Audience: As stated before, direct eye contact is a powerful and effective communicator. In public speaking, where there may be ten people or a hundred people or more, speakers should scan the entire audience to make a personal connection when making key points. This gives individuals in the audience the perception that they're getting personal attention. Scanning from left to right or right to left across the audience may be referred to as the "Light House Beacon." As the *Light House Beacon*, facilitators should sweep the audience with their eyes, resting only one to three seconds or less on each person (unless one is in a dialogue mode). This ensures attention and engagement.

Active Listening: It is said that the reason human beings have two ears and one mouth is so that they can listen more and speak less. This skill is critical for facilitators because they must simultaneously play many roles while managing the current situation and thinking of next steps to come. A basic technique called *The Listening Ladder* helps facilitators in this important aspect: *Look at the person speaking to you. Ask questions. Don't interrupt or be interrupted. Don't change the subject. Empathize. Respond verbally and nonverbally.*

"Color" in Your Voice: Voice timbre is a powerful medium of communication when speaking, presenting, or managing any other activity of a given session. Speak loud enough to throw your voice to the back of the room so that the words are clear to one and all. Vary your tone and pitch and repeat key phrases and learning points with a different vocal emphasis. This may be referred to as putting "color in your voice." This concept is particularly impactful when telling stories, using quotations, and expressing relevant metaphors. Use the *Power of Pause*. Pause at the various key intervals and emphasize sparkle and freshness in your voice. The audience draws energy from the facilitator's voice.

Body Language and Enthusiasm: Appropriate use of gestures expresses emotion through the body to make a point or convey a particular feeling. Using hands, pointing with the fingers, raising eye brows, looking around, shaking your head, and other gestures convey messages through a "visual language" which, when combined with color in your voice and pausing with purpose, enhances the impact of what is being communicated to the audience. I use a gesture of clapping my hands loudly when I want to show my passion for making a point. It grabs the attention of the participants and promotes an environment of enthusiasm.

Mannerisms: Check your dress, hair, and clothing before standing up and presenting. Avoid close or tense body postures. Be aware of your verbal tics and practice eliminating the non-words such as "uh," "you know," and others. Great speakers don't use non-words. It is important to greet the participants as they arrive. This concept may be referred to as *connection before content*.

Be aware of the cultural norms of the local geography. Respect diversity of geographies, people and cultures. For example, some Eastern cultures have a very respectful way of handing out their business cards. They hold it with both hands, card text facing the recipient and present it with a slight bow. The recipients reciprocate with the similar gesture.

Avoid referencing politics, religion, ethnicity, war, or any other topic of contention or sensitivity (unless the session topic is one of these issues). I use metaphors and narrate lessons of war relevant to my topics *only* after asking permission from the audience.

Discussion and Debate: This is an integral part of group sessions. To solve problems, develop solutions, and improve products and services, healthy discussion is critical. Several techniques and tools are designed by the facilitator in the Prepare Process step. Here are some key considerations for facilitating discussion:

- *Questioning:* Avoid closed questions such as, "Who can tell me on which date...?" Instead use open question such as, "What might be the timeframe for...?"

- *Lubricators:* Use verbal and nonverbal lubricators that demonstrate your attention to the one speaking. Also, most participants' questions may not be questions! Clarify and promote dialogue by using the reflective or deflective approach. For example:
  - ✓ **Verbal**: "I see." or "That is interesting."
  - ✓ **Nonverbal**: Nodding, leaning forward, and constant eye contact.
  - ✓ **Reflective**: "If I understand correctly, you are asking..."
  - ✓ **Deflective**: Address the group, saying, "How does the rest of the group feel about...?" or to the individual, "You have obviously done some thinking on this. What's your view on...?"

Gratitude: A facilitator's session has many enablers who contribute to the success of every phase of the process. The session coordinator, the wait staff who served breakfast and lunch, the hotel staff who helped with the audio system, and others deserve expressions of thanks because they "facilitated" their end of the service. Usually, when a session concludes, the participants close their laptops and pack their briefcases and off they go. The support staff is almost invisible to them. I make it a practice to call all the support staff before the wrap-up and publically acknowledge their contribution so that the participants may give a round of applause as a visible gesture of their appreciation. It is not just good manners, but it's good for the soul of everyone whose energy flowed in that session—one and all. Robert Louis Stevenson said, "The man who forgets to be grateful has fallen asleep in life."

Learning on the Fly: In *FYI, For Your Improvement, A Development and Coaching Guide,* Michael M. Lombardo and Robert W. Eichinger have identified Learning on the Fly as a crucial competency and describe it thus:

> *Most of us are good at applying what we have seen and done in the past. Most of us can apply solutions that have worked for us before. We are all pretty good at solving problems we've seen before. A rarer skill is doing things for the first time. Solving problems we've never seen before. Trying solutions we have never tried before. Analyzing problems in new contexts and in new ways. With the increasing pace of change, being quick to learn and apply first time solutions is becoming a crucial skill. It involves taking risks, being less than perfect, discarding the past, going against the grain, and cutting new paths. The one who is skilled in this competency:*

- ✓ *Learns quickly when facing new problems*
- ✓ *Is a relentless and versatile learner*
- ✓ *Is open to change*
- ✓ *Analyzes both successes and failures for clues to improvement*
- ✓ *Experiments and will try anything to find solutions*
- ✓ *Enjoys the challenge of unfamiliar tasks*
- ✓ *Quickly grasps the essence and the underlying structure of anything.*

Being a leader of the facilitation process and the session, you have the obligation to develop and possess the *Learning on the Fly* attributes outlined above. I also refer to this capability as the *Learning Agility* of a Facilitator, the ability to rapidly respond to change by understanding the current situation quickly and determining possibilities for action through new information. To inculcate these attributes, the facilitator must be an avid reader of a variety of subjects, have a library of resources such as methods, techniques and tools to draw from on a short notice, and have the ability to research and network with other professionals as and when needed.

Genius ... is the capacity to see ten things where the ordinary man sees one.
~ Ezra Pound, American expatriate poet and critic

Influencing Others: As a facilitator you wear multiple hats: educator, trainer, consultant, and even coach and mentor. Participants will look up to you and observe your behavior, your actions, and how you lead them in a session. This leaves an impact on the participants that they may take away as a learning experience and a technique to apply somewhere else in their own work engagements. In essence, you are leaving your legacy at every step. This means you have a tremendous responsibility to say and do the right things.

Dale Carnegie's *How to Win Friends and Influence People* outlines some attributes that should be considered in the role of a facilitator.

- ✓ Be sincere. Do not promise anything that you cannot deliver.

- ✓ Be empathetic. Ask yourself what it is the other person really wants *(e.g., objectives identified by the workshop manager and participants).*

- ✓ Consider the benefit the person *(group/participants)* will receive from doing what you suggest.

- ✓ Match those benefits to other person's *(group's/participant's)* wants.

- ✓ When you make your request, put it in a form that will convey to the other person *(group/participants)* the idea that s/he personally will benefit.

When I was writing this section of the chapter, the sixteen-year-old Pakistani advocate of education for girls in oppressive environments, Malala Yousafzai, was making a powerful speech at the United Nations. In closing her emotional and enthusiastic speech advocating the rights of children, she raised her index finger and said, "One child, one teacher, one book, and one pen can change the world." With passion in her voice, she said this while moving her body along with the pointed index figure as she scanned the audience from one end of the hall to the other.

This is an excellent example of the points made in this section: Malala opened her speech with humbleness, showing good manners, and she made eye contact with the entire audience and connected with them. She used color in her voice and through body language demonstrated enthusiasm. She very gracefully showed gratitude to all those who helped her recover from the shot fired point blank at her head by terrorists for speaking up for girls' education in Pakistan. Watching her speak, I was impressed by the number of attributes discussed in this chapter that this young woman displayed.

SELF-ASSESSMENT

In the Self-Awareness and Style piece of the Facilitation Leadership Framework outlined in Figure 4.1, take a few moments and with a pencil identify in "Your Notes" the items you believe you may wish to explore for learning and improvement. This can become input to your development plan described in Chapter 11.

Your Notes:

SKILLS AND COMPETENCIES

FOUNDATIONAL SKILL SET

The following seven foundational skills are essential for anyone in the role of a facilitator. To develop these skills, facilitators need to be aware of their personal strengths and weaknesses and then diligently work on acquiring and practicing those competencies for their professional selves. *Facilitators must be at their best while facilitating sessions.* This is the measure of their competency:

- ✓ Active Listening
- ✓ Questioning
- ✓ Information Gathering and Analysis
- ✓ Public Speaking
- ✓ Presentation Skills
- ✓ Intervening (Summarizing and Paraphrasing)
- ✓ Managing Group Dynamics.

COMPREHENSIVE SKILL SET

For facilitators to continue a professional journey of this art and craft, the International Association of Facilitators (IAF) has developed Core Facilitator's Competencies. In addition, they have a professional certification in place which is outlined below and is also referenced in Chapter 12.

BACKGROUND

The International Association of Facilitators (IAF™) is the worldwide professional body established to promote, support and advance the art and practice of professional facilitation through methods exchange, professional growth, practical research and collegial networking. In response to the needs of members and their customers, IAF established the Professional Facilitator Certification Program. The Professional Facilitator Certification Program provides successful candidates with the professional credential *"IAF Certified™ Professional Facilitator—CPF."* This credential is the leading indicator that the facilitator is competent in each of the basic facilitator competencies. The Core Facilitator Competencies© IAF™ 2003 document provides an overview of the competency framework that is the basis of the CPF certification.

The competency framework described in the Core Facilitator Competencies was developed over several years by IAF with the support of IAF members and facilitators from all over the world. The competencies reflected in the document and assessed in the Certification Process, form the basic set of skills, knowledge, and behaviors that facilitators must have in order to be successful facilitating in a wide variety of environments. Copies of this document are available free of charge from the IAF web site (http://www.iaf-world.org) or from the certification program administrator, at certify@iaf-world.org. (Reference: Foundational Facilitator Competencies© IAF™, 2003, Version 1.0)

THE COMPETENCIES

A. CREATE COLLABORATIVE CLIENT RELATIONSHIPS

1) Develop working partnerships

   ☐ Clarify mutual commitment
   ☐ Develop consensus on tasks, deliverables, roles and responsibilities
   ☐ Demonstrate collaborative values and processes such as in co-facilitation.

2) Design and customize applications to meet client needs

   ☐ Analyze organizational environment
   ☐ Diagnose client need
   ☐ Create appropriate designs to achieve intended outcomes
   ☐ Predefine a quality product and outcomes with client.

3) Manage multi-session events effectively

   ☐ Contract with client for scope and deliverables
   ☐ Develop event plan
   ☐ Deliver event successfully
   ☐ Assess / evaluate client satisfaction at all stages of the event / project.

B. PLAN APPROPRIATE GROUP PROCESSES

1) Select clear methods and processes that

☐ Foster open participation with respect for client culture, norms and participant diversity

☐ Engage the participation of those with varied learning / thinking styles

☐ Achieve a high quality product / outcome that meets the client needs.

2) Prepare time and space to support group process

☐ Arrange physical space to support the purpose of the meeting
☐ Plan effective use of time
☐ Provide effective atmosphere and drama for sessions.

C. CREATE AND SUSTAIN A PARTICIPATORY ENVIRONMENT

1) Demonstrate effective participatory and interpersonal communication skills

☐ Apply a variety of participatory processes
☐ Demonstrate effective verbal communication skills
☐ Develop rapport with participants
☐ Practice active listening
☐ Demonstrate ability to observe and provide feedback to participants.

2) Honor and recognize diversity, ensuring inclusiveness

☐ Create opportunities for participants to benefit from the diversity of the group
☐ Cultivate cultural awareness and sensitivity.

3) Manage group conflict

☐ Help individuals identify and review underlying assumptions
☐ Recognize conflict and its role within group learning / maturity
☐ Provide a safe environment for conflict to surface
☐ Manage disruptive group behavior
☐ Support the group through resolution of conflict.

4) Evoke group creativity

   ☐ Draw out participants of all learning/thinking styles
   ☐ Encourage creative thinking
   ☐ Accept all ideas
   ☐ Use approaches that best fit needs and abilities of the group
   ☐ Stimulate and tap group energy.

D. GUIDE GROUP TO APPROPRIATE AND USEFUL OUTCOMES

1) Guide the group with clear methods and processes

   ☐ Establish clear context for the session
   ☐ Actively listen, question and summarize to elicit the sense of the group
   ☐ Recognize tangents and redirect to the task
   ☐ Manage small and large group process.

2) Facilitate group self-awareness about its task

   ☐ Vary the pace of activities according to needs of group
   ☐ Identify information the group needs, and draw out data and insight from the group
   ☐ Help the group synthesize patterns, trends, root causes, frameworks for action
   ☐ Assist the group in reflection on its experience.

3) Guide the group to consensus and desired outcomes

   ☐ Use a variety of approaches to achieve group consensus
   ☐ Use a variety of approaches to meet group objectives
   ☐ Adapt processes to changing situations and needs of the group
   ☐ Assess and communicate group progress
   ☐ Foster task completion.

E. BUILD AND MAINTAIN PROFESSIONAL KNOWLEDGE

1) Maintain a base of knowledge

   ☐ Knowledgeable in management, organizational systems and development, group development, psychology, and conflict resolution

☐ Understand dynamics of change
☐ Understand learning/ thinking theory.

2) Know a range of facilitation methods

☐ Understand problem solving and decision-making models
☐ Understand a variety of group methods and techniques
☐ Know consequences of misuse of group methods
☐ Distinguish process from task and content
☐ Learn new processes, methods, and models in support of client's changing/emerging needs.

3) Maintain professional standing

☐ Engage in ongoing study / learning related to our field
☐ Continuously gain awareness of new information in our profession
☐ Practice reflection and learning
☐ Build personal industry knowledge and networks
☐ Maintain certification.

F. MODEL POSITIVE PROFESSIONAL ATTITUDE

1) Practice self-assessment and self-awareness

☐ Reflect on behavior and results
☐ Maintain congruence between actions and personal and professional values
☐ Modify personal behavior / style to reflect the needs of the group
☐ Cultivate understanding of one's own values and their potential impact on work with clients.

2) Act with integrity

☐ Demonstrate a belief in the group and its possibilities
☐ Approach situations with authenticity and a positive attitude
☐ Describe situations as the facilitator sees them and inquire into different views
☐ Model professional boundaries and ethics (as described in the ethics and values statement).

3) Trust group potential and model neutrality

☐ Honor the wisdom of the group
☐ Encourage trust in the capacity and experience of others
☐ Vigilant to minimize influence on group outcomes
☐ Maintain an objective, non-defensive, non-judgmental stance.

SELF-ASSESSMENT

Check off each item in the competencies checklist with a "+" sign if you are good at the skill and a "-" sign if you need development. This can be integrated into your development plan, described in Chapter 12.

HELPFUL HINTS

Leadership, Values, and Ethics permeate every aspect of Self-Awareness & Style and Skills & Competencies. Therefore, to achieve professional excellence, it is incumbent upon facilitators, in all their roles, to adopt, strive for, and practice these dimensions in every engagement. Over a period of time, these attributes become habits and become embedded in the psyche of good facilitators. ***Bringing who you are to what you do*** is a "Brand" for which you are respected and recognized. Facilitation leadership is a rewarding and satisfying journey.

Chapter 5
Engagers and Energizers

If your actions inspire others to dream more, learn more, do more and become more, you are a leader.
~ John Quincy Adams

Engagers are physical activities, mental activities or concepts that, when integrated into meetings, sessions and workshops, enhance the involvement of participants in the purpose of their activity.

Energizers are physical activities, mental activities or conceptual exercises that hold fast the attention of participants during a session. These are integrated into meetings, sessions and workshops to enhance the experience and alertness of the participants.

When designed in agendas, *engagers* enhance the involvement of the participants and *energizers* hold the attention of the participants. These two concepts complement each other and sometimes overlap in that an engager can also serve the purpose of being an energizer and vice-versa. Collectively, these are integrated in the main session agenda items to ensure the effectiveness of the participants to deliver optimal outcomes. Numerous types of engagers and energizers may have several integration points in session agendas designed by facilitators to maximize their effectiveness in specific activities.

Facilitation of workshops outlined in the *Mahal Facilitation Framework* is a proven process that, if executed professionally, results in successful outcomes. As stated in the previous chapter, a facilitator is also an educator, trainer, consultant and a session leader—all in one role.

In this chapter, principles and practical applications of theories are identified that engage participants to maximize their contributions to the success of workshops. Two Gurus of the industry have provided us with elegant yet simple ideas of energizers and engagers. It is up to us, as facilitators, to apply these concepts in practical facilitation. The two theories are: Adult Learning Theory by Dr. Malcolm Shepherd Knowles, who is considered the father of Adult Education; and Dr. Howard Gardner's Multiple Intelligences Theory, which defines methods to engage participants. Engagers and energizers include:

- Adult Learning Theory
- Multiple Intelligences Framework
- Integration Points in Agenda Activities
- Principles and Phrases ("Artie-Facts")
- Facilitator's Mantra.

ADULT LEARNING THEORY

Dr. Malcolm Shepherd Knowles is considered the father of Adult Education and Learning Theory via the notion of Andragogy. While Pedagogy is defined as the art and science of teaching children, Andragogy is defined as the art and science of educating and transferring learning to adults. Andragogy makes the following six assumptions about the design of learning. As theorized by Dr. Knowles, the six assumptions underlying andragogy are:

1) Self-concept
2) Experience
3) Readiness to learn depends on need
4) Problem-centered focus
5) Internal motivation
6) Adults need to know why they need to know something

Self-concept: Self-concept refers to adults becoming more self-directed and independent as they mature. Adults typically prefer to choose what they want to learn, when they want to learn, and how they want to learn. This assumption means that educators can provide more choices for learners, such as allowing them to design their own tests, and providing a collaborative learning environment that fosters mutual respect.

Experience: Adult learners have a wealth of life experiences that they bring with them into new learning experiences. Because of this, they are able to contribute richness to class discussions and are considered valuable resources for learning from and with each other. Some of the experiences, though, may cause misinformation or biases related to the new learning and must be clarified so as not to cause a barrier to the new learning.

Readiness to learn depends on need: Whether or not adults are ready to learn depends on what they need to know in order to deal with life situations. Life situations that compel adults to learn include such things as learning to care for a child who has been diagnosed with a disease or learning to cook healthy meals to prevent health risks.

Problem-centered focus: Adults need to see the immediate application of learning. Therefore, they pursue learning opportunities that will enable them to solve problems.

Internal motivation: Adults will seek learning opportunities due to specific external motivators, but the more potent motivators (self-esteem, better quality of life, self-actualization, and so on) are internal.

Adults need to know why they need to learn something: Adults need to know what's in it for them—how this new knowledge will solve a problem or be immediately applied.

In practical terms, andragogy means that instruction for adults needs to focus more on the process and less on the content being taught. Strategies such as case studies, role playing, simulations, and self-evaluation are most useful to engage adults both in learning workshops and in general meetings, sessions and workshops.

MULTIPLE INTELLIGENCES FRAMEWORK

The psychology of learning and their application via behaviors has been studied and knowledge and theories have accumulated over a long period of time in human history. The Theory of Multiple Intelligences, was developed by psychologist Howard Gardner in the late seventies and early eighties, enhanced in the nineties, and published in his book, *Frames of Mind.* Dr. Gardner proposes that individuals possess eight or more relatively autonomous intelligences. Individuals draw on these intelligences, individually and corporately, to create products and solve problems that are relevant to the societies in which they live (Gardner, 1983, 1993, 1999, 2006b, 2006c).

Figure 5.1 – Multiple Intelligences Framework

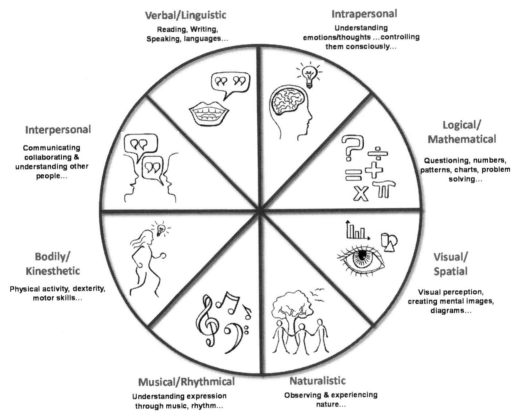

Source: Howard Gardener's Multiple Intelligences, Frames of Mind

Gardner's eight identified intelligences (Gardner, 1999) include:

1. Linguistic intelligence
2. Logico-mathematical intelligence
3. Spatial intelligence
4. Musical intelligence
5. Bodily-kinesthetic intelligence

6. Naturalist intelligence
7. Interpersonal intelligence
8. Intrapersonal intelligence.

Table 5.1 – Multiple Intelligences Description

Verbal/Linguistic	An ability to analyze information and create products involving oral and written language such as speeches, books, and memos.
Logical/Mathematical	An ability to develop equations and proofs, make calculations, and solve abstract problems.
Visual/Spatial	An ability to recognize and manipulate large-scale and fine-grained spatial images.
Musical/Rhythmical	An ability to produce, remember, and make meaning of different patterns of sound.
Naturalistic	An ability to identify and distinguish among different types of plants, animals, and weather formations that are found in the natural world.
Bodily/Kinesthetic	An ability to use one's own body to create products or solve problems.
Interpersonal	An ability to recognize and understand other people's moods, desires, motivations, and intentions.
Intrapersonal	An ability to recognize and understand his or her own moods, desires, motivations, and intentions.

He also proposed three distinct uses of the term "intelligence":

1. A property of all human beings (All of us possess these eight or nine intelligences)

2. A dimension on which human beings differ (No two people—not even identical twins—possess exactly the same profile of intelligences)

3. The way in which one carries out a task in virtue of one's goals (Joe may have a lot of musical intelligence but his interpretation of that Bach partita made little sense to us).

(Reference: Multiple Intelligences: The First Thirty Years, Howard Gardner, Harvard Graduate School of Education, © Howard Gardner, 2011.)

A detailed understanding of the evaluation of learning psychology and related sciences by many experts, including Dr. Howard Gardner, is ubiquitous and is out of scope of this book. In the context of facilitation, Gardner's Multiple

Intelligences have a practical application in managing group dynamics and optimizing both learning effectiveness and engagement of participants in the process of facilitation. The practical usage of the Multiple Intelligences is outlined in the following section.

MULTIPLE INTELLIGENCES USAGE IN WORKSHOPS

Hundreds and thousands of engagers, energizers and their combinations can be found in numerous books and practiced by facilitators from their own libraries. In the previous section we discussed what these are and where we might use them in sessions. Now, we focus on how to easily identify their types so that when we design agenda activities we will find their appropriate uses.

While it is not the only way to identify engagers/energizers for use in agendas, the most logical reference for identifying appropriate engagers and energizers is Dr. Howard Gardner's Multiple Intelligences Framework discussed earlier. The engagers and energizers may not fit exactly into the eight types of intelligences, but they do provide some context for identifying and incorporating them into the design of workshop agendas.

The concept of multiple intelligences is complementary, in that when you use one concept it may include one or more of the other concepts. For example: When participants are paired up to discuss the topic at hand and instructed to take a walk in the garden while talking, three intelligences are at work: Naturalistic, Bodily/Kinesthetic and Interpersonal.

Notwithstanding the formal role of a facilitator, I believe that facilitators are in the "entertainment business." They must use engagers and energizers to engage, energize and thus "entertain" using a variety of techniques that hold the attention of participants and promote better learning and solutions creation. The "entertainment" must be clean, dignified, and relevant to the mission of the session.

Verbal/Linguistic

Application Examples: Stories, debates, lectures, large and small group discussions, brainstorming, crossword puzzles, word games, audiotapes. Have the participants read from workbooks and participant materials rather than the facilitator reading it for them. Use metaphors, analogies, quotations, poems, humor, and stories to make a learning point or inspire ideas for developing solutions. I maintain a library of such items to draw from. Giving examples of your own stories or stories of historical events and personalities can be very effective. When using a metaphor or story about a war, ask permission of the audience first, because some people find these to be offensive. Avoid politics, religion, ethnicity, nationalism, and any other controversial or sensitive topic. Use phrases in the local language of the geography and culture. When I conduct session in Latin America, I research phrases in Spanish that may make a learning point while being entertaining. Show relevant videos and cartoons.

Logical/Mathematical

Application Examples: Numbers and patterns; deductive thinking; scientific demonstrations; logical and mathematical problem-solving exercises; logical, sequential presentations of content; computer programming. Create and provide questions or quizzes relevant to the topic at hand. Use games that show logic and define patterns. A variety of puzzles and experiential exercises are available in the marketplace to promote engagement. To test retention and reinforce learning create a workshop Jeopardy-like game show. Create documents about the topic with fill-in-the-blanks where the participants may collaborate with other team members to guess or generate data relevant to the learning or problem solving. This serves as the *Intrapersonal* intelligence type as well.

Visual/Spatial

Application Examples: Visuals, graphs, charts, diagrams and maps, visualization, presentations, mind mapping and visual organizers, painting, collages, visual arts, graphic symbols. Use the "rich picture" exercise. These are photographic cards that are distributed to the participants to create their own story or metaphor to express their understanding of the topic. For creating a strategy or vision, or for describing a process, break the participants into small groups, and have them draw a picture on a flip chart using multiple colored markers that represent the scenario under consideration. This serves as the *Interpersonal* intelligence type as well.

Music/Rhythmic

Application Examples: Singing, putting information into chants, hearing songs that teach, using music in the background, playing all kinds of musical instruments, linking old tunes with new concepts. Music is a way to create and change mood of the participants. When participants arrive in the room it is a good practice to have some soft music playing in the background. This helps them ease into the session. Similarly the music can be played during breaks and occasionally in thinking exercises (be aware that, in some cases, there are those who find music distracting). It is believed that music with about sixty beats a minute is generally soothing to the mind because the average resting heart is sixty seconds a minute. (The music of Handel, Vivaldi, Bach, and others of the 1600–1760 era of Western Baroque music falls in this category.)

Naturalistic

Application Examples: Field trips, outdoor activities, activities that help map connections, hands-on experiments, activity write-ups, walks in the park discussing topics covered in the workshop, and having natural lighting and plants in the room. Connecting with nature improves comprehension and promotes engagement and wellbeing. While planning the workshop, look to reserve a facilitation-friendly room or facility. One of the criteria should be that the room has natural lighting and plants. (Many hotel conference rooms are without any windows or natural lighting and are like modern-day dungeons where people spend a whole day without the benefit of fresh air or natural lighting.) Periodically, send the participants outside to a garden for a discussion, to brainstorm ideas, or to find solutions relevant to the topic under consideration.

After lunch, participants tend to be a bit lethargic. I use this as an opportunity to pair up participants and send them out for a nine-minute walk—a technique that I learned from Eric Jenson. It is called a "GLP walk" forming three questions. 1) What am I **G**rateful about? 2) What I have **L**earned so far in the session? 3) What is my **P**romise going forward? As they walk, one person shares the three answers with the second person and the second one then shares with the first. If the participants have not worked together before, this gives them an opportunity to network and reinforce their learning from the morning (they don't report out upon returning). This serves as the *Interpersonal* and *Bodily/Kinesthetic* intelligence types as well.

Bodily/Kinesthetic

 Application Examples: Creative movement, dance and physical awareness exercises; hands-on learning; competitive and cooperative games; using body language, gestures, and hand signals to communicate; breathing exercises. Every thirty minutes or so have the participants get up from their chairs and do an exercise. It is not only common sense but also proven by studies that physical movements are very healthy for body and mind. More oxygen goes to the brain when we get up and move around (it is believed to be twenty percent more oxygen).

When preparing the workshop agenda, design an activity that gets participants up and moving after about thirty minutes in inactivity. For example, a brainstorming activity using sticky notes that the participants generate and get up to place on a wall chart, or putting participants in groups to work around a flip chart producing ideas together. This serves as the *Interpersonal* intelligence type as well.

Create opportunities to stretch and breathe using a variety of exercises that are commonly available or that you have created on your own. I occasionally ask participants to stand up and perform the first stance of Tai Chi. (Caution: excuse those participants who may be physically challenged.) Think of magic tricks which may present a learning opportunity as well as creating movement, such juggling or using a rope trick to represent three dimensions of project management: Time, Resources and Scope. Laughing exercises are another tool that creates a mood of fun and relieves stress.

Interpersonal

Application Examples: Discussion and learning in a groups or sub-teams, paired sharing, conflict mediation, role playing, interactive games and

exercises, group and peer teaching, group brainstorming sessions, social gatherings, simulations. To promote this aspect of the intelligence, periodically have small groups brainstorm for solutions. The objective of this type of intelligence is to promote collaboration and cooperation among the participants. Brainstorming exercises and working in small groups to discuss and generate ideas are some of the examples of this type of intelligence. Use of Ideation Cards promotes dialogue, discussion and debate. Exercises where you ask the participants to create diagrams or maps on flip charts, serves the purpose of the *Visual/Spatial* intelligence type as well.

Intrapersonal

Application Examples: Independent study; self-paced learning; private time for study, reflection, or meditation; reflection and journal-keeping time; personal connections; self-esteem activities. Periodically during particular topics, ask participants to reflect on their own thoughts first and then report out or participate in a group brainstorming. The objective of this type of intelligence is to promote self-reflection and private space and time for learning or solving a problem through idea generation. Many brainstorming exercises have a step where the individuals first generate ideas themselves and then collaborate with others to prioritize options. Self-paced learning, independent study and meditation can be used both as engagers and energizers.

Often, it helps learners and participants in work sessions to use their idle hands and fingers on activities that allow them to think better and concentrate on the topic at hand. There are a variety of learning aids and so-called "thinkertoys" that facilitators can provide to the participants to promote latent self-reflection while actively participating in discussions. In my workshops I always provide items that are individually packed and are take away gifts for the participants. This serves to keep these items hygienic, by not allowing them to be reused in other workshops.

COMPLEMENTARY ENGAGEMENT TOOLS

Thiagi (aka Sivasailam Thiagarajan, Ph. D.), is the founder of The Thiagi Group, which develops games, simulations and performance-based experiential activities products for use in training. The games products are for effectiveness of engagement while having fun. Reference: www.thiagi.com.

INTEGRATION POINTS IN AGENDA ACTIVITIES

The following are some of the typical usages of engagers and energizers in the design of session/workshop activities. When designing the ROA, facilitators should identify and incorporate the most suitable items from among those shown here.

ICEBREAKER

An icebreaker is a ship or boat built for breaking passage through icy waters. In terms of people, it is a technique for easing tension or relieving shyness at a gathering of strangers. In sessions, icebreakers are used at the beginning of an activity such as the introduction of attendees. Icebreakers serve as engagers and can be energizers if used as a creative exercise.

KICK OFF

A kick off is used in sports to score a goal or gain ground by kicking a ball. In sessions, one of the first activities is typically a Kick Off by a senior executive to define the expected results and set the tone to inspire participants toward a common objective. This may be in the form of a presentation, video, or a speech. This is a form of an engager.

CONTEXT/FRAMING

Prior to the introduction of a new training topic or an agenda work item in a group session, the facilitator or the workshop manager sets the context of the topic about to be started. This is also referred to as "Framing" the topic. It provides an overall idea or picture of the new topic through the use of words, a story, a metaphor, or a relevant cartoon or video. This activity helps the participants prepare their minds with a scenario around the topic at hand. This is a form of an engager.

STATE CHANGE

State Change is a term commonly used to describe transitions between activities in a session. In training or learning transfer workshops or work sessions, there are several entry points for State Change such as the opening of a session or returning from breaks. The facilitator uses an engager or an energizer on these entry points to send a message to the participants to drop what they were doing and get ready to participate in the next activity. This can be a ritual established by the facilitator to get the attention of the participants. For example: "Please turn to your neighbor and say, 'Welcome back from break.' " or shutting off the music if it has been playing during the break.

SPECIAL BREAKS

Generally there are several breaks in a session: comfort breaks, coffee/tea breaks, lunch breaks, and others. It is common for participant to have low energy during afternoons, especially after lunch. Facilitators may send the participants in pairs to take a walk outside for few minutes with an assignment to review the morning's discussions on the topic of training or to solve a problem. Depending on the nature of the session and the audience, these breaks could be used for meditation activities or physical stretching exercises such as Tai Chi.

OPENING AND CLOSING

The opening of a session or the initiation of a new activity presents an opportunity to use engagers such as the use of a relevant story, a metaphor, a quiz, or a recap of previous activities' outcomes. The closing is equally important in order for the facilitator to end the session memorably by using an energizer that sends the participants off with a good memory of their experience in the session. It can be a celebration of the session or a successful conclusion to the project.

PRINCIPLES AND PHRASES, OR "ARTIE-FACTS"

To optimize the engagement of participants and to promote effective knowledge transfer for learners in any type of session, there are proven concepts that I have used over the years with success. These are a collection of phrases that pass on profound learning points to the participants while grounding them in sound principles that are consistent with adult learning and engagement concepts. When I facilitate workshops, I use what I call "Artie-Facts", a play on my Americanized name of Artie.

Participants have fun with them and they often include these Artie-Facts in their own library of tools. Here are some proven principles and useful phrases that may be used at any appropriate time during the facilitation of workshops where participants learn and are "entertained" at the same time. Such phrases become part of your "Style" and thus your "Brand" and leave a memorable experience in the minds of the participants.

MAKE "THE ROUNDS" BEFORE YOU MAKE THE ROUNDS

 In the medical profession when medical students are going through various stages of learning such as internship and residency, they make a lot of "rounds," meaning learning and conducting patient treatment processes and protocols to hone their skills. Eventually when they complete the training programs and get their license to practicing medicine, they start making their own "rounds," meaning visiting and examining the health of the patients under their charge.

"Make the rounds before you make the rounds" means that trainees must learn proper skills before they start practice on their own. I use this as a metaphor for the facilitator to gain agreements from all the relevant stakeholders in the Engage and Prepare steps of the Facilitation Process, so that when sessions are being facilitated, their expectations are well understood by the participants, other stakeholders, and the facilitators themselves. This is a critical success factor for the facilitator to deliver expected outcomes.

YOU ARE YOUR BEST TOOL

A competent facilitator has a library of methods, techniques and tools that can be used as appropriate for the topic at hand. Invariably there are situations that call for quick changes in approach and the facilitator has to think quickly and seamlessly transition to another method or tool that might work better. Your thinking and capability as a facilitator is the best tool above all others. Since it is such an important asset, facilitators should continually experiment, learn and improve their own toolkits.

CONNECTION BEFORE CONTENT

Before any meeting or work session of any kind, an introduction of the participants is essential. It is also important to clearly outline who is playing what role in a workshop. The participants need to know who among the attendees are playing the role of the session manager, the sponsor, the facilitator, and other roles. This promotes openness and a level of comfort among participants. After this is done, the content of the session is introduced.

VOICE IN THE ROOM (ACTIVATION PHENOMENON)

Human psychology is such that individuals attending a workshop need to be recognized in their own rights. During the opening of a session when introductions are being made, ask the participants to say something personal about themselves in addition to the standard, but important, "name, department, and organizational role statements." This demonstrates to the attendees that they are important and inspires them to be more participative, thus adding more value. If this is not done, they are likely to be less engaged and may not provide valuable input.

In his book *The Checklist Manifesto: How To Get Things Right*, Dr. Atul Gawande, who promotes the concept of checklists in operating rooms around the world, writes "The investigators at Johns Hopkins and elsewhere had observed that when nurses were given a chance to say their names and mention their concerns at the beginning of a case, they were more likely to note problems and offer solutions. The researchers called it an *Activation Phenomenon*. Giving people a chance to say something at the start seemed to activate their sense of participation and responsibility and their willingness to speak up."

MORE OF THEM AND LESS OF YOU IS BETTER

 Adults learn by doing and prefer hands-on engagement for solving problems or developing solutions. Whether the type of session is a knowledge transfer or a workshop, design the agenda activities in a way that most of the work is done by the participants and not by the session leader. This strategy promotes ownership by the participants and through this approach they are more engaged and energized, which is one of the objectives in a successful session.

DON'T BE A SAGE ON THE STAGE, BE A GUIDE ON THE SIDE

 This phase complements the one discussed before: More of them and less of you is better. Adults would rather be shown why they should do something and then provided guidelines to do an experiential activity or knowledge transfer. This is consistent with Dr. Knowles' theory of Andragogy as the art and science of educating and transferring learning to adults. Transform lectures into learning exercises and then guide the participants as a coach rather than as a sage on the stage.

LITTLE LEARNING IS BIG LEARNING

 Every bit of learning, no matter how small it may be, adds value to the receiver's knowledge. Little learning makes a big difference when participants in work sessions discuss, debate, and formulate new ideas. Therefore, along with the main topics of interest, pass along any other complementary learning as well. This section on Principles and Phrases is an example of how little learning is big learning.

FACILITATOR IS IN THE "ENTERTAINMENT" BUSINESS

Preparation of a work session and conducting it for success requires preparation, preparation and preparation, and the rest is theatrics—drama. I like to say that three-fourths is preparation and one-fourth is theatrics. Theatrics means using engagers, energizers, and relevant methods, techniques and tools to lead a session to a successful outcome. The facilitator is in the "entertainment" business. It's a different type of entertainment and stage, but a stage it is. Among others, storytelling, using humor, and a positive attitude should be the hallmark of a good facilitator.

BE A LIGHTHOUSE BEACON

As discussed in the Facilitation Leadership Framework, making constant eye contact and continually gauging audience perceptions provides the facilitator with state-of-the-session information. Based on these perceptions the facilitator can make adjustments and use tools such as engagers and energizers as needed and appropriate. Make it a habit to scan the audience as a lighthouse beacon.

ARE YOU COMFORTABLE WITH THIS?

This is an open ended question that I ask the groups throughout sessions at various logical points to ensure engagement and understanding of the topic being facilitated. It is better to avoid phrases such as "Do you understand?" that can be a bit condescending and close-ended.

TO ADULTS, GIVE ONE INSTRUCTION AT A TIME

When giving instructions about a training exercise; or work session exercise, give one instruction at a time. Adults are better at processing one instruction at a time; and once they understand what has to be done, they process the next one. Too much too fast may not stick.

PROCESS CHECK!

When I want to give instructions to a group and need their attention, I use the phrase "Process Check!" with color in my voice so everyone understands that I want to tell them something important.

ATTENTION GRABBERS (CLAPPING WITH PASSION)

In numerous occasions throughout sessions when I want to emphasize a point or learning, I clap my hands loudly. This grabs the attention of the participants and also shows my passion about the topic I wish to share with them. This, or any other such gesture to grab attention, becomes a ritual in the session.

TORIAEZU: IT'S OKAY FOR NOW!

In Japanese slang language, the term Toriaezu stands for *It's Okay for Now!* In Japan, some organizations use this phrase to build consensus when they have arrived at a certain stage of discussion and debate. One person calls out "Toriaezu" while bowing down per their social custom of respect. If all agree that it is okay for now, they call out "Toriaezu" with a bow as well. The topic gets closed and they move on to the next agenda item. I use this in all of my workshops to check with the group to determine whether they are ready to close a topic and move on. I find this method to be successful and the groups have fun with this approach.

KEEP CALM AND CARRY ON

During the battle of Britain in the Second World War, when London was being devastated with destruction and death, the British Government placed posters all over the city with the slogan: "Keep Calm and Carry On." This was to encourage people to stand up to the challenge and inspire them to go about their lives. In a work session, many things can go wrong ranging from facility issues and equipment problems to lack of full participation by attendees, difficult situations or people, and even to attendee personal issues. I find this phrase very useful in the role of a facilitator. No matter what happens in a workshop due to any reason whatsoever, a facilitator must keep calm and carry on.

CREATE AN HONORABLE CLOSE TO THE WORKSHOP

Occasionally a work session may not go as planned. Due to various reasons, the session agenda may have to be drastically changed and even canceled by the manager or the sponsor. In such cases the facilitator must always re-contract the agenda activities with the workshop manager/sponsor to accommodate any changes they might wish. The changed agenda may call for ending the workshop. If this occurs, the facilitator must begin wrapping up the closing items of the agenda such as Next Steps, Communication Plan, and agreement on the follow-up documentation of the workshop covered thus far. Then thank the participants and hand over the workshop to the manager/sponsor to formally close. This is an honorable way of wrapping up a session where unexpected issues cause it not to proceed further. Remember, the facilitator is responsible for the process and context, not the content. In conclusion of this chapter, let me share with you *The Facilitator's Mantra* inspired by my colleague Vince Arecchi.

Figure 5.2 – Facilitator's Mantra

Don't look for trouble
Throughout the facilitation process, pay attention to detail while keeping the big picture in mind. Stay within the professionalism of the art and craft of facilitation; and maintain upright behavior.

Don't let them see you sweat
The facilitator "stands alone" while facilitating a session. When unexpected situations arise manage those wisely using tactics, honest responses, integrity of intent. Always demonstrate self-confidence.

Keep calm and carry on
In any adverse situation, maintain your composure and deliver the agreed outcomes with patience, courage and professionalism.

Chapter 6
Tools

You are your best tool!
~ Unknown Author

In any type of work, there are two key concepts that are fundamental to success: The knowledge of the tools and techniques that exist to help you do your work and the skills to use them effectively. In this chapter, the frameworks, methods or methodologies, techniques, and tools are often referred to simply as "Tools" for ease of explanation. Also, the terms "meetings", "work sessions", and "learning sessions" may be referred to as "workshops".

For the four types of facilitation defined in the *Mahal Facilitation Framework*, while some tools are common to all, there are many that are type specific. For example, the basic agenda design of OARRs (Objective, Agenda, Roles and Rules), are common to all types, but specific methods may be type dependent:

- For *Strategies and Solutions*, strategic planning and problem solving methods are needed

- For *Programs and Processes*, project and process management methods are needed

- For *Learning and Development*, knowledge transfer methods are needed

- For *Cooperation and Collaboration*, team effectiveness methods are needed.

It would be a daunting task to identify and classify all possible methodologies, techniques and tools of the many professional practices in the four categories of the framework. That is outside the scope of this book.

In this section I have identified techniques and tools that may be commonly used in a variety of situations and session types. Consider this as a starter and foundational kit for a facilitator to work from. Each of the techniques has a description and process steps of how to go about using it, along with a template. While there are many ways each of the techniques can be used and improvised, I have included one proven usage to introduce the concept. Listed in the Resources Chapter are many other sources for methodologies, techniques and tools for your use as you progress in your practice.

In Chapter 7: Workshop Environment, there is a comprehensive list of supplies a facilitator should have on hand. A few of these supplies are outlined here as these are referenced in this chapter.

- *Cards, Meta-Cards, and Sticky Notes* are supplies used for writing ideas and data. These paper items come in many sizes and colors

- *Markers and Pens* are writing instruments for flip charts, cards and others. They come in many types, colors and sizes

- *Wall Charts and Flip Charts*: Wall charts are large sheets of paper that can be displayed on the facilitation room walls, and flip charts are standard items used in work sessions.

In the examples of tools we are about to explore, the concepts of adult learning methods and multiple intelligences—as discussed in an earlier chapter—are implied. When you use these tools, you may want to maximize the use of those concepts and principles.

COMMON TECHNIQUES THAT ENABLE OTHER METHODS, TECHNIQUES AND TOOLS

Workshops typically consist of these stages: *information gathering, analyses and synthesis, and action plans*. These may vary according to the subject matter and professional practice situations being dealt with. Each of these is generic in nature and used in just about every methodology, technique or tool one may encounter. Brainstorming types and the KJ Method are described in this section.

For a general brainstorming exercise, Figure 6.1, 6.2, and 6.3 visually show how brainstorming is done in stages.

- *Brainstorming* is the first stage, with participants generating their ideas on the topic of focus on sticky notes—one idea per sticky note. It is a technique that helps groups generate large amounts of information about any topic of interest for the purpose of further analysis. It is typically followed by the KJ Method of clustering the information.

- *Affinity Diagram (KJ Method)* is the next stage and is used to observe affinity among like ideas, and cluster them into themes relevant to the topic under study. This is a collaborative team effort to agree on the labels of the themes to make them meaningful to the audience. This technique helps organize large amounts of data/information into manageable, understandable themes and is used in conjunction with brainstorming. It is typically followed by further analysis and actions.

- *Analysis and Actions* is the third stage, where agreement is reached on the priority of these themes so that action can be taken to develop and implement agreed solutions. One method is "Dotocracy," a democratic method where majority rules. A set of sticky dots (or simply "dots") of any color are distributed to the participants to vote on their personal preference. They can distribute the given set of dots across many clusters or they may place all of their dots on one cluster. This method is very common and is widely used in organizations, and depends on the professional practice and unique purpose of the analysis—actions, initiatives, or projects may be created to achieve desired results.

The three following scenarios visually describe what the exercise output may look like; the data used is fictitious to illustrate learning points. Figure 6.1 shows how participants may identify ideas of interest and place them on a wall chart.

Figure 6.1 – Brainstorming with sticky-notes or cards

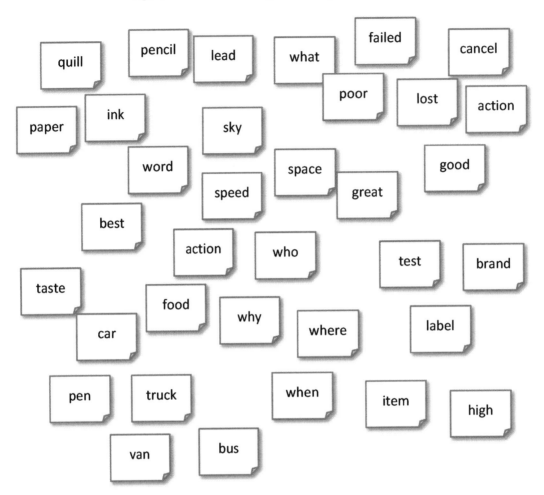

Figure 6.2 shows how participants may cluster like items into themes and label them with a meaningful title.

Figure 6.2 – Affinity Diagram (KJ Method): Clustering into themes

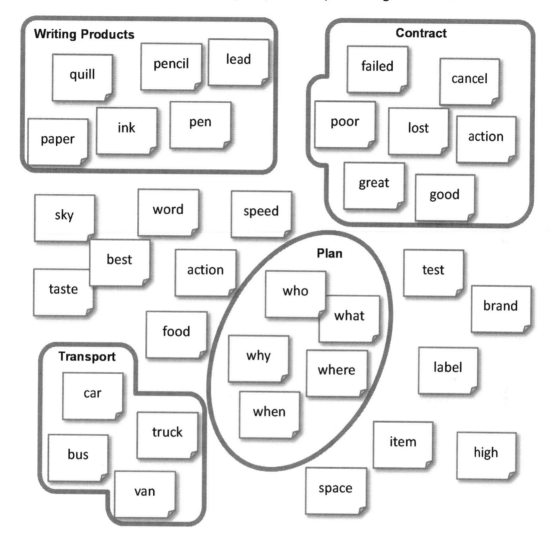

Figure 6.3 demonstrates the use of dots to prioritize clusters for actions.

Figure 6.3 – Analysis and Actions: Prioritizing using dots

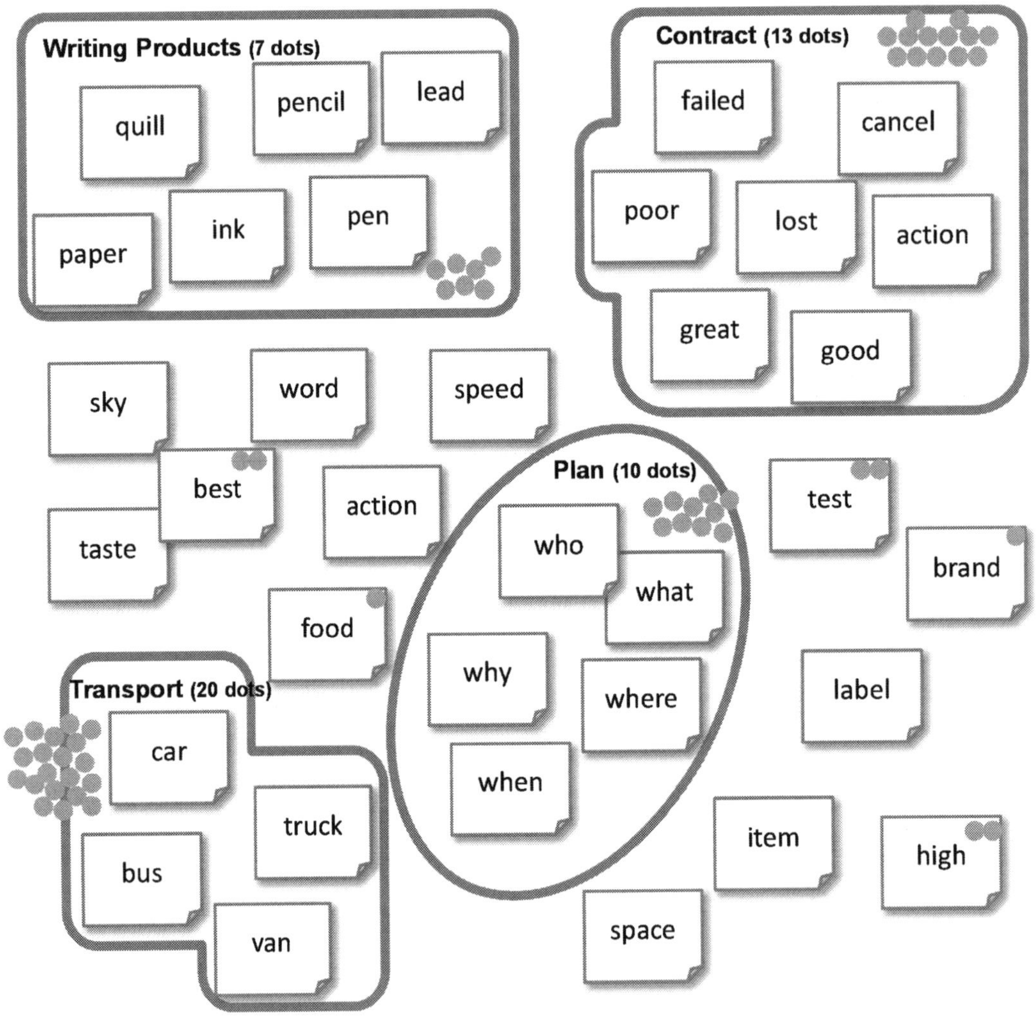

Writing Products (7 dots)
quill
pencil
lead
ink
pen
paper

Contract (13 dots)
failed
cancel
poor
lost
action
great
good

sky
word
speed
best
action
taste
food

Plan (10 dots)
who
what
why
where
when

test
brand
label
item
high
space

Transport (20 dots)
car
truck
bus
van

BRAINSTORMING

Since brainstorming in its many forms is the most common tool used in meetings and work sessions for gathering information, idea generation, and problem solving, it is useful to understand its origin, theory, and the types of brainstorming that can be used in a variety of situations.

Advertising executive Alex F. Osborn began developing methods for creative problem solving in 1939. He was frustrated by employees' inability to develop creative ideas individually for ad campaigns. In response, he began hosting group-thinking sessions and discovered a significant improvement in the quality and quantity of ideas produced by employees. Osborn outlined the method in his 1953 book *Applied Imagination*.

Brainstorming is a group or individual creativity technique that is used to find solutions to specific problems by gathering a list of ideas that are spontaneously contributed by its member(s). Osborn claimed that brainstorming was more effective than individuals working alone in generating ideas, although more recent research has questioned this conclusion. Today, the term is used as a catch all for all group ideation sessions.

Principles

Osborn claimed that two principles contribute to "ideative efficacy." 1) Defer judgment, and 2) Reach for quantity.

Rules

Following these two principals were his four general rules of brainstorming, established with the intention to:

- Reduce social inhibitions among group members
- Stimulate idea generation
- Increase overall creativity of the group.

Osborn's Four General Rules of Brainstorming:

1. *Focus on quantity:* This rule is a means of enhancing divergent production, aiming to facilitate problem solving through the maxim "quantity breeds quality." The assumption is that the greater the number of ideas generated, the greater the chance of producing a radical and effective solution.

2. *Withhold criticism*: In brainstorming, criticism of ideas generated should be put on hold. Instead, participants should focus on extending or adding to ideas, reserving criticism for a later "critical stage" of the process. By suspending judgment, participants will feel free to generate unusual ideas.

3. *Welcome unusual ideas*: To get a good and long list of ideas, unusual ideas are welcomed. They come from looking at problems from new perspectives and suspending assumptions. These new ways of thinking may provide better solutions.

4. *Combine and improve ideas:* Good ideas may be combined to form a single "better" good idea, as suggested by the slogan "1+1=3." It is believed to stimulate the building of ideas by a process of association.

Applications

Osborn notes that brainstorming should address a specific question. He held that sessions addressing multiple questions were inefficient. Further, the problem must require the generation of ideas rather than judgment. He uses examples such as generating possible names for a product as proper brainstorming material, whereas analytical judgments such as whether or not to marry do not have any need for brainstorming.

Brainstorming Groups

Osborn envisioned groups of around twelve participants, including both experts and novices. Participants are encouraged to provide wild and unexpected answers. Ideas receive no criticism or discussion. The group simply provides ideas that might lead to a solution and applies no analytical judgment as to feasibility. The judgments are reserved for a later date and action.

Criticism

Over the years there has been some criticism of the brainstorming technique in that individuals, when working in groups, may withhold their individual ideas and therefore "free ride" with others without fully participating, and thus undermine brainstorming. To prevent this possibility, ask the participants to first reflect on their own thoughts individually and then contribute their ideas to the larger group collectively.

Brainstorming Methods—Some Examples

Nominal Group Technique

Participants are asked to write their ideas anonymously. The facilitator collects the ideas and the group votes on each idea. The vote can be as simple as a show of hands in favor of a given idea. This process is called distillation.

After distillation, the top ranked ideas may be sent back to the group or to subgroups for further brainstorming. For example, one group may work on the color required in a product while another group may work on the size, and so on. Each subgroup will come back to the whole group for ranking the listed ideas. Ideas that were previously dropped may be brought forward again once the group has re-evaluated the ideas.

It is important that the facilitator be trained in this process before attempting to facilitate this technique. The group should be primed and encouraged to embrace the process. Like all team efforts, it may take a few practice sessions to train the team in the method before tackling the important ideas.

Group Passing Technique

Each person in a circular group writes down one idea and passes the piece of paper to the next person, who adds some thoughts. This continues until everyone gets his or her original piece of paper back. By this time, it is likely that the group will have extensively elaborated on each idea.

The group may also create an "idea book" and post a distribution list or routing slip to the front of the book. On the first page is a description of the problem. The first person to receive the book lists his or her ideas and then routes the book to the next person on the distribution list. The second person can log new ideas or add to the ideas of the previous person. This continues until the distribution list is exhausted. A follow-up "read out" meeting is then held to discuss the ideas logged in the book. This technique takes longer, but it allows individuals time to think deeply about the problem.

Team Idea Mapping Method

This method of brainstorming works by the method of association. It may improve collaboration and increase the quantity of ideas, and is designed so that all attendees participate and no ideas are rejected.

The process begins with a well-defined topic. Each participant brainstorms individually, then all the ideas are merged onto one large idea map. During this consolidation phase, participants may discover a common understanding of the issues as they share the meanings behind their ideas. During this sharing, new ideas may arise by association, and they are added to the map as well. Once all the ideas are captured, the group can prioritize and/or take action.

Electronic Brainstorming

This is a computerized version of the manual brainstorming technique and is typically supported by an electronic meeting system (EMS). Simpler forms can also be done via email and may be browser based, or peer-to-peer software can be used. With an electronic meeting system, participants share a list of ideas over a network. Ideas are entered independently. Contributions become immediately visible to all and are typically anonymous to encourage openness and reduce personal prejudice. Modern EMS also supports asynchronous brainstorming sessions over extended periods of time as well as typical follow-up activities in the creative problem solving process such as categorization of ideas, elimination of duplicates, assessment and discussion of prioritized or controversial ideas.

Individual Brainstorming

Individual brainstorming is the use of brainstorming in solitary. It typically includes such techniques as free writing, free speaking, word association, and drawing a mind map (a visual note taking technique in which people diagram their thoughts). Individual brainstorming is a useful method in creative writing and has been shown to be superior to traditional group brainstorming.

Questions Brainstorming

This process involves brainstorming the questions, rather than trying to come up with immediate answers and short-term solutions. Theoretically, this technique should not inhibit participation as there is no need to provide solutions. The answers for developing questions come from predetermined problems to be solved. Once the list of questions is set it may be necessary to prioritize them to reach to the best solution in an orderly way. "Questorming" is another phrase for this mode of inquiry, which was developed at MIT in the

1950s for getting a group of participants to come up with more creative solutions to problems.

Affinity Diagram (KJ Method)

The Affinity Diagram, aka KJ Method, is a special kind of brainstorming tool that is used to organize large amounts of data and information into groupings based on their natural relationship and the affinity of the topic for analysis. While information grouping has been done for a long time in the history of mankind, in the 1960s the Japanese anthropologist Jiro Kawakita formalized it as a technique. It is also known as KJ diagram/method, after Jiro Kawakita.

When to Use the KJ Method

The KJ Method is effective during brainstorming activities when large amounts of information are gathered and the information needs to be organized in a way that groups gain deeper insights by clustering the data into natural or logical themes. This is typically done using paper cards or sticky notes. The themes are then used to further create activities for project initiatives, or for achieving desired results. The process of this exercise is:

1. Teams from diverse backgrounds or cross-functional areas relevant to the topic at hand brainstorm ideas to gather information on meta-cards/sticky notes and place them on a wall chart.

2. Team members then look for logical affinity of the data among the individual cards and cluster them, forming "themes." Each theme is then given a title or a label for common understanding by the participants.

3. Based on the purpose of the exercise, teams then conduct further analysis, which may include prioritization of the themes to create initiatives for desired actions.

TOOLS CATALOGUE

For facilitating sessions of all types and topics, the number of methods, techniques and tools can run into the hundreds, if not thousands.

Nevertheless, it is still practical for the reader of this book to understand and learn the use of commonly used tools across a variety of situations. Once learned, a facilitator will be able to combine and improvise these tools to have even wider applications across facilitation needs. In this section a starter kit of tools is compiled for general facilitation needs.

In Table 6.1, the first column introduces the purpose of the tools listed alphabetically; the second column has the tool title and a unique identifier, followed by a brief description. Each of the tools in this catalogue has detailed instructions in how to use them in Chapter 12. The tool titles and the identifiers in Table 6.1 are cross referenced in Chapter 12.

Table 6.1 – Tools Catalogue

Purpose	Tool
Assessment for Developing Strategies and Solutions	**SWOT Analysis (Tool #1)** SWOT (Strengths, Weaknesses, Opportunities and Threats) Analysis is an assessment technique that helps a group understand the current state of an area of interest and then determine actions for a future state. This assessment can be conducted for an organizational unit, business area or product or a service—or any other topic of interest.
Assessment for Knowledge Sharing and Continuous Improvement	**After Action Review (AAR) (Tool #2)** After Action Review (AAR) is a knowledge management and continuous improvement technique. It may be conducted after a project is completed, a class has concluded, or a work session has finished. This assessment helps determine what went well and what can be improved in future.
Banners and Charts	**Banners And Charts (Tool #3)** Most of learning is non-conscious learning, or learning without trying to learn. Among the most effective engagement tools are banners or charts put up on the walls for the participants to have a visual throughout the workshop. These large banners/charts of three feet by four feet may include methodology frameworks, inspirational information, and other relevant graphics to "educate" the participants.
Creative Visualization	**Rich Picture (Tool #4)** Rich Picture is a team exercise used by the group of participants to create a visual of what they may see as the current state or the future state of things they may be analyzing. This is also an effective icebreaker and a team collaboration exercise.

Purpose	Tool
	Picture Simulation (Tool #5) Picture Simulation is a team exercise used by the participants to create a visual scenario using pictures that metaphorically represent their role, their situation, or any activity of interest the individuals or teams may want to share and communicate with others. This can serve as an icebreaker and is a way to consolidate and confirm understanding of some topic at hand.
	Graphic Templates (Tool #6) Graphic templates are visual tools for information gathering and for documenting and presenting work session outputs in an engaging and interesting format. These templates are generally created by artists and digitized for use by enabling editing. Also see Chapter 10.
Communication	**Communication Guideline (Tool #7)** A facilitator must communicate with clients, workshop participants, management, and other stakeholders. A basic set of communication guidelines are essential to use as a checklist when sending written communication or when the workshop outputs are disseminated.
Data Model	**Data Model (Tool #8)** The data model provides a common language among the business users, managers, business analysts, data analysts, process analysts, and technology analysts to have a meaningful dialogue around the information requirements of getting work done and creating systems applications.
Decision Making	**Dotocracy (Tool #9)** In brainstorming exercises where a large amount of data is gathered, there is generally a need to decide and prioritize items that matter most for change or implementation. There are numerous ways of decision making. Using "Dots" (sticky dots), the colored labels, as a tool for building consensus and decision making is very effective in workshops. This is called "Dotocracy".
Group Dynamics	**Managing Challenging Participants And Situations (Tool #10)** The success of a session (meeting, training or solutions facilitation), depends on the productive participation of the attendees. Participants may present a variety of behaviors in the session causing disruption. A facilitator must manage challenging participants and situations effectively to ensure harmony of the session so that attendees are fully engaged to achieve the agreed objective.

Purpose	Tool
	Body Language (Tool #11) Body language also plays a major role. Different from spoken words, body language is the non-conscious and conscious transmission and interpretation of feelings, attitudes, and moods, through body posture, movement, physical state, position, and relationship to other bodies, objects and surroundings.
Ideation / Innovation	**Lotus Blossom (Tool #12)** The Lotus Blossom concept developed by Yasuo Matsumura of Japan, is a technique of ideation for new ideas, problem solving and exploring options for implementing existing solutions. In the Lotus Blossom, you start with a problem or area of concern in the center core of the Lotus Blossom template. Ideas for possible solutions are then generated around the core area of concern.
	Biomimicry (Tool #13) Biomimicry (from *bios*, meaning life, and *mimesis*, meaning to imitate) or learning from nature, is a design discipline that seeks sustainable solutions by emulating nature's time-tested patterns and strategies.
Information Gathering	**Brainstorming (Tool #14)** Brainstorming in its many forms is the most common tool used in meetings and work sessions for gathering information, generating ideas, and solving problems. It is typically followed by the KJ Method of clustering the information into themes for actions.
Information Identification	**Information Identification Guide (Tool #15)** Organizational "objects" or components are entities that constitute an organization. These are the parts that make the organization whole. When information is to be analyzed for a variety of reasons, those entities need be recognized, understood, documented, and communicated in a methodical manner. This is an effective technique for identify objects of interest. Examples: Processes, Systems, Roles, etc.
Introductions	**Voice In The Room (Tool #16)** In any meeting or session the participants must share who they are, who they represent, and why they are there. This is essential to creating a cohesive team for the duration of their participation. In addition to this idea, one must add an additional concept to promote the ideas of Voice-in-the-Room as discussed in Chapter 5. Examples include Icebreaker tools and Personal Shields.

Purpose	Tool
Laughing Exercise	**Laughing Therapy (Tool #17)** It is a well-known and proven fact that laughing is good for health and healing when used in good humor and as enjoyment. This exercise, when practiced in workshops, creates a relaxed and positive energy while promoting better engagement, team building and celebration of success.
Library of Resources	**Personal Library Of Facilitation Resources (Tool #18)** Individuals planning to be great teachers and passionate facilitators must have a comprehensive library available to them at all times. This includes a systematic plan for reading, collecting, cataloging, and maintaining a library, containing artifacts that include stories, quotations, articles, methods, techniques, tools, and more.
Listening Skill	**Listening Ladder (Tool #19)** The facilitator must be a good listener throughout the facilitation process and its phases: Contract, Prepare, During the Session, Conclude and Evaluate. Good listening ensures that you don't miss out or misunderstand what the client or participants say. Listening Ladder is a useful technique to be aware of and to sharpen your listening skills.
Presentation	**Presentation Skills (Tool #20)** Making presentations is inherent to a facilitator's role. Facilitators must be aware of presentation fundamentals and build competency to be effective in this role. Good presentation skills include understanding the purpose and audience, and organizing materials to deliver them in an engaging and effective manner.
Problem Solving	**Brainwriting (Tool #21)** Brainwriting is a way to solve problems using intuition. Individuals find a quiet area where they can think and reflect on the challenge that needs resolution. By concentrating on the question to be addressed and thinking through possible solutions, an individual arrives at possible options. These are presented to the larger group for inclusion in brainstorming exercises.
	Lateral Thinking (Tool #22) Lateral thinking is a technique of solving problems through an indirect and creative approach, using reasoning that is not immediately obvious and involving ideas that may not be obtainable by using only traditional step-by-step logic.

Purpose	Tool
Process Improvement	**Process Scope Diagram (Tool #23)** Simply put, a process may be defined as "how work gets done," a series of logical activities that produce an outcome for stakeholders. To analyze a business process for improvement, the first step is to understand all the components that constitute a process and create a Process Scope Diagram. Then conduct a "health check" to identify areas of improvement and plan changes to the process. **Process Map (Tool #24)** Processes are a series of activities that produce products or provide services for stakeholders. To understand how these steps flow and pass the output of one to become the input of the next, a visual diagram is very effective and desirable. These diagrams are called Process Models or, simply, Process Maps. They are typically developed after the Process Scope Diagram has been created.
Prioritization of Options	**Priority Matrix (Tool #25)** In brainstorming exercises where a large amount of data is gathered, there is generally a need to prioritize the items of the greatest importance to enable change or implementation. A Priority Matrix helps classify information based on level of effort and perceived value.
Questions Development	**Appreciative Inquiry And Kipling's "Framework" (Tool #26)** Two techniques of framing questions are outlined in this section: Appreciative Inquiry is a way of asking questions that focuses on what is good and can be better rather than on the problems only. Rudyard Kipling's poem *The Elephant's Child* has a practical framework for creating a list of questions.
Questions Brainstorming	**Questions Brainstorming (Tool #27)** This approach works very well when an organization wants to launch a new product or service. There may be many unknowns ranging from cost, profit, technology, logistics, etc. At this stage they don't know what they don't know. Questions Brainstorming is a very effective approach to developing the right questions to be addressed in an organized way. This technique is sometimes called Q-Storming.
Relaxation	**Relaxation Response – Meditation (Tool #28)** In facilitation there are many situations where participants need be relaxed in order to effectively engage in a session. One of the most widely recognized methods of relaxation is meditation. For participants in work sessions to relax, they need to be aware and watchful of what is happening by being alert and in the moment.

Purpose	Tool
Responsibility Charting	**<u>RACI (Tool #29)</u>** RACI (Responsible, Accountable, Consulted, and Informed) responsibility charting is a technique used for establishing roles and responsibilities of cross-functional work teams. This approach enables team members to systematically define activities and to identify decision points and the relationships of those activities and decisions to each of their roles, thus leaving no ambiguity about how work is to be accomplished.
Root Cause Analysis	**<u>Ishikawa (A.K.A. "Fishbone") (Tool #30)</u>** Ishikawa (a.k.a. "Fishbone") is a trouble-shooting technique that is topic-specific for determining causes and their appropriate fixes. One example is cause and effect analysis using the Ishikawa Method (a.k.a. Fishbone Method). Using a template that looks like a fishbone, a brainstorming exercise is conducted to identify root causes of certain outcomes. This analysis becomes the basis for identifying a solution.
Storytelling	**<u>Stories And Such (Tool #31)</u>** Whether it is a religious institution, a non-profit/for-profit organization, or any group in society, stories are powerful tools for communicating ideas and messages. In facilitation, storytelling is extremely effective for opening sessions, framing the topics of focus, and inspiring and engaging participants. These stories can range from commercial, historical, spiritual, and geographical in nature to any possible genre you can think of. Storytelling is an art and must be practiced by facilitators.
Strategy Development	**<u>Strategy Development And Value Proposition (Tool #32)</u>** All organizations and organizational units achieve their vision through the development and execution of their strategies. The strategies begin by defining the Value Proposition in terms of products and services, followed by all the supporting enablers such as people, processes, technology and infrastructure. There are numerous approaches to developing a strategy. This is a practical and easy to understand approach for workshop settings.
Thinking and Decision Making	**<u>Six Thinking Hats (Tool #33)</u>** Six Thinking Hats was created by Edward de Bono in his book *Six Thinking Hats*. *Six Thinking Hats* is an important and powerful technique for information gathering and decision making. It is used to look at decisions from a number of important perspectives. This forces you to move outside your habitual thinking style, and helps you to get a more rounded view of a situation. It allows necessary emotion and skepticism to be brought into what would otherwise be purely rational decisions. It opens up the opportunity for creativity within Decision Making.

Purpose	Tool
Visual Dictionary	**<u>Visual Dictionary (Tool #34)</u>** Visuals are very effective tools for the mind to make meetings, facilitation, and training interesting and engaging. While everyone is not a professional artist, there is an artist in everyone. We all have the ability to draw simple icons and images on flip charts, presentations, and charts that are relevant to the topic at hand. This provides an alternative to computer-generated visuals. This library is a starter kit which that can be copied and drawn. After some practice you can add your own images to the dictionary.
Voice Care	**<u>Voice Care: Tips On Caring For Your Voice (Tool #35)</u>** For facilitators (including trainers and speakers), talking for long and uninterrupted periods, particularly in multi-day sessions, can be very fatiguing to one's vocal cords, so the "trick" is to try to rest them at various intervals. Of course, this is easy to say but how do you do this when you're conducting an all-day workshop? Carol Weiss Riches, a member of the National Association of Teachers of Singing (NATS) presents very useful information and common sense strategies in Chapter 12.

HELPFUL HINTS

You are your best tool. The term "best tool" may mean different things to different people. In the context of a facilitator's role, consider the following criteria to be the "best tool." Build a comprehensive library of tools and by experimenting and improvising, continuously create newer and even hybrid tools that may have innovative uses in your workshops. This can only happen by reading, learning, observing other masters of this craft, and taking calculated risks by trying them out. Master the tools of your trade and use the right tool for the right purpose at the right time. This will make you your Best Tool.

Chapter 7
Workshop Environment

Plan your work and work your plan!
~ Author Unknown

The success of a meeting, group workshop, or training session depends a lot on the facility, the seating arrangement, the food, the ambience, and other important considerations. It is the responsibility of the facilitator to identify the requirements for the workshop environment to the client during the preparation phase of the facilitation process. It is also wise for the facilitator to check the facility ahead of time if possible and go there to set up the room ahead of the workshop start time. The desirable aspects of a workshop environment are a facilitation-friendly room, proper seating setup, working equipment, adequate and appropriate supplies, and safety and security. Before we go into the details of a facilitation-friendly environment, let's identify basic guidelines that should govern the workshop environment.

GUIDELINES FOR FACILITATION-FRIENDLY FACILITY

Space: The facility should be large enough to host the participants in a way that they are comfortable in seating and doing team exercises around the room without being claustrophobic (tight space inhibits full participation). Any special needs considerations must be respected.

Lighting: Natural lighting in the room is preferred because it promotes better engagement of the participants. (Most hotel meeting rooms are like "dungeons" with no natural lighting; they are generally designed for the convenience of food caterers rather than the convenience of the participants).

Wall Space: Plenty of free wall space is required in order to hang wall charts and wall paper for conducting hands-on exercises. (Be careful that markers are not used directly on the paper in case the color bleeds.)

Equipment: All equipment such as seats, tables, projection screens, overhead projectors, and flip chart easels should be in good working order. Support staff should be available to provide technical assistance.

Food: The facility should have breakfast, coffee/tea, lunch, and afternoon snacks available. Napoleon Bonaparte observed that "an army marches on its belly." Likewise the workshop participants are more attentive and engaged when food and beverages are available during the session.

ROOM SETUP

Depending on the type of workshop, plan ahead for an appropriate seating arrangement. See Table 7.1 for suitable options and patterns in planning seating.

Table 7.1 – Seating Patterns

Pattern	Advantages	Disadvantages
Conference	Good for meetings, problem solving and planning discussions. Implies the need for a lead person.	Only the person in charge of the session may "lead." Promotes formality. Movement for exercises is limited.
Classroom	Facilitator/Trainer controls the session with visuals accessible to all. May be good for computer-based training.	All participants cannot see each other, which inhibits open discussion. Difficult to form small teams for exercises.
V-Shape	Facilitator controls the session with visuals accessible to all. Participants can turnaround easily and have discussions in teams.	All participants cannot see each other, which inhibits open discussion to some extent. Difficult to form small teams from across the tables.

Pattern	Advantages	Disadvantages
U-Shape	Promotes group discussion by all participants. The facilitator can have closer proximity to all. The visuals are accessible.	Some participants may not be able to make eye contact with others. Difficult to mix and match small teams for exercises.
Semicircle (No desks)	Promotes open discussion. Led by the facilitator. Good for sensitive topics and relevant problem solving. Visuals/presentation are accessible to all.	Participants look up to the facilitator to lead and may not initiate dialogue on their own.
Clusters	Promotes collaboration and teamwork in each of the clusters. If there are reasonable numbers of chairs that face the front then everyone can have a good view of the facilitator and the visuals/presentations.	Too many chairs around each table would require some participants to always have to turn their bodies and heads toward the front, causing discomfort.
Round	Promotes equal participation, group discussion and problem solving. Participants can see each other. Facilitator steps out and guides from outside the circle. Good for discussion on sensitive topics and problem solving (table "barriers" are eliminated). The facilitator may sit in the circle and stay passive, letting the participants take the lead.	Visuals and presentations are difficult for all participants to see. Is limiting in the event the group size has to be expanded.

Aside from the need to facilitate very large group of people—which is not in the scope of this book—an average workshop size for one facilitator to handle would be twelve to sixteen participants (plus or minus two). If the participants exceed twenty (plus or minus two) in number, a co-facilitator may be required. The rule of thumb is one facilitator for up to sixteen to eighteen participants (this count depends on the nature of the topic and the workshop).

The room should be prepared well in advance of the arrival of participants so that when they arrive, they feel welcomed and ready do the work or to learn, as the case may be. Play appropriate background music. Have a welcome chart that is colorful and inviting at the entrance with the title of the workshop and the date(s). Make flip charts ahead of time and display them on the walls, including the one for workshop guidelines and rules.

a) *Workshop Effectiveness Guidelines (Table 7.2) Chart.* These are sometimes referred to as *Rules*. As a facilitator I decide what guidelines to establish. However, I do ask the participants if they would like to add to the pre-made list. These pre-made guidelines avoid having to create them from scratch during the workshop.

b) *Parking Lot Chart.* This refers to a chart that is typically used during workshops to jot down items that need to be addressed at a later stage or during breaks. Instead of parking lot, I sometimes prefer to use the title *Ice Box.* I explain that the purpose of this chart is to write down items that need be addressed later—or, rather, keep them "fresh." I do this to differentiate myself from those who have been using the Parking Lot for years.

c) *Jargon Chart.* People tend to use their organization-specific acronyms, which in many cases, are not even common knowledge among their peers. I introduce this as a rule that whenever participants use an acronym or some unique phrase it is their responsibility to write the full word/definition on a sticky note and place it on the jargon chart. This becomes their workshop dictionary and is documented with the deliverables.

d) *Next Steps Chart.* The next steps chart is meant to identify the actions to be agreed upon at the end of a session. The pre-made chart saves time at a later stage of the session.

e) *Name Tent Cards.* Provide name tent cards and markers for each of the participants and ask them to write their names on both sides of the tent card and place them on the table in front of them. Having them write their names on both side of the tent card helps those who are sitting behind to know the names of those in front of them. This is particularly helpful in a classroom-style seating arrangement.

f) *Agenda Chart.* The agenda can be made into a large chart and placed on the wall for common reference as well as being made available in the room. Even when agendas have been electronically communicated, many people walk in without a hard copy or don't have their laptop with them. They will expect the agenda to be available at the workshop.

g) *Learning Aids.* I always provide items that participants can "play" with during a session. This helps them in their concentration as "the hands want to do something." The items should be individually packaged and are not meant to be shared with others. They are giveaways for the participants to take with them. Avoid silly putty or "play items" that people share because those can be unhygienic (if someone has a cold, the items may pass on the germs). Also avoid items such as Kush Balls and such because people will throw them at each other and may cause injury to someone.

h) *Table.* Prior to a session, place on the participant's workspace, the workbook, a writing pad, a pen/pencil, a learning aid "toy," a name tent card, and a water bottle or a glass (with water available in a pitcher). Make sure that the participants have comfortable elbow space and that their space is not crammed.

EQUIPMENT

These days, facilitators and participants bring their laptops and clients often provide the projectors to cut costs. (Hotels tend to charge too much for the use of their projectors.) In addition to having your presentation files on your laptop, carry the files on a flash drive as a backup solution. If your laptop malfunctions, the files can be loaded on a temporary/borrowed one. Another good practice is to send an e-mail to yourself, attaching the presentation files. Ensure that you have enough flip charts, with easels, to conduct team exercises. Security is an important consideration for times when the meeting room is not in use, such as when participants take their lunch breaks. Check with the facility staff regarding the safety policy. The room may need to be locked for breaks to ensure that laptops and other items of value are secured.

FOOD

The food arrangement is typically handled by the client. The facilitator must work with the client to make sure that the food is healthy and meets the needs of the participants. The availability of coffee, tea, and other beverages throughout the duration of the workshop is preferred. A buffet lunch catered in the meeting room saves time versus walking to the cafeteria for a sit-down lunch. Afternoon snacks should be healthy snacks such as fruit, rather than the cookies, biscuits, and brownies that people generally prefer. The sugar content of these foods tends to make participants lethargic and the facilitator is then challenged to keep them attentive and participative for the remainder of the session.

WORKSHOP ENVIRONMENT CHECKLIST

- ☐ Sufficient access to the facility prior to the workshop time
- ☐ Safe place to be (ensure emergency exits)
- ☐ Seating pattern (and comfort)
- ☐ Lighting quality (including natural light)
- ☐ Air quality (humidity between 60% and 80% and temperature between 66° and 74°)
- ☐ Location of rest room facilities
- ☐ Equipment, technology, white boards, flip charts with easels
- ☐ Participant workbooks/handouts and learning aids
- ☐ Wall Charts (Welcome, Ice Box/Parking Lot, Jargon, Agenda, and other charts)
- ☐ Posters (relevant to the topic as well as inspirational and motivational)
- ☐ Name tent cards and markers
- ☐ Water, food and beverages
- ☐ Supplies
- ☐ Live plants (if possible)

☐   Music (mild and soothing).

FUTURISTIC FACILITATION ROOM

With more awareness of the value of facilitation, progressive and forward-looking organizations should think about the designs and patterns of facilitation rooms to optimize the engagement of the participants, whether for meetings, group facilitations, or transfer of knowledge. These rooms should enable adult learning methods including use of engagers and energizers, and have multimedia technology, natural lighting, flexible and configurable/portable seating with desks, usable wall space for white-boarding and hanging charts, and all relevant supplies readily available.

WORKSHOP EFFECTIVENESS GUIDELINES

Table 7.2: Workshop Effectiveness Guidelines, contains suggested ideas for managing a workshop. Facilitators must come prepared with these guidelines already created, and communicate them at the beginning of the workshop. A printed chart placed on the wall is helpful in periodically reminding the participants of agreed upon rules.

Table 7.2 – Workshop Effectiveness Guidelines

Guidelines for Workshop	Rational
Respect the value of time.	Establish strict standards for starting and returning from breaks. The facilitator must set an example by always being punctual. (As the saying goes, one may have a watch but still not know the value of time).
Participate Actively: You will get out what you will put into the session.	Ensure that the participants understand that they have a stake in the outcome of the session.
Respect diverse opinions.	This promotes participation by all.
Hold one conversation at a time.	This helps avoid distractions and disengagement by others.
Use laptops on breaks only, unless required by the session or for note taking.	Unless laptops are required for the session, limiting their use helps lessen distractions. Some people use their laptops for copious note taking. This exception should be allowed by making everyone aware of this option.
Keep cell/mobile phones ON, but take them outside for	There is always a chance of a personal or professional emergency for an individual. The facilitator should not take

Guidelines for Workshop	Rational
responding to calls.	on the responsibility for such unforeseen circumstances.
Keep work areas clear of all trash during the workshop.	Participants tend to leave their empty coffee cups and snack plates lying around on the tables. Instructing them to clear their trash during breaks promotes cleanliness and order on tables that are shared with others.
Don't leave any organizational proprietary material lying around in the room after closing. Take it away and dispose of it appropriately.	Particularly in hotel conference rooms, leaving organizations' documents exposes the documents to risk. Industrial intelligence, aka spying, is real. Help participants mitigate the risk of exposing important information.
Any others?	Ask the participants if they would like to add any additional guidelines.

SUPPLIES CHECKLIST

Supplies are a critical enabler to any workshop; the success of the outcome depends on the timely availability of relevant supplies. In the preparation phase of the facilitation process, a complete list of needed supplies is identified through the development of the Running Order Agenda (ROA). For an engaging and interactive one- or two-day workshop with around sixteen participants, a complete set of supplies might fill a small suitcase on wheels.

There are facilitators and trainers who take pride in stating that they travel around the world leading sessions using only their laptops. It is clear that either they don't understand adult learning and engagement principles and practices that maximize effectiveness, or they are lazy and take the easy way out. They do injustice to their participants, their sponsors, and their craft, not to mention to their own development.

Internal facilitators in organizations should have a small facilitation kit that they can easily take into conference rooms—sometimes on short notice. The supplies kit is one important aspect of the professionalism of a facilitator. A suggested supplies checklist that can be customized by any facilitator is outlined here. (Supplies in this list include activity reminders as well).

PRE-WORKSHOP ACTIVITIES
☐ Contact Information (contact person, role, phone number, e-mail, etc.)
☐ Facilitator's Running Order Agenda (ROA)

☐ Participant Agenda (multiple copies)
☐ Requirements for a facilitation-friendly facility and other relevant requirements
☐ Requirements for food and beverages
☐ Communication to participants by the client/manager/sponsor
☐ Pre-work instructions to the participants
☐ Presentation files, participants workbooks
☐ Travel and lodging arrangements
☐ Workshop supplies.

IN-SESSION SETUP ITEMS
☐ Participant notebooks (training), handouts (facilitation)
☐ Agenda copies
☐ Wall charts, banners
☐ List of attendees
☐ Name tent cards
☐ Sign-in sheet
☐ Evaluation forms
☐ Business cards and marketing material.

Note: Try to use environmentally friendly material where possible, such as recycled paper that promotes sustainability.

IN-SESSION ACTIVITY SUPPORT ITEMS
☐ Facilitator's kit
☐ Learning aids (facilitation "toys" with purpose)
☐ Paper rolls (48 inches x 24 yards)
☐ Paper cutting knife
☐ Masking tape "artists' non-stick" and/or painters blue-tape (also Duct tape as backup)
☐ Markers of all sizes (water soluble markers to avoid damage to clothes)
☐ Sticky notes of all sizes (largest to smallest sizes)
☐ Sticky dots of various colors
☐ Glue stick and pushpins
☐ Pads of paper and pens/pencils
☐ Engagers and Energizers (e.g., creativity aids)
☐ Camera with charger

- ☐ Laptop equipment with charger; wireless remote
- ☐ Backup flash drive with presentation files
- ☐ Music speakers.

PERSONAL SUPPORT ITEMS
- ☐ Water bottles
- ☐ Snacks, throat soothers
- ☐ "Entertainers Secret"—for dry throat (this is available in select pharmacies)
- ☐ Band-Aids
- ☐ Hand sanitizer
- ☐ Toothbrush and toothpaste (to keep mouth fresh after meals).

The evening before and on the day of facilitation, avoid eating onions, garlic, etc., which may carry an offensive smell.

HELPFUL HINTS

- Always verify the workshop facility by seeing it yourself, if possible. Even if you request a facilitation-friendly room by giving all the details, be mindful that it is not always easy for others to visualize your specific needs.
- During the breaks, you won't always have time to eat snacks or the luxury of taking a leisurely lunch because, as the facilitator, you are always arranging charts and other items for the next activity. Therefore, pack your own snacks to eat on the fly in the event of time constraints.
- Have you ever heard the saying, "Pack your own parachute"? Well, you should pack your own supplies. One critical missing supply item can inhibit your performance and the quality of the output—in addition to causing frustration over the lack of a needed tool.

Chapter 8
Virtual Facilitation

Chapter By Angela Gallogly

As virtual facilitators, we have the capacity to transform the organizations we are working with to share information and ideas more completely, to decide and implement more successfully and to move through changes more creatively.
~ Cheryl Kartes, CTF and ToP Mentor Trainer

With the globalization of many organizations and an increasing prevalence of remote and virtual teaming, virtual facilitation has become more of the norm than the exception. Many facilitators confess to initial skepticism when an opportunity to facilitate virtually appears. How can the engagement, energy and collaboration essential to an effective facilitated event be replicated in the sterile confines of an online meeting?

Fortunately, experience and technology are demonstrating that not only is virtual facilitation a suitable alternative to traditional face-to-face facilitation, it can be a more advantageous option in some cases. Virtual facilitation can overcome the boundaries of geography, physical space and budgetary constraints. It can allow different facets of an organization the opportunity to come together in a virtual forum to achieve session goals efficiently and economically.

Virtual facilitation can be successfully applied to all elements of the Mahal Facilitation Framework: *Strategies and Solutions* to set direction, *Programs and Processes* to optimize execution, *Learning and Development* to enhance Human Capital and build competencies, and *Cooperation and Collaboration* to enhance engagement. Virtual sessions can take many forms: telephone conferencing, video conferencing and collaborative groupware/web-based tools. It is important to note that the type of virtual setting used can vastly impact the way the event is planned and facilitated.

Facilitators that are inexperienced with a virtual setting often make the mistake of creating a Running Order Agenda (ROA) based on a face-to-face session and attempting to use it in a virtual session. This approach is flawed. Just as a running order is customized to each event, organization, session objective, and so on, so must a virtual session be customized to the virtual setting. Some of the components listed in Chapter 3: Facilitation Process will differ in a session that is facilitated virtually. Therefore, the ROA of a virtual meeting must be different.

There are certainly challenges with virtual facilitation that must be addressed. Awareness of the potential pitfalls is important so that preventative measures can be planned and implemented. *Engagement, Relationship, Communication, and Technology* are some of the more common challenges, as depicted in Figure 8.1.

Figure 8.1 – Virtual Facilitation Framework

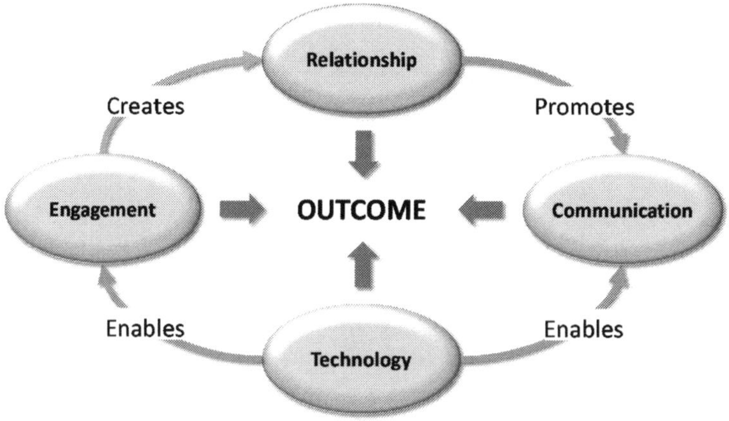

Engagement creates Relationships; Relationships promote Communication; Technology enables Engagement and Communication; and all four factors deliver desired Outcome.

ENGAGEMENT

The importance of engagement was established in Chapter 5. Adults learn best through experience, and this is particularly important within a virtual session. Many participants succumb to the temptation to multi-task during a virtual session. They check e-mail, look at their phones, read items on their desk, and more. The ability to multi-task is a myth. Adults can certainly move from one area of focus to another quickly, but no one can successfully focus on two things simultaneously. Any time participants allow their attention to be pulled away from the facilitated session, engagement is diminished.

The facilitator must imbed tools and techniques into the curriculum that will keep the attention of the group. It is also important to establish session ground rules that discourage multi-tasking. Much of the groupware available provides assistance with this challenge. For example, some display a symbol or an icon by a participant's name when that participant has selected a different screen on the computer monitor. If the facilitator sees that several people have begun to stray from the groupware screen, he or she can call a "process check" and encourage participants to reengage.

The facilitator can reference the participant list to ensure that every person is included in discussion. Each person can be called on to provide input or answer questions. Using peoples' names promotes focus and participation. If participants know they might be called on at any moment, they will be far more likely to listen intently. The facilitator can assign roles such as timekeeper or note taker to promote involvement. Additionally, most groupware includes chatting panels, annotation tools, virtual white boarding, polling, and testing functionality. These are excellent for promoting engagement. Participants should be engaged early and repeatedly throughout the session.

It is beyond the scope of this book to compare and contrast all of the virtual tools and platforms that are available, but it is important to note that there are many options and variations on the market. Technology is constantly changing and improving. If virtual facilitation is new to an organization, the facilitator may have the opportunity to influence the decision of what virtual platforms will be used. Each tool has different functionalities and costs and should be well researched before licensed. Look for free trials and testing opportunities when analyzing platform candidates. If a tool is already licensed by the organization, fully explore the tool's functionality. Many organizations fail to maximize the use of the tools already available.

Beyond technology, the facilitator must imbed more traditional methods of engagement, including visuals, questioning techniques, and experiential activities. The Adult Learning theory of Dr. Malcolm Shepherd Knowles and the Multiple Intelligences theory of Dr. Howard Gardner still apply. The inexperienced virtual facilitator must resist the risk of becoming a presenter rather than a facilitator.

The virtual facilitator should keep session length to no more than two hours, if possible. Even the most well-intentioned participant can lose focus if the session runs longer. If logistics make a lengthier session necessary, breaks should be planned every hour. Encourage participants to get up and move during breaks, increasing oxygen flow and creating a more alert contributor.

RELATIONSHIP

Icebreakers are intended to help participants get to know one another enough to feel comfortable participating in session activities. The best results are achieved when participants feel comfortable sharing their perspectives and honest opinions. This personal connection can be more challenging in a virtual environment. Therefore, the facilitator must provide time in the agenda for this connection to take place.

It is also helpful to invite only those participants that are essential to the meeting. The bigger the group, the more difficult it is for people to connect. Additionally, larger groups are more vulnerable to disengagement. Audio conferencing and groupware tools can allow a hundred or more participants, but this is only suitable for presentations or short briefings, not for a session where facilitation is truly required. The key to preventing these obstacles is awareness and preparation. Table 8.1 outlines potential solutions for the challenges of virtual facilitation. This is not an all-inclusive list but is intended to help generate ideas for the facilitator planning a virtual session.

COMMUNICATION

Communication can be more challenging when facilitating virtually, especially if the virtual setting lacks video conferencing. Without video, the ability to communicate nonverbally is lost. Communication experts have differing opinions on the actual percentage of communication that takes place via body language, but nearly all agree that it is greater than fifty percent. This means that a virtual facilitator has lost the ability to dynamically read the "cues" of the participants, and participants have lost the same ability to communicate nonverbally with the facilitator and with other session attendees.

Groupware attempts to compensate for this gap by providing feedback tools. Symbols (often referred to as emoticons) can be selected to indicate agreement, confusion, approval, etc. The facilitator can train participants in the use of these tools and encourage their use within the session. The icons are typically displayed next to the participant's name, allowing the facilitator to get instant, nonverbal feedback from participants. With or without the use of groupware, the facilitator should remember that any time nonverbal cues are missing, more detailed and thorough communication is needed to ensure understanding. This will take more time and should be accounted for in the running order.

TECHNOLOGY

Communication can also be more challenging due to technology malfunctions. Facilitators should anticipate the possibility of audio feedback delays and the potential for background noise that can often occur during audio conferencing. Virtual facilitators often create session rules for communicating virtually. For example: participants should state their names before speaking and should avoid speaking over one another. In groupware settings, attendees can use the "raised hand" symbol to indicate the desire to speak.

Participants need to have the appropriate hardware, software and online connections required by the virtual tool being used. Additionally, both the facilitator and participants should be trained and comfortable with the technology. Facilitators must be sensitive to the fact that some people are uncomfortable with new technology, especially if they have been accustomed to in-person meetings in the past. To maximize participation, facilitators should help these individuals by providing training at the beginning of the agenda and providing encouragement and positive reinforcement throughout the session.

Table 8.1 – Virtual Facilitation Framework Checklist

Virtual Challenge	Potential Solutions
Engagement	☐ Call participants by name ☐ Assign roles such as timekeeper and note taker ☐ Include ground rules that discourage multi-tasking ☐ Design activities that require participation by all ☐ Create questions that involve all session participants ☐ In groupware, use virtual whiteboards, chatting panels, annotation tools, polling, and quizzing ☐ Provide breaks ☐ Keep sessions as brief as possible (no more than two hours)
Relationship	☐ Create an icebreaker that helps participants connect ☐ If using groupware or audio conferencing, divide larger groups into breakout teams for discussion ☐ Plan for both facilitators and participants to share photos of themselves if video conferencing isn't available ☐ Share stories and personal experiences to build rapport
Communication	☐ Speak more slowly ☐ Use visual aids ☐ Check for understanding ☐ Use Groupware feedback tools that mimic body language
Technology	☐ Understand technical requirements and communicate to participants ☐ Practice using technology prior to session ☐ Ensure participants have set up and tested technology prior to session, if possible ☐ Imbed opportunities for participants to practice using the virtual tool at the beginning of session

An important caution related to the use of virtual technology: with all of the functionality available, facilitators often make the mistake of over-stimulating their participants. It is possible to play music, show a visual, animate text, annotate, and speak all at the same time, but research shows this can actually hinder the absorption of the content. It's simply too much input to process. When planning to use these functionalities, less is more. For example, show a visual and speak, *or* show text and allow participants to read. It is fine to use all of the technology, but resist using it all at once.

Last, the facilitator should create contingency plans for technology failures.

PREPARATION

Preparation for virtual events can be more time consuming than for face-to-face sessions. Many facilitators estimate preparation to take twice as long as for a face-to-face session, particularly if the facilitator is new to virtual facilitation. The preparation of the agenda and running order must be detailed and thorough. A practice session using the audio, video or groupware is recommended. Does the video or audio have a delay? Do the videos, visuals or polling questions function as planned? For a successful session, the facilitator must feel comfortable with both the content and the technology. Whether the setting is face-to-face or virtual, a lack of preparation can become a barrier to the success of the session.

MEETING CLOSE AND FOLLOW-UP

As with any facilitated event, the meeting close and follow-up is important. If actions are required from meeting participants, they should be clearly communicated and documented. The facilitator should communicate what form of follow-up documentation should be expected: action lists, notes, summary reports, saved whiteboard files, or other documentation. One of the biggest values of groupware is the ability to save working files and whiteboards. Groupware sessions and video/audio conferences can be recorded and replayed for reference, if needed. *Note:* if the facilitator plans to record the event, it should be pointed out to all session participants.

GLOBAL FACILITATION

Since virtual meetings can span large geographic areas, the virtual meeting should be scheduled with all impacted time zones in mind. Select a time that is most central for all participants. If meetings will be recurring, rotate the time when they are scheduled to assist participants in each time zone. If facilitating globally, be aware of potential cultural and language differences. If there are language differences, allow additional time in the agenda for communication. In these situations, paraphrasing and checking for understanding are essential to effective communication. (Refer to Chapter 9 for more information on cross-cultural facilitation.)

COMPETENCE

Becoming an effective virtual facilitator is no different than developing any other facilitation skill. With every virtual session, facilitators gain experience and build confidence. It can be valuable to build opportunities for feedback into the first few facilitated sessions. Ask participants what worked well in a session and what would have made it better. Facilitators should also take time for self-reflection and evaluation. What went well, and what should be changed or adjusted in the future? Recall Chapter 2 and the definition of competency (the combination of knowledge, skills, and motivation/attitude). It can be beneficial to view the introduction of the virtual platform as an exciting opportunity rather than a difficult situation or obstacle.

THE VALUE

Consider the many benefits of virtual facilitation: less travel, less expense, increased inclusiveness, and the opportunity to explore new ways of working together, to name only a few. Virtual facilitation can provide tremendous value for an organization, but it also provides rewards for the facilitator. There is an opportunity to build new skills and grow in the facilitator role. The virtual world is truly limitless in terms of opportunities for creativity and collaboration.

Compare Table 8.2 with the in-class running order described in Chapter 3 Table 3.7. Note the different methods, techniques and tools that have been planned to accommodate the virtual setting. The training objectives and content remain the same.

Table 8.2 – Virtual Running Order Agenda Example

		Virtual SWOT Analysis Training		
Date and Time:		DD, Month, YYYY 10:00 AM to 11:30 AM – US EST (1.5 Hours)		
Location:		Online Groupware Room		
Objective:		To provide training to Human Resource employees in the use of SWOT Analysis: (Strengths, Weaknesses, Opportunities and Threats).		
Roles:		Workshop Sponsor: VP of Human Resources, Manager ABC, Coordinator DEF, Participants, HR Staff, Facilitator *Name 1*		
Online Setup:		Have a welcome visual displayed. Prepare a virtual whiteboard for parking lot. Prepare and upload slide presentation.		
Preparation:		Research history of SWOT. Prepare a PowerPoint deck on SWOT. Confirm session invites. Provide agenda and handouts in PDF to HR project manager prior to session for distribution. Test all groupware functionality. Complete online practice session to run through content with the technology.		
	Topic	**Description and Deliverable**	**Estimated Time**	**Resources**
		State Change		
1	Kick-off	Purpose of the workshop and expected outcomes by VP of HR. (Engager)	5 minutes 10am-10:05am	Executive presentation in PowerPoint
2	Groupware Training	Poll participants to gauge level of experience with groupware. Demonstrate use of feedback and annotation tools to participants. Have all participants practice using these tools. (Engager)	5 minutes 10:05am-10:10am	Software tools
3	Introductions	(Engager/Energizer) Facilitator: Display a map of the United States. Participants shares their name and role within the organization. Then they use annotation tool to place a checkmark where they live. Participants share one fun fact about their community/city that others might not know. Facilitator shows photo of self and introduces self and background.	10 minutes 10:10am-10:20am	US map Digital photo

4	Review SWOT Definition	SWOT definition and purpose. (Framing) Phrase: "Do you know what the biggest room in the world is?" (Pause) "Room for improvement." SWOT is a proven tool that helps identify strengths, weaknesses, opportunities and threats. Give examples. (Engager) Ask participants to click green checkmark (feedback tool) if they are following and comfortable with pace.	10 minutes 10:20-10:30am	Software tools
	Comfort Break	Encourage participants to stand up, stretch, and take a short walk.	7 minutes 10:30-10:37am	
	State Change	(Energizer) As participants return to online session, encourage them to use annotation tools to complete an online word search or crossword puzzle together as quickly as possible. Puzzle will have key SWOT terms and definitions.	3 minutes 10:37-10:40	Electronic puzzle
5	SWOT Instructions	(Activity) By the Facilitator The origin/history of SWOT as a tool commonly used. Variation of SWOT is SPOT (P stands for Problems) when to use which is important (Call on specific participants to ask what might be the reason for one versus the other). Show how S is to leveraged, W is to be converted to S, O is to be leveraged and T to be minimized. SWOT can be used to create improvement actions with time frames. Check for understanding using groupware polling, feedback and annotation tools.	30 minutes 10:40-11:10am	Presentation Slides
6	Summarize/ QA	(Engager) Ask each person to think of one area in HR where they may be able to use SWOT for continuous improvement. (Energizer) Have each person present their contribution and type it on the virtual whiteboard.	10 minutes 11:10-11:20am	Virtual whiteboard with headings
7	Wrap-Up & Next Steps	Identify any next steps and thank the participants for their time. Create a memorable close using a story and a related or symbolic visual (Engager).	10 minutes 11:20-11:30am	Story, visual

#	Item	Description/Steps
	Supporting Enablers	
A	Techniques and Templates	SWOT Template
B	Presentation Slides/Charts	PowerPoint deck, prepared virtual white boards with headings
C	Equipment	PC, groupware, phone or headset with microphone for VOIP audio. Time Zones Clock
D	Engagers/Energizers	Electronic games, map, photos, story library
E	Supplies	Notebook, pen, highlighter
F	Participant Notebook/Handouts	PDF with SWOT template
G	Post Workshop Actions	TBD in the workshop
H	Communications	HR Project Manager will send out the groupware invite, agenda and electronic materials to all participants. Will also arrange for HR VP to kick off the workshop.
I	Logistics	Quiet workspace to lead virtual session, reliable technology and adequate broadband. Time Zones considerations.

HELPFUL HINTS

- A virtual session, like any facilitated event, has inherent challenges. Awareness, followed by planning and preparation, are key to minimizing these obstacles.

- For a successful session, the facilitator must feel comfortable with both the content and the technology. Run through the facilitation plan, the Running Order Agenda and the Participants Agenda using the technology that will be used in the session.

- Embrace virtual facilitation as an opportunity rather than a challenge. Create opportunities for participant feedback and strive to continuously improve.

Chapter 9
Cross-Cultural Facilitation

Chapter by Catherine Mercer Bing

Do unto others as THEY would have you do unto THEM.
~ Author Unknown

With globalization, employees around the world are interacting more often with each other, both virtually and in face-to-face work sessions. Even in companies that are not global, multiculturalism in the workplace is a business imperative that must be understood and managed effectively. All four aspects of the Mahal Facilitation Framework: *Strategies and Solutions, Programs and Process, Learning and Development,* and *Cooperation and Collaboration* are impacted by cross cultural considerations. They all require communication and since learning is pervasive in these areas, this chapter focuses on the foundations of design and delivery of materials, specifically taking into account the aspects of culture that impact learning and effective communication.

The "Golden Rule" often quoted as *"do unto others as you would have them do unto you."* is all about how *you* want to be treated. In the cross cultural world, we need to treat people the way *they* want to be treated. The definition of "respectful" for a person in one culture may in fact be disrespectful to someone from another culture. This could include shaking hands (men and women do not shake hands in certain cultures) or it might be making direct eye contact (in other cultures this is extremely rude), and so forth. The quotation at the beginning of this chapter: *"Do unto others as THEY would have you do unto THEM,"* sets the tone of this chapter.

The concepts and principles introduced in this chapter focus on all aspects of learning, program design, and development—they apply equally to facilitation of workshops. The chapter also will include some activities to use when developing trainers and facilitators who work in multi-cultural settings. Let's start with an example of why culture is an important topic to include in this publication.

EXAMPLE OF CULTURAL BLUNDERS IN LEARNING FACILITATION

Zoe McWinters has been asked by Rhonda McCarthy to teach a half-day class in Project Management. She appreciates being recognized for her expertise and works very hard to create a half-day program with a PowerPoint presentation on the topic and some participant exercise materials as handouts.

Zoe is opening her program with a little exercise that helps participants get to know each other. She has a mixed cultural class. She introduces the program with what she calls an "icebreaker" by asking each individual to introduce himself/herself and tell the class their most important achievement.

When it gets to Zeng Ding's turn, he simply says his name and that his achievement is that he was selected to attend the class. He then looks at the floor. Zoe encourages him to tell more about his experiences and achievements by saying, "Zeng, I am sure you accomplished some achievements that are more important than attending this class, please tell us about just one thing so we all can get to know you better." He continues to look at the floor and the silence becomes uncomfortable. She waits until the silence gets unbearable, shrugs her shoulders then calls on the next person in the class. About a third of the remaining participants choose to say that their greatest accomplishment is being in the class.

For the next exercise, Zoe asks questions specific to the pre-work and gets about three or four people (out of fifteen) who are eager to share their answers. After calling on those participants a couple of times each, she comments, "I am sure some of the rest of you know these answers too. Don't be shy. Mariza, do you know the answer to my question?" Mariza does not answer, so Zoe calls on one of three participants who seem to know all the answers.

*Early in the program Zoe is asked by one of the participants what PMBOK®
(Project Management Body of Knowledge) stands for. She praises the
participant who asks and says, "There are a lot of acronyms in this business. If
I use any you do not know, please ask me to clarify them." She gets no other
questions about acronyms during the session.*

*At the break and within earshot of some of the participants, she complains
bitterly to a male colleague that the class is not very responsive. She suggests
that maybe it is because they are not from the US but from various cultures that
they are just not prepared for the content. She is anxious that she is falling
behind in covering the materials and now will have to speed up the program
delivery.*

*After the break, she starts right on time and calls out to the participants who
are not in the class when she wants to start. After the break she attempts to
lighten things up a bit by telling a humorous story about an older gentleman
who felt he was too old to learn new things, but eventually was proved
wrong…a few in her class responds with a laughs, but for most, the story seems
not to have the intended effect.*

*Zoe continues to provide exercises for practice in the subject matter and puts
participants into small groups to present their findings. They seem to work
better without her involvement. She ends the morning with a high level of
frustration, but is glad she got through all the materials in the time she was
assigned. When her evaluations come back she is surprised that she got pretty
good marks even from the students who did not seem very involved in the
learning.*

(Test Yourself) Questions:

What did Zoe not do well? Provide some specific examples.

What did Zoe do well? Provide some specific examples.

(See the end of the chapter for the answers.)

This example clearly illustrates the frustration for facilitators and learners
and highlights the need for general cultural sensitivity in any learning
situation. When learners are culturally diverse, a lack of cultural

metacognition on the part of the facilitator leads to making things more difficult—not easier as facilitation implies.

This example is full of cultural missteps. The outcome of the session was to be learning. However, the facilitator focused on her preferences (which were culturally bound to what works for her or in her culture). She employed methodologies and questioning techniques she had used in similar situations with mono-cultural learners. She did not understanding the cultural drivers for the people who attended this program. She showed a lack of respect for the learner and did not understand how to engage them to learn. So, instead of learning, she may have caused headquarters Human Resources to lose respect (face) and she may have contributed to frustrating the employees who attended her session rather than making learning easier.

We use this example to point out how easy it is to be perceived as "culturally insensitive." Here are just some of her errors:

1. Zoe called on each person and asked them to reveal something about themselves—in group orientated countries this is highly unusual and very difficult.

2. Zoe embarrassed Zeng Ding by calling on him and pushing for a "better answer." In some countries education is highly valued so he was correct that this program may have been his greatest accomplishment.

3. She misread his looking down after answering—which in his culture is a sign of respect.

4. She focused on getting the materials completed in the time frame not on whether the learning actually took place.

5. She missed the discomfort she caused when she talked about an older gentleman learner being wrong.

6. She mistook the meaning of the silence. (Did she think it was disinterest or inability?) So she concentrated on those participants were willing to offer their individual opinion.

To repeat...to facilitate is to "make easy." In making it easy for learners, we must better understand what cultural values and experiences the participants bring to a learning scenario. Effective facilitators will adjust to the learning styles of their participants. To be a good facilitator in multi-cultural learning situations and workshops, we must have a sense of what makes learning and involvement easier for participants.

Our cultural values, learned early and deeply embedded, drive what we think is acceptable behavior throughout each stage of creating and delivering a learning situation. If we, as professionals are not careful, we will allow our unconscious bias to define *how* we design and deliver learning opportunities. We will base the "how we do what we do" on our preferences, not those of others—thus making it more difficult for them and easier for us. To prevent this we need to start with some basic culture terminology.

CULTURE TERMINOLOGY

Cultural dimension are complex and do not exist in isolation. However, we need to start with some basic culture terminology so we understand what Zoe missed in her facilitation. Dr. Geert Hofsgtede has done some of the widest and longitudinal research in the cultural field and his dimensions and orientations will be used as the framework to talk about culture in this chapter.

Figure 9.1 – Cross-Cultural Facilitation Framework

"Cultural Metacognition refers to a person's reflective thinking about his or her cultural assumptions. Cultural metacognition seems to have a strong effect on how people effectively collaborate across cultures." (Harvard Assistant Professor Roy Y.A. Chua)

Dr. Geert Hofsgtede's research highlights five dimensions:

1. Individualism (Individual or Group Orientation)
2. Power Distance (Hierarchical or Participative Orientations)
3. Certainty (Need for Certainty or Tolerance for Ambiguity)
4. Achievement (Achievement or Quality of Life Orientation)
5. Time Orientation (Long or Short Term Orientation).

These terms will be used and examples given to help facilitate understanding for the reader.

TERM DEFINITIONS

Cultural definition: Culture is the collective programming of the mind that distinguishes the members of one group or category of people from others.

Individualism Dimension: Individualism is the degree to which decisions are made for the benefit of the individual, or for the benefit of the group. The orientations for this dimension are Individual or Group Orientation.

Power Distance Dimension: Power Distance is the degree to which inequality or distance between those in charge and the less powerful (subordinates) is accepted. The orientations for this dimension are Hierarchical or Participative Orientation.

Certainty Dimension: Certainty is the extent to which people prefer rules, regulations and controls, or are more comfortable with unstructured, ambiguous or unpredictable situations. The orientations for this dimension are Need for Certainty or Tolerance for Ambiguity Orientation.

Achievement Dimension: Achievement is defined as the degree to which we focus on goal achievement and work or quality of life and caring for others. The orientations for this dimension are Achievement or Quality of Life Orientation.

Time Orientation Dimension: Time Orientation the extent to which members of a society are prepared to adapt themselves to reach a desirable future, or the extent to which they take their guidance from the past and focus on fulfilling their present needs and desires. The orientations for this dimension are Long Term or Short Term Orientation.

CULTURE APPLIED TO LEARNING

In the world of learning and development, the definition of "facilitator" is, "…one that helps to bring about an outcome (as learning, productivity, or communication) by providing indirect or unobtrusive assistance, guidance, or supervision (for example, the workshop's facilitator kept discussion flowing smoothly…)." While training is a type of facilitation (learning transfer); it can be different in application from general facilitation in some cultures.

- A trainer is defined as "a person who teaches" implying that the trainer possesses the knowledge and "owns" the learning. A subject matter expert who is introducing his/her specialty to others is a good example of this.

- The difference with facilitation is that facilitators create an environment where the learning can take place. This implies that the learner owns the learning. The facilitator creates the scenarios for thinking things through and helping the learners come to conclusions without necessarily being "told" the answers.

This is an important distinction when working across cultures. In more of the Western cultures, it is incumbent on the students to be responsible for their learning.

In many High Power Distance cultures, it is the professional who is responsible to make sure learning occurs. In India, for example, for thousands of years under their caste system, the Brahmins were held in highest regard. People of this caste were found in professions including Hindu priests, artists, teachers, technicians. And not unlike the religious leaders in Early Europe, they were educated and could read. In many parts of the world, teachers—and learning—are still held in high regard. In India, due to cultural nuances such as deference to elders and deference to those who are better educated, there is still pressure on those delivering the learning materials to "own" the learning. It is incumbent upon them to assure the students learn.

An Aspect of Power Distance

Hierarchical Orientation = Employees are expected to follow through as ordered; they are less likely to suggest solutions for problems unless specifically asked/told.

Participative Orientation = Employees are expected to go to managers to report on progress and suggest approaches to problem solving.

In Western cultures, it is more incumbent on the students to be responsible for their learning.

OTHER DIFFERENCES

You might be surprised that in some countries, class discussion is not the norm and, in fact, it is uncomfortable for certain students to speak up or challenge other students' opinions. This is likely due to Group Orientation (as opposed to Individual Orientation). When a culture values harmony, there is less likelihood of challenging discussions.

There is less likelihood of learners (or employees for that matter) asking challenging questions or bringing up challenging issues. There is a preference for a group response and opinion, rather than an individual one. Small group work in learning situations is very comfortable. In many Western schools, small group work or students helping other students is still seen as "cheating." (Thus reinforcing the Individual and Achievement Orientations – do it yourself attitudes in Western countries and competing against others as opposed to Group and Quality of Life Orientations which include behaviors such as cooperation and helping each other – typical in Asian and other cultures.)

An Aspect of Achievement

Achievement Orientation = Assertiveness, competitiveness and ambition are virtues.

Quality of Life Orientation = Modesty, solidarity, and helping others are virtues.

TENSION BETWEEN INDIVIDUAL OR GROUP ORIENTATIONS:

In collectivistic [Group Oriented] cultures, people will assess themselves in terms of their ability to maintain harmonious relationships with others. One's identity is the group: the family, neighborhood, school, or the company where one works. Words for the concepts identity and personality in terms of a person separate from the context do not even exist in the Chinese and Japanese languages. (Source: Cross-Cultural Consumer Behavior: A Review of Research Findings. Journal of International Consumer Marketing, 23:181–192, 2011 ©2011 Marieke de Mooij and Geert Hofstede).

Again in the West, we expect people to have and express their own opinions, but this is not the case in much of the rest of the world. As an example, a consultant was providing a program for the Biostatistics and Clinical Programming department of a major global pharmaceutical company. The class was in held in the US where over 70 percent of the members of the department were of Chinese descent. The class was being observed by an American who attended due to an interest in the subject. At the first break he approached the facilitator and said, "I noticed that you are reluctant to call on anyone in the class and you keep putting them into small groups. Why don't you just call on people?"

He was unfamiliar with the scenario that if an instructor were to call on an individual and that individual did not know the answer it would be the instructor who lost face, not just the student. He was uncomfortable with the approach to attend to the preferences of the learners – to come up with a group opinion rather than an individual one. If he has been the instructor, the learner would not have had it easy.

An Aspect of Individualism

Individual Orientation = Speaking one's mind is a characteristic of an honest person.

Group Orientation = Harmony should always be maintained and direct confrontations avoided.

TENSION BETWEEN TASK AND RELATIONSHIP

This same person then asked, "Well wouldn't it be faster to get through the materials if you just called on one person instead of spending time letting them discuss in small groups?" Here he was expressing a lack of understanding of the difference between task and relationship.

An Aspect of Individualism

Individual Orientation = Task prevails over relationship.

Group Orientation = Relationship prevails over task.

He felt that the need to get through the material (the task) was more important than making sure the students were comfortable, which consists of getting to know and trust their learning colleagues better through small group interactions.

STAGES FOR DEVELOPING LEARNING IN TRAINING OR WORKSHOPS

In the learning and development world, there are a series of steps to assure that the investment in attendees is effective and ensures change. Let's focus on each stage of the process of creating learning situations and workshops. We will look at each through the lenses of culture and "facilitation"—making it easy.

These stages include:

1. Data Gathering/Needs Assessment
2. Program Design
3. Methodology Selection
4. Delivery Style
5. Creation of Participant Learning Materials.

STAGE 1: DATA GATHERING/NEEDS ASSESSMENT

To design an effective learning situation it is most helpful if the outcomes required are made clear to the designers (to make it easier for them to succeed in their part of the process). Of course this process of gathering information involves people in the company who are typically not the "end user" (learners). They might be the department head, a functional head, supervisors, or executives, in addition to the learners. If we are going to facilitate a needs assessment/data gathering conversation, how do we make it easy for them to provide information? Here are a few culturally nuanced ideas on how to be effective as well as culturally appropriate:

A. For those with a more Individual Orientation and Participative Orientation—they might prefer to just answer an emailed set of questions.

B. For someone who prefers a more hierarchical approach:
   1. Arrange a formal introduction to that person by someone at his/her level before trying to collect information.
   2. Treat the person with the information with the utmost respect.
   3. Behave formally when conversing.

C. If the interviewee has a Need for Certainty (as opposed to a Tolerance or Ambiguity)
   1. You will be more effective if you provide the questions you intend to ask well in advance so they know what to expect.
   2. Clearly express how long you need to spend with them so they know what to expect.
   3. Make clear what you will do with the information they give you in advance of the collection of the data.

STAGE 2: PROGRAM DESIGN

Designing effective training requires a thorough understanding of the needs of the trainees. And knowing what outcomes are expected helps inform content and the design methodologies used. Modification becomes even more critical to the success of a training program when it is presented to audiences of different nationalities or audiences of multiple cultural backgrounds within a single program.

Once the issues and sponsor-determined outcomes have been clarified, the program design begins. Now you need to think about the learners and what will make it easier for them. What is different when design of learning is cross-cultural?

An Aspect of the Certainty Dimension

Need for Certainty = Comfortable in structured environments.

Tolerance for Ambiguity Orientation = Trying new approaches is encouraged.

Things to consider:

- Amount of clarity varies (Need for Certainty). Note: Need for Certainty and Tolerance for Ambiguity are orientations describing the Certainty Dimension.

- Process expectations may differ (Power Distance).

- Expectations of leader responsibilities may differ (Power Distance).

- More difficult to build relationships (Individualism).

- Communication is more difficult.
  - o English is an acquired language for many and they may have learned British English so there is greater likelihood for misinterpretation.
  - o Accents may be more difficult to understand.

- Thinking processes may differ (convergent vs. divergent thinking).

- Willingness to disagree/differ/discuss may differ.

Here are some strategies:

A. Many cultures expect and want a lot of context, background and history. Others want "the bottom line." Western designers tend to forget the importance of providing much more information than they think is needed. Appendices, pre-readings (both of which are task focused) and discussion groups or focus groups prior to the formal session (relationship oriented) and various other techniques help bring the learners to the same understanding of context in ways that meet their cultural preferences.

B. In high Need for Certainty Cultures, training takes longer, sometimes as much as twice as long.

C. In high Power Distance Cultures, the program and the presenter need to be introduced by the sponsor (a senior executive) to give "weight" to the importance of the time spent.

STAGE 3: METHODOLOGY SELECTION

In choosing methodologies, designers of domestic programs already understand the importance of sensitivity to the needs and preferences of the trainee. Designers must consider regional preferences, levels within an organization, and/or differences between functions.

Senior management usually wants training in shorter bursts rather than full days. Middle management and lower levels of the organization seem to prefer the opportunity to practice what they learn, which takes more time than many executives are willing to give. Short trigger stories, which are designed to stimulate thinking and learning, should contain different content for training software engineers than they would for those in marketing, customer service, or facilities management.

Program designers use information about the variety of cultural approach preferences, as measured by assessments like ITAP International, Inc.'s Culture in the Workplace Questionnaire™ (to CWQ), to help inform their choice of varied methodologies for activities.

Both trainers/instructors and facilitators cannot assume that all participants in a learning situation come with the same framework, understanding, context, willingness to learn, and so forth. Anyone who has conducted learning sessions (or managed more than one person at a time) will tell you that everyone is different. A tactic that may work with one person may completely fail when used with another. This is most true when working with or helping people from a variety of cultural backgrounds. Here is what you might want to do differently to align with various cultural orientations:

- Need for Certainty. Prepare a detailed agenda and distribute it in advance. Include time allotments and stick to the time schedule. Make sure you leave ample time for all the activities and debriefs. Put more time in the schedule rather than cramming too much into the program.

- Allocate more time for every topic/stage.

- Limit the topics to be covered and list them using simple, clear sentences.

- Clearly define outcomes desired.

- Give adequate notice of the session (more than you might usually give).

- Send program materials out well in advance for review. People who speak English as an acquired language may need extra time to make sure they understand what will be covered. They may read English better them they speak it and they may need time (in advance of the program) to review the materials.

- Do not assume that because a particular methodology typically works well in your home country that it also will work well in a multi-cultural setting. One example of an activity that works well with participants who have an Individual and Participative Orientation is Brainstorming. This does not work well in "cultures of silence" with those who have a group orientation. It also may not work well if there are multiple levels of employees in the session. If participants have a preference for hierarchy, the higher level employees will be deferred to by the others.

STAGE 4: DELIVERY STYLE

In formal learning situations, facilitation is defined quite differently than training. Simply put, training is more about "telling" and facilitation is more about "leading the thinking process to better understanding through unobtrusive guidance." Facilitators tend to be neutral individuals who act as a catalyst for the group of learners. Trainers may be subject matter experts who are sharing their knowledge to groups of learners.

Understanding cultural national preferences is a critical part of knowing your international audiences. Delivery style preferences vary greatly from country to country. What is different?

- In countries with cultural preferences for hierarchy (like Japan or France), "good" training tends to be defined as a transfer of information and knowledge from the professor to the students with limited interaction with the students. In hierarchical countries, training design tends to incorporate a higher proportion of lectures.

- People who have a preference for hierarchy may expect and prefer the facilitator to lecture (tell) rather than facilitate.

- People may not participate until invited (or until there is silence to give respect). Others may talk over or interrupt those who are trying to be what is deemed as polite in their cultures.

- Preference for in-person (relationships) vs. technology (task) may vary.

- Lack of familiarity with or preferences for certain tools/techniques (not all societies have the same level of technology available to them even in the work place).

- People may not know of, or be comfortable with, certain learning approaches, or may not prefer them.

- Lack of understanding will not necessarily mean questions are asked (Group or Hierarchical Orientations).

- Many may speak English as an acquired language (and therefore lose much of the nuance that native speakers take for granted).

- You might want to consider having an interpreter. Please note that interpreters are different from translators. Interpreters will *interpret* what they think you mean, rather than translate directly/exactly.

- If you use an interpreter, count on at least doubling the time for the program.

- If you have natural cultural groups, allow natural culture groups to discuss the nuances in their mother tongue for periods of time to make sure they understand nuances. Give them time to ask questions in English.

An Aspect of the Time Orientation

Long Term Orientation = Success over a long time horizon is valued.

Short Term Orientation = Quick results are expected.

What you might want to do differently:

- Allow for social networking time (Group Orientation).

- Have senior executives speak (Hierarchical Orientation).

- Be patient (Long term and Quality of Life Orientation). Note: Long and Short Term Orientations are orientations describing the Time Orientation Dimension.

- Allow pauses (thinking/responding time especially for those who need to translate).

- Use clear, concise words/sentences (simple words and phrases that get the point across and do not confuse people).

- Explain in more than one way.

- Allow for small group work vs. individual work (Group Orientation).

- Do more explanation and provide examples (Need for Certainty).

- Call on participants (Participative Orientation) or explain that you intend to go around the room expecting everyone to participate (more hierarchical because you delegated each person the responsibility to speak).

- Share more information and context (Need for Certainty).

- Use "signpost" language. Tell them in advance what is coming up next. For example you might say, "After the break of ten minutes, we will be ..." Think of this as serving the same purpose as road signs so that you know in advance what is happening.

- Now a word about e-learning. Internet and computer usage varies significantly from country to country. Some countries, like the U.S., Canada and Scandinavian countries, have embraced these technologies and are pushing for more learning via technology (task focused). Technology comfort and usage in other countries (even in developed countries like France and Italy) is usually limited to younger generations. As a result, on-line training programs designed for mid-level executives are likely to be received rather more positively in the U.S. but could be received quite negatively in France or Italy.

- Make sure that the audience has the infrastructure, the knowledge of how to use it, and the willingness to use it before investing in on-line delivery.

STAGE 5: CREATION OF PARTICIPANT LEARNING MATERIALS

A. Use lots of visuals (simple words and expressive graphics) for those who speak English as an acquired language.

B. Make sure the colors and other graphics are universally understood and inoffensive.

C. Translate the materials into the mother tongue of the participants. If you translate the materials make *sure* you have someone other than the original translator/translation company do a back translation so you can be sure the initial translation was accurate.

D. Use and refer to page numbers to help them follow along.

E. Many cultures need more context than Americans typically do (we like bullet points and short answers). Use appendices and handouts to provide this so that those who need it, have it and others can glance through.

F. Like politics, almost all examples provided within programs should be locally derived. To cite Martin Luther King Jr. as an ideal for leadership is meaningful to Americans, but means less to the French or the Japanese.

G. Ask a learning professional or resource expert to go through the program content and materials outline to provide more appropriate examples.

REVIEW OF ZOE'S SITUATION

Refer to the case study at the beginning of this chapter.

Test Yourself:

What did Zoe do well? (Provide specific examples.) **What did Zoe not do well?** (Provide specific examples.) The Answers to the questions are below.

What did Zoe do well?

*   Zoe did not realize it, but putting them into small groups worked better than calling on individuals to answer questions.

*   By company standards she got a good evaluation. (In Asia, one is likely to get a good evaluation to create harmony and not cause anyone to lose face.)

*   She praised one participant by asking for an explanation of the acronym PMBOK® (Project Management Body of Knowledge).

What did Zoe not do well? She:

*   Did not plan enough time for the program. When you have non-English speakers in a program give yourself more time for them to learn.

- Did not introduce her expertise (she is displaying Tolerance for Ambiguity Orientation). She would have been more respected if she'd had a senior executive introduce her (Hierarchical Orientation).

- Used the term icebreaker which does not translate at all meaningfully in some cultures.

- Used an icebreaker that is more effective in cultures comfortable with pointing out their accomplishments.

- Used PowerPoint slides, which tend to have little context. Some cultures need a lot more information than others do especially when they speak English as an acquired language.

- Did not understand naming conventions in some Asian cultures (last name first) and called Mr. Zeng by his last name because it was first in the sequence of names.

- Did not understand what an honor it might actually have been for Ding to have been selected to attend this session.

- Lost face by her individual questions because if the student does not know the answer the trainer loses as much face as the learner.

- Recommended that everyone ask questions like the one participant who asked for an explanation of the acronym PMBOK® (Project Management Body of Knowledge). Speaking up and asking questions may seem like challenging the leader in some cultures—it is better to remain silent.

- Complained about her class within earshot of others (rude in almost any culture) and this caused them to lose face. She also assumed they were not prepared, which may not have been the issue at all.

- Focused on being on time rather than assuming the learning has taken place.

- Made a comment about an "older gentleman," which could have been perceived as disrespectful to the elderly.

- Assumed that her evaluations were an accurate reflection of her doing a good job.

HELPFUL HINTS

Culture is deeply embedded and values that drive workplace behaviors are not easily changed. Recognize that people are going to do things differently from the way you might do them. Different is not necessarily better or worse—it may just be different. Respect others and their approaches. They, too, want to succeed and are for the most part. They want to do an effective job. Find ways to reconcile how to work together that takes into account the differences in your approaches. Clearly outline what is expected in some detail (Need for Certainty). That and clear, frequent communication are very helpful approaches in identifying differences and working to find ways to honor, yet reconcile those differences.

First and foremost, *know your audience!* If you cannot really know who they are (culturally) then, as in any facilitation activity, carefully watch the audience. If what you are doing does not work, or does not work for some of them then switch it up. Talk about learning and cultural style differences so that everyone knows why you are doing things a little differently. Get them into small groups to talk about and present what they are thinking should change.

Professor Roy Y.J. Chua, Assistant Professor, Organizational Behavior Unit, Harvard Business School says, "Managing cultural friction not only creates a harmonious workplace, but ensures you reap the benefits of multiculturalism at its best." (Source: Blanding, Michael, Cultural Disharmony Undermines Workplace Creativity, Harvard Business School Working Knowledge Magazine, 09 Dec 2013.)

Chapter 10
Visual Facilitation

A process cannot be understood by stopping it. Understanding must move
with the flow of the process, must join it and flow with it.
~ From "Dune" by Frank Herbert

Visual Facilitation, also known as Graphics Facilitation is the process of gathering information in a group setting to create a hand drawn compelling picture that communicates the vision or business objectives of an organizational entity. This technique can be used for depicting the history of an organization as well. Incorporating visuals elicits participation, ownership, and creativity from all group members. The use of graphics is collaborative and ensures an outcome that participants are more likely to support. David Sibbet, the founder of Grove Consultants International, is a master facilitator and a pioneer of visual facilitation—the use of large-scale, interactive graphics to support group process in meetings, teams and organizations. His techniques of visual processes, strategic visioning, and creative future-oriented symposia have become a professional practice in their own right.

The use of computer-generated graphics such as animation, story boarding, and similar visual tools aside, the focus of this chapter is visual facilitation. Visual facilitation is the art and craft of creating graphics for effective communication by capturing stories and ideas from the minds of participants through hand drawn images. These techniques can be used by any worker, manager, executive, or workshop participant, without any formal training in art. And with practice, employees can become good at applying hand drawn graphics in problem solving or ideations. In some cases, expert artists are engaged to create graphics and two are shown here:

   a) Graphics Reporting, where an artist watches the progress of a meeting or a work session and is asked to create visual drawings for communication to employees, customers or other stakeholders.

b) Visual Facilitation, where an artist who is well versed in creating business visions, strategies, programs, and so on, is engaged to partner with team members, or with the team leader and his/her team, to create a visual story in the workshop with collective collaboration. This process is driven by a formal methodology which is outlined in this chapter.

THE BENEFITS OF USING GRAPHICS

From ancient times, various cultures developed petroglyphs, cave drawings, stone carvings, and wood carvings such as totem poles to tell a story or convey a specific message for the benefit of future generations. Similarly, visuals and visual narratives today bring organizational messages to life through collaborative creation of their organizational "stories." This includes vision and strategy development, game plan implementation, process mapping, and innovation ideas that are used as a powerful communication to inspire and motivate teams to a higher level of performance. In addition these visuals become an asset for marketing and sales to their customers and consumers.

In workshops, participants are asked to describe their ways of working to develop formal business processes. Even standalone graphic templates are created to make the presentations interesting by putting the graphics in reusable PowerPoint slides. Organizations use graphic outputs for creating visual messages through animation, online portals, communication kits, product campaigns, customer engagement kits, and other outputs to educate their employees and influence customers, stakeholders, and communities to promote their products and services.

Graphic facilitation has multifaceted uses that may be incorporated in meetings, training sessions, group workshops, and general transfer of knowledge. Regardless of the purpose of the graphics, use of color enhances their message and engages the right side of the brain, promoting creativity. Graphics facilitation can be successfully applied to all elements of the Mahal Facilitation Framework: *Strategies and Solutions*, *Programs and Processes*, *Learning and Development*, and *Cooperation and Collaboration*.

VISUAL/GRAPHICS FACILITATION

Organizations have many possible uses for graphics facilitation. In this chapter you are introduced to five approaches for graphics facilitation application. These methods range from simple to more advanced techniques:

1. Personal Graphics Kit
2. Group Graphics Exercises
3. Reusable Graphic Templates
4. Graphics Recording
5. Visual Facilitation.

Depending on the best use of the graphics, several options are available to the facilitator. The meeting facilitator can draw the graphics based on verbal input from the group using simple techniques such as drawing stick figures, dollar icons, circles, squares, arrows, and so on.

Another option is to have the participants draw the graphics using only pictures and no text. Again, drawings can be simple and participants should be instructed to use graphic symbols to make the picture more meaningful and interesting as a communication tool. For example, using circles for meetings, squares for output documents, and arrows for projects and linking them on a timeline creates a visual that works like a roadmap for a traveler. Objectives and milestones can then be easily added to the picture. This can be done using flip charts or sheets of paper attached to the walls of the meeting room.

A professional graphics recorder can be brought in to graphically record the pictorial vision of what is happening during the meeting. For the most advanced graphics facilitation a graphics artist-facilitator (a business "storyteller") is engaged who is well versed in organizational ways of working and understands what business outcomes generally are and how best to communicate those points throughout the organization and sometimes externally to customers as well.

1. PERSONAL GRAPHICS KIT

Everyone in an organization who facilitates meetings and workshops of any kind, with little practice, can use graphics to make the session interesting and engaging in terms of describing concepts, challenges and objectives of the session. Graphics can be drawn on flip charts, wall charts, participant handouts, and even dropped in PowerPoint presentations. Chapter 12 discusses a tool called Visual Dictionary (Tool #34), which can be used as a starting kit. Beyond this, the possibilities are unlimited. One good source of this idea and its learning possibilities is Dan Roam's book *The Back of a Napkin: Solving Problems and Selling Ideas with Pictures*. Following is an example of this approach.

Figure 10.1 – Visual Dictionary Example

2. GROUP GRAPHICS EXERCISES

When work teams come together to develop strategies, solutions, programs, and processes, they generally have differing viewpoints of how work gets done. Facilitators, in order to establish a baseline, may ask the group to use multiple colors and draw icons, symbols, and other visuals to depict their collective understanding. In addition to serving as an icebreaker, this method promotes collaboration among team members. They enjoy doing this type of exercise. The output of this exercise then becomes an important input to the next steps of the planned workshop. The tool is described in more detail in Chapter 12 Tool #4.

Following is an example of this approach. A group is describing their transportation organization's process of package delivery. The packages are picked up from the shipping customer and transported via trucks and by air, and are delivered to the receiving customer. There is no text used and the drawing is multi-colored (the source diagram of this example is in color). There are other variations of this technique, such as creating stories using pictures cut out from magazines.

Figure 10.2 – Group Creative Visualization "Rich Picture"

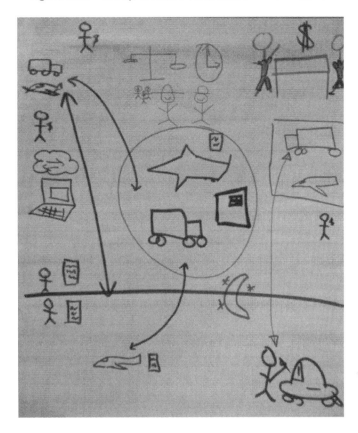

3. REUSABLE GRAPHIC TEMPLATES

In addition to the power of computer generated graphics displayed through software such as PowerPoint, there is another approach to computer generated graphics: hand drawn diagrams by an expert artist. Organizations, particularly centers of excellence, can create hand drawn graphics of their commonly used templates and then digitize them to be used in PowerPoint in an editable format. This way, the entire organization can use them over and over for their new initiatives and projects. Following is an example of this approach. This standard template for project planning may be used by everyone in an organization. (By Artist-Facilitator Kevin Woodson of Visual Ink Creative.)

Figure 10.3 – Reusable Graphic Template in PowerPoint

4. GRAPHICS RECORDING

This activity involves a trained and experienced artist in graphics drawing who captures discussions or meeting proceedings in real-time—but only in the background—without actively participating in conversations. Typically, a large sheet of paper is placed on the wall where the artist can see the participants and hear their conversations clearly. The artist has to be very fast in capturing the essence of what is being said and metaphorically represent that "story" on the paper. For this activity, the team leader must provide orientation to the artist by sharing the agenda for the session, communicating the expected outcome, outlining who the audience is for this deliverable.

The graphic story thus created, in addition to becoming an institutional memory asset, is an effective tool for communicating ideas, vision, strategies, and more to the intended audience. For example: a large organization's Human Resources Department wanted to brainstorm the changing demographics in the work force to assess how they might impact future strategies of filling their talent pipeline. The artist drew a "picture" of the organization's work force history along with possible changes in the future and how to prepare for sourcing and adopting new measurements such as human capital and knowledge management. After the picture was colored and digitalized, the team leader wrote a narrative to describe the graphic story, which was then shared to all human resource leaders throughout the organization.

5. VISUAL FACILITATION

A visual process for facilitating strategy, solutions development, and collaborative communication is the most efficient approach for workshop participants to understand the same message and to realize how they, themselves, fit in the big picture. The visuals move the process along more quickly and give all members of the group a say. The visual process helps groups get "unstuck" by illustrating the progress in a clear picture that highlights weak points and invites the most innovative thinking.

Graphic flow charts (or "process maps") provide a high-level perspective on organizational ways of working. When used appropriately for planning, visuals can bring critical elements of a strategy to life. When group members illustrate the story of a process, strategy, marketing plan, or company vision from A to Z, by providing their input to the drawings, they take ownership and have pride in what they do or what they plan to do.

There are several ways in which graphics professionals contribute to the process of graphics facilitation. They include creating graphics in advance, and drawing in real-time while a meeting is in progress with a follow up of coloring and fine tuning. In this section, the methodology used by Visual Ink Creative of California is outlined below along with example visuals.

Graphic Templates prepared by trained graphics facilitators in advance of a session are valuable tools for capturing information using icons, symbols and colors in a group setting. A graphics professional can meet in advance with a small leadership team (or a sales team as an example) and draft a visual—a drawing that represents about 80 percent of what the visual will look like (sometimes called a "straw dog"). The finished product represents what the leadership team sees as the vision of where they want to end up in three or five years (or the biggest challenges to achieving that goal). A graphic template that is prepared in advance has several uses:

1. The graphic clearly communicates the process described in the visual.

2. If the visual was illustrated on large sheets of paper on walls, fold-outs can be rendered and handed to participants to open up for reference during meetings.

3. Standalone templates (editable PowerPoint slides) can be generated showing the vision, process or project, or to create an agenda. Because these templates are 'editable,' they can be re-used by modifying them for specific projects and presentations in the future.

The visual facilitation methodology involves the following steps.

Foundation and Vision

Strategy development teams work cross-functionally, virtually, and in meetings for intense development sessions. These teams are held together by a big picture that defines their purpose, challenge, and goals.

Figure 10.4 – Visual Story "Big Picture" Organizational Strategy

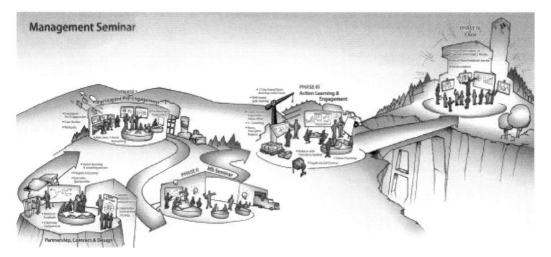

Foundational Input

A basic visual framework helps teams define the common challenge. Before meeting with the strategy team, the graphics professional works with leaders to develop an understanding of the challenge and the current situation. Working virtually, they use PowerPoint presentations, interviews, and white papers to design the initial framework that the team uses as a first step in building strategy.

Team Participation

By building on the visual foundation, the team creates its own map of success. When the team meets, the graphics professional uses the foundational material created up front as a launching-off point for new ideas, collaboration, and focus. They work with the strategy teams in focused workshops to create an initial live vision, spending a day or two designing the future together. The live vision clearly speaks to the big picture strategy and allows individuals to understand how and where they fit in. As the strategy evolves, the initial vision is used to reach out to experts beyond the core strategy development team.

Iteration

The vision integrated into the Big Picture becomes the dynamic guiding document for strategy. Once the team's initial vision is on the wall, it begins to evolve into a bigger picture, encompassing key elements of the strategy. The resulting Big Picture incorporates a vast amount of knowledge from the team, subject matter experts, and key leaders in the context of the vision. As the Big Picture evolves over several weeks or even months, it includes input across an organization and creates enthusiasm around the subject or issue.

Drill Down

As the Big Picture and vision gain support, strategists delve into the details. This phase is referred to as a drill down or deep dive because focused teams concentrate in depth on critical pieces of the big picture. See Figure 10.5. Drill down uncovers the details to support the big picture story. From the big picture story, it's easy to develop the next level of elements because the common visual language has already been developed and agreed to by team members. Following are some examples of the byproducts at this stage.

- *Customer Storyboards*: See the customer's profile and walk in his or her shoes
- *Visual Prototyping*: Design and test business strategy quickly
- *Strategy Roadmap*: What happens when, and who is responsible
- *Other Byproducts*: Visualize supply chain, program management, stakeholders, market segments, and industry trends.

Figure 10.5 – Drill Down Action Learning

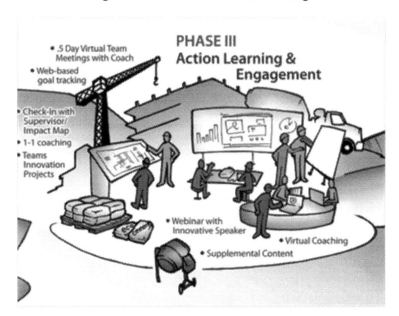

Agenda Example

To engage an artist for this type of graphics facilitation, the team leader and the participating work groups plan an agenda design to conduct the above mentioned steps of the methodology. Following is a high-level example of such approach.

- Leader/Sponsor presents the topic and scope and identifies the expectations of the outcome, then kicks off the initiative and motivates the team.

- Artist Facilitator leads and guides small groups to develop their ideas around the topic (keeping in mind the audience and planed outcomes).

- Teams report out their ideas and concepts about the topic.

- Facilitator creates a combined graphic view by synthesizing the ideas presented by the teams (with their help); any gaps are addressed.

- Facilitator iterates the refinement of the graphics deliverable—as many times as needed until the client is satisfied with the outcome.

- The team leader and the teams plan an approach for rollout of the "story".

Rollout

The strategy is rolled out in phases to larger audiences. Each approach is different for varying target audiences and desired objectives. The Road Map visuals are used to create communications including messages, scripts, executive presentations, animated videos, and training materials.

The Big Picture is used for the homepage of a website. For example a large international organization developed a big picture of the Business Change Methodology. The methodology showed the entire process in a visual metaphor of an education system improvement in a town.

In the Deep Dive phase, each of the methodology phases is shown with actions and deliverables.

In the Roll Out phase, the methodology process is made into large wall boards for education teams working on change projects and each of the team members receives a folded smaller version of the Big Picture.

To implement this methodology across the world, an expert methodologist's voice is recorded along the flow of the map so that employees can learn it as part of their eLearning resource.

HELPFUL HINTS

It has been said that a picture is worth a thousand words. Whether you have artistic aptitude or not, learning basic drawings and using them in workshops can be a very powerful way of solving problems, communicating ideas, inspiring others, and gaining consensus. Transfer of knowledge and workshops will be more interesting and engaging for participants with the use of visuals. Take the first step and begin using graphics in your meetings and workshops. You will enjoy it and so will your participants. Just do it.

Chapter 11
Self-Development

Self-Development is Self-Accountability.
~ Artie Mahal, Author, Educator and Facilitator

DEVELOPING YOUR COMPETENCIES

The justification for developing the competency of Facilitation is well-explained in Chapter 2, Value Proposition. As a reminder, Facilitation includes conducting meetings, delivering training, transfer of knowledge, and group sessions for specific purposes. Those purposes fall under one of the four categories of facilitation needs as shown in the *Mahal Facilitation Framework* in Chapter 1, Facilitation Framework.

As stated in the Introduction of this book while more and more organizations are formally recognizing facilitation as one of their core competency models, a majority have yet to grasp the concept that facilitation is a critical enabling competency. So, in many cases you are responsible for your own development in facilitation competency. You will develop and grow in your role as a professional facilitator in your organization while preparing for the day when you become a free agent/consultant. No matter what your professional track might be, facilitation skills, which are transferable, will expand your horizon to new possibilities you may not even have envisioned yet.

So, how do you go about self-development? Recall the 70/20/10 learning framework from Chapter 1 where 10 percent of learning comes from formal training such as reading books, attending seminars, and online and formal education; 20 percent comes from others (including one-to-one learning from your managers, peers, and other professionals); and 70 percent comes by doing—applying facilitation tools every time you find an opportunity. And the opportunities are everywhere. Keep a keen eye out to identify them and take charge by volunteering, not only in your own department or circle, but outside of your areas as well.

In the earlier stages of learning facilitation, there is generally a fear of failure in front of your managers and peers. This can be easily managed by the following strategy: Simply start using the facilitation concepts and tools in every meeting or group collaboration work—without making any special announcement that you are facilitating. Just do it.

Also, seek out opportunities in community events where they have similar needs as that of the business organizations, but can't afford to pay in most cases. Volunteer and take the lead in conducting facilitated sessions *pro bono*. You will be able to practice in non-threatening and less risky environments. And, giving back to the community generates good feeling and goodwill and can be very rewarding personally.

There are three tools provided in this chapter: A checklist to identify opportunities; a development plan template to formally take charge of your own planning and monitoring your progress in facilitation competency, and a Self-development Mantra, a strategy for developing core competencies to be successful in the dynamic changing work environment. American President Calvin Coolidge observed, *"We cannot do everything at once; but we can do something at once."* So, take the first step and plan a road map of development for yourself.

DEVELOPMENT OPPORTUNITIES

Review the foundational skillset list and the checklist of skills in the International Association of Facilitator's Foundational Competencies found in the Core Competencies section of Chapter 4. Identify areas of improvement and self-development. Use this same checklist when completing Table 11.1.

Next, identify some areas in the list below where you may find or create opportunities to facilitate.

Your Organization/Business	Community
☐ Meetings	☐ Non-Profit Organizations
☐ Focus Groups	☐ Religious Organizations
☐ Volunteer in Training Delivery	☐ Governmental/Political Events
☐ Workshops for Solutions	☐ Schools, Colleges
☐ Lunch and Learn Sessions	☐ Fraternal Organizations
☐ Organizational Events	☐ Toastmasters
☐ Others?	☐ Others?

In the opportunities listed above, in addition to seeking the role of leading sessions, consider working as a co-facilitator with an experienced facilitator—to gain confidence and skill. This can be a very effective developmental approach for the beginners.

MY DEVELOPMENT PLAN

To plan your competency development, fill out Table 11.1, and diligently implement actions for development.

Table 11.1 – My Development Plan Template

Development Plan	Competency: Identify Skill/Competency
Goal: Finish the sentence, "I need to change from (current state of behavior, skill or knowledge) to (desired future state)."	
From:	*I need to change from…*
To:	*I need to change to…*
Learning Events and Self-Help: How can I gain insights about achieving the Goal (reading, courses, self-study, others)? Identify names of books, materials and other resources. (10%)*	
Other People: How can I collaborate and learn from others: observation, coaching, mentorship and gaining feedback. Identify names and resources. (20%)*	
Assignments: Determine task, project and job assignments that will allow me to gain experience and practice the new behavior, skill or knowledge. State why, what, how, where, when and with whom. (70%)*	
Other Experiences: Choose experiences that can build skills and behavior in the desired competency: what, where and how.	
Monitor/Evaluation: How will I monitor the progress of the plan? Establish milestones or checkpoints. How will I know I have reached the Goal? State who you will ask and what you will ask.	
*Refer to 70/20/10 Learning Framework	

This is a snapshot in time. Periodically review your plan and update and maintain an inventory of your skills and competencies.

MY FACILITATION JOURNEY

Near the beginning of this book, I have included a section about My Personal Facilitation Journey, in which I narrate how I didn't know what "facilitation" was or how I could initiate that learning. Having been exposed to Gary Rush's facilitation boot-camp, I came back excited about the possibilities of facilitating meetings and workshops. As I sought opportunities to apply my learning and gain experience in facilitation, I also had the "fear of facilitation"—fear of failing in front of my peers and my managers but, more importantly, the fear of looking like a novice in front of session participants.

To overcome this feeling, I sought opportunities outside of my work, in community organizations where I could practice and hone my skills. I found a few opportunities to lead small sessions, three of which included my *Gurudwara* (Sikh Temple), a non-profit organization for physically challenged people, and an organization that provided grief counseling to children in need. At these places, it didn't matter if I made mistakes or looked like an inexperienced session leader. I did this work *pro bono*, which fed my soul and gave value to those organizations. My big break came unexpectedly in the New Jersey Historical Commission, an entity of the State Government that promotes the history of the State and provides guidance and funds for historic preservation.

I was appointed to the New Jersey Historical Commission by Governor Christine "Christie" Todd Whitman, as an honorary member. Among the ten honorary commissioners were historians, legislators, and community service people. As I was new and not really a professional historian, I was appointed to this role based on my past service, as a member of the Ethnic Advisory Council to the state under two previous governors and I was expected to learn and contribute well.

After the first meeting, I told my wife that I thought that by accepting the commission I had taken on more than I was qualified for—that it was out of my comfort level. In the beginning, I attended the meetings of the commission without saying or contributing very much. A few months after my appointment, the chairman of the commission, a surgeon, called an emergency meeting to tell us that due to budget constraints, several million dollars were going to be pulled back from the Historical Commission, impacting several initiatives that were already underway. We commissioners were very concerned and brainstormed various options for convincing the Secretary of State of the importance of the work we were chartered to do.

As a newly minted facilitator, I knew the processes involved in strategic planning: developing a mission and vision, and the execution of strategies to achieve desired outcomes. I asked a simple question, "Do we have a mission and a supporting vision that defines why we exist and what our objectives are in terms of New Jersey Historic Commissions services?" One or two experienced commissioners replied that there was a mission statement in place but that no vision had been defined in the previous few years. My response was, "Then we don't have anything to show to the Secretary of State and the Governor that shows the value we are adding and what we plan to achieve."

It was clear that we did not have a story to tell, so how could we ask for our funding back? The commissioners asked what we should do. I suggested that we hold a two-day workshop to refresh the mission, create a future vision, and show programs and projects in progress. Then we could package this vision and our supporting achievements and present them to the Secretary of State. In other words, we would market our organization to the State in order to preserve the funding.

The commission unanimously agreed and I was asked to prepare the workshop, facilitate it, and produce a five-year plan document. The workshop was a success and the five-year plan was presented and publicized. Based on this effort, the commission did get a portion of our funding back and we commissioners were again working on our planned initiatives. For the first time I felt that I had added value as a commissioner even though I lacked academic history education. The confidence I gained by designing and facilitating the workshop with successful outputs and outcomes helped me engage more effectively in my business workshops. The "fear of facilitation" was diminishing and I now believed in myself and behaved in front of groups as an experienced professional session leader.

After about six months, I received a call from the Secretary of State's office requesting me to come to Trenton, the State Capital, and meet with the Secretary of State. Upon arriving on the appointed date, I discovered that I was the only commissioner invited to this meeting. I wondered if I was being removed from the commission to be replaced by a professional historian, a professor, or another academic person. The Secretary of State called me into her nice large office, offered me a cup of coffee, and after some small talk broke the news. "The Governor and I were impressed by how you conducted the workshop and led the commissioners to create a vision for the Historical Commission. We are proud of you and would like you to become the chairman of the commission." (They had planned to retire the surgeon from his term of office.)

I was in shock. Here I was, thinking I was being handed a pink-slip and, to my amazement, I was being offered a leadership role. I told the Secretary of State that I was honored to be asked to head the commission, but that my job consumed extensive travel time and I was not sure if I should accept such responsibility. The Secretary of State asked me to think it over and get back to her in a week. She also informed me that, since there was paid staff in the historic commission's office, I could delegate to them and ease my share of work. After much deliberation, I accepted the role and conveyed my decision to the Secretary of State. Within a few days (two days before Christmas), a formal invitation to the appointment of chairman of the commission was sent to me. I was in my glory and happy to have been given such an honor at the State level.

On Christmas Eve, I had a pain in my chest and went to the emergency room. It turned out that I had blockage in couple of my coronary arteries, which resulted in heart by-pass surgery. I now felt that between my demanding job and the recovery process from the heart surgery, I would not be able to do justice to the role of commission chairman. I sent my regrets and turned down the position. The Secretary of State sent me flowers along with good wishes for recovery, and expressed that she and the Governor respected my decision. I had missed or, rather, let go of a once-in-a-lifetime opportunity to serve in a position of responsibility at that level.

This experience of mine has lessons: To obtain experience, work *pro bono* in non-profit institutions where they welcome this type of service. As you gain confidence and experience, begin applying the relevant tools in your place of business. The profession of facilitation, which includes consulting, training, and much more, opens up windows of opportunities beyond the sphere of your current job and, possibly, your imagination. As the pioneers dared to travel to unknown areas and discovered new lands, rivers and mountains that were beyond their imagining, you, too, can venture forth and see where your new-found knowledge of facilitation will take you.

SELF-DEVELOPMENT MANTRA

Gary Rush stated in the Foreword of this book: Facilitation skills are the skillset of the twenty-first century for all professionals. In addition to developing facilitation skills, it is incumbent upon facilitators and all professionals, regardless of their industry or practice, to continuously educate themselves on the ever-changing and complex dynamics of the workplace.

Six factors form the foundational imperatives for surviving and thriving in the workforce. I call it the *Self-Development Mantra: How to Write, Speak, Learn, Think, Present, and Network.*

LEARN TO WRITE

The quality of a facilitator's writing is a reflection of the levels of performance one might expect from him/her as a facilitator. With all of today's electronic tools, the art and craft of writing using proper grammar has become diluted and casual. While the speed of writing in simple terms may be productive, it does not replace the effectiveness of good and professional writing. Facilitators must write proposals, memos, position papers, document work outputs, and more.

Strategy: Learn to write concisely and clearly. Business writing workshops and classes are very useful in improving this skill. In addition, creative writing skills help in formulating your own stories and anecdotes which can be used in a variety of situations.

LEARN TO SPEAK

You are judged by who you are and by how you speak. My father drilled in me this statement: *"One of the most important things in life is what to say, how to say it, and when to say it."* Regardless of your accent or ethnic background, your choice of words and vocabulary make the difference in speaking with confidence. Accents represent an interesting variety in the diversity of people in the global work environment.

Strategy: Learn how to speak well and with confidence in meetings and work sessions. Toastmasters International is a good resource for sharpening this skill.

LEARN TO LEARN

Learning to learn is a skill unto itself. Learning is about acquiring knowledge about something and then becoming good at it by application. Through Nature's tools of our senses (sight, smell, taste, touch, and hearing) we learn continuously. But learning for the advancement of our profession requires deliberate and planned reading on a variety of topics, as well as watching multimedia content, taking classes, conversing with others, and deducing your own concepts of knowledge and wisdom. *"The only person who is educated is the one who has learned how to learn and change."* – Carl Rogers, American psychologist.

Strategy: In addition to reading professional material, read about a variety of topics through books, periodicals, etc. Even reading children's books inspire concepts and stories which facilitators can use effectively. The 70/20/10 learning framework described in this book is a proven approach for learning by design.

LEARN TO THINK

Critical thinking is another skill for the twenty-first century. To make sound decisions in a complex and dynamic environment, professionals need a methodical approach to deducing meaning or "connecting dots" using the information at hand. Critical Thinking is defined by Anne Pauker Kreitzberg and Charles B. Kreitzberg of Cognetics Interactive thus: *"Critical Thinking is the process of understanding a situation, problem, or body of knowledge as deeply and accurately as possible. In an organizational setting, the challenge is to be able to do this with imperfect information and accounting for the 'human element' of individual differences, team dynamics and organizational realities. The goal is to use the best information available, given the situation, to make the decisions that lead to appropriate and effective action."*

Strategy: Learn and *practice critical thinking* concepts, principals and methods.

LEARN TO PRESENT

Present both yourself and the topic at hand with confidence, integrity and credibility. In Chapter 4 practical tools have been discussed under the Self-Awareness and Style of the Facilitation Leadership Framework. *"The human brain is a wonderful organ. It starts to work as soon as you are born and doesn't stop until you get up to deliver a speech."* – George Jessel, American actor.

Strategy: Practice, practice, practice. And by sincerely valuing your craft, become your own Brand: "Bringing who you are to what you do."

LEARN TO NETWORK

Network, Network, Network. In the changing dynamics of a global economy, the work environment has become more challenging, both for getting jobs and succeeding in existing roles. On average, a new person in the workforce is predicted to change jobs five to seven times in his/her career. Gone are the days when organization promoted "job security." Today, employees feel perpetual "job *in*security" in work environments. Columnist Dr. George Crane made a profound statement: *"There is no future in any job. The future lies in the person who holds the job."*

While it is important to possessing the necessary skills and qualifications for getting and sustaining your job, networking with people—both inside and outside your work environment—is critical for ensuring gainful employment. *"Goodwill is the one and only asset that competition cannot undersell or destroy."* Ludwig Börne, German political writer and satirist.

The Network illustration is symbolic of the effort one must put into building meaningful relationships. Individual need to put twice the effort to reach out and "give" something (double arrow) before they can hope to "get" something (single arrow) in return.

Strategy: Networking does not happen by accident. While some people are natural at making connections and connecting the dots to leverage mutual benefits, others must make it a habit to learn how to network with sincerity.

IAF's Facilitator Certification Program

In any of the facilitation roles—a Facilitator, a Learning Facilitator, or A Facilitative Leader—as a part of your development and professional progress, you may want to consider becoming "Certified Professional Facilitator" - IAF-CPF©. The following information on the certificate program is sourced from The International Association of Facilitators (IAF) (http://www.iaf-world.org/).

The International Association of Facilitators (IAF) has met the need for standards in facilitator certification. In 1990, an international team of IAF members identified the core competencies required to facilitate group interaction. This team's efforts resulted in the IAF competency model and assessment process.

The assessment process is based on rigorous peer review of knowledge, experience and demonstration of skills. The IAF Certified™ Professional Facilitator designation indicates attainment of these core competencies. The professional facilitator designation offers clients an assurance that those who are certified are qualified to design and provide basic group facilitation services.

WHAT'S IN IT FOR YOU?
As a successful certification candidate you will:

- Receive a certificate that entitles you to use the IAF designation: Certified Professional Facilitator©.

- Test your facilitation skills against a set of professionally developed competencies recognized by your peers.

- Receive individual *and* confidential feedback from independent professional facilitators.

- Join a respected and developing group of professional facilitators.

- Gain competitive advantage by being listed on the IAF Website as a CPF, a Certified Professional Facilitator©.

CERTIFIED PROFESSIONAL FACILITATOR—IAF-CPF©
Facilitation is a rapidly expanding, worldwide profession that plays a key role in helping shape the world we live in. Today, facilitation plays a vital part in the workings of businesses, governments, and communities across the globe. With facilitation cast in such an important leadership role, a very important question arises: how does an organization assess the capability of the facilitator they hire to do the job?

As early as 1998, IAF recognized that there was no clear way for clients to assess the capability of those who offered facilitation services. With facilitation becoming a crucial tool for accelerating productivity and strategic alignment in organizations, a reliable and accurate assessment tool was needed. IAF, a worldwide professional body established to promote, support and advance the art and practice of professional facilitation, sought to answer that need. A worldwide team of dedicated IAF members identified the core facilitation competencies required for skillful facilitation of meetings and workshops, and upon those core competencies, the IAF assessment based certification program was created. IAF now offers the IAF Facilitator Certification program to facilitators all over the world. Assessments in core facilitation competencies are offered in all IAF regions with the number of offerings based upon demand.

A BRIEF OVERVIEW OF THE FACILITATOR CERTIFICATION PROCESS

- The process begins when you receive your IAF Facilitator Certification Information/Application packet. Within the packet you will find a complete Process Overview, information on the core competencies, and all the application materials and information needed, including the cost.

- Your first step toward certification begins with the completion of an application and the payment of an application fee. This is followed by the submission of a resume, and evidence of your professional training and experience.

- Two Accredited Assessors are assigned to each candidate.

- These assessors review the application documents for evidence of professional experience and the facilitator competencies.

- Successful candidates are then invited to an "Assessment Day" for further testing and demonstration of their skills against the competencies.

During the Assessment Day, candidates:

- Are interviewed by his/her assigned assessors to further explore and test their application.

- Conduct a practical workshop on a preselected issue. This workshop is designed to evaluate the candidate's practical capabilities in working with the core competencies and is presented for their assigned assessors and other independent assessors.

- Are provided a final interview and feedback session with their assigned assessors after which candidates are informed of the outcome of their application for certification.

For more information about the certification process, read *IAF-CPF Certification Process Overview and the Facilitator Core Competencies.*

The Professional Facilitator Certification Program provides successful candidates with the professional credential *"IAF Certified™ Professional Facilitator – CPF."*

HELPFUL HINTS

- As you build your knowledge, skills and competency in your facilitation practice, document the inventory of your learning. This will inspire you to continue progressing. Update an internal or external resume.

- When you meet facilitators through attending seminars or online study, make a contacts list. This becomes a virtual community of peers who can provide valuable feedback, advice and guidance. Even experienced facilitators have a need to bounce ideas off of others in their profession.

- Build your own library of tools for easy access when needed.

- Seek opportunities to make presentations or teach facilitation skills to others. Teaching others helps our own selves to become sharper in the craft.

Chapter 12
Tools Library

It's best to have your tools with you.
If you don't, you're apt to find something you didn't expect and get discouraged.
~ Stephen King, On Writing: A Memoir of the Craft

This chapter is a follow-up to Chapter 6. In that chapter, basic concepts of facilitation such as brainstorming were introduced along with a catalogue of 35 tools. Recall Table 6.1 (Tools Catalogue). In this chapter each of those 35 tools is described in detail for their application by a facilitator. While some on the list may require more expertise than others, most can be used with practice. Consider this as a starter and foundational kit for a facilitator to work from. Each of the techniques has a description and process steps for how to go about using it, along with a template and examples in some cases. These tools can be improvised for a variety of sessions and uses. Each of the tools on the following pages has a header which has a unique identifier that corresponds to the Tools Catalogue in Chapter 6.

SWOT ANALYSIS (TOOL #1)

SWOT (Strength, Weaknesses, Opportunities, and Threats) Analysis can be conducted for the current state of any organization or any part of an organization, including process, roles, and products and services. You conduct a brainstorming exercise with relevant stakeholders around the four quadrants as shown in Figure 12.1. Then do a clustering of ideas (affinity analysis) to determine themes. The themes are organized into strategies or projects and initiatives. These are prioritized and assigned time frames and ownership for their implementation.

Figure 12.1 – SWOT Framework

Strengths (Leverage)	Weaknesses (Convert into Strengths & Opportunities)
Threats (Minimize & Convert into Opportunities)	Opportunities (Leverage)

Strengths and Weakness are generally internal; Threats and Opportunities are generally external to the organization in scope of the assessment. Strengths need to be leveraged more. Weaknesses that matter most must be converted into strengths. Opportunities are the quick wins and other improvement ideas which must be leveraged. Threats are the constraints that must be managed/minimized and/or converted into strengths.

The SWOT Analysis technique is credited to Albert S. Humphrey, an American business and management consultant who specialized in organizational management and cultural change in sixties and seventies.

PROCESS

1. Identify/determine and agree on the scope of the area to be analyzed (an organizational unit, product or service, or other area).

2. Create a SWOT template on a wall-chart. Provide large or medium-size sticky notes along with appropriate markers. Frame (explain) the concept of SWOT—its purpose and the expected outcomes. Write two data items on each sticky-note: An item above the line and the implication below the line as in Figure 12.2.

Figure 12.2 – Sticky Note Structure

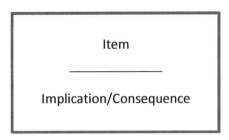

Item
_____
Implication/Consequence

For example, if SWOT is being conducted for a Recruit and Hire Process of an organization, one Post-It may have as a weakness item: *Poor Selection of Candidates* and the implication would be *Less Competent Employees in the Organization.* This concept of capturing two bits of data: *Item* and *Implication/Consequence* for analysis is my contribution to this technique. In the same exercise this enriches the value of the data gathered by thinking deeper about an issue. Instead of SWOT, in some cases a variation can be used: SPOT—Strengths, Problems, Opportunities and Threats. In cases where strategies are to be developed, "Weakness" may be used, whereas if a product or a service is being analyzed, "Problem" may be used. Note: In some cases the sticky notes can be used in four colors—one color for each quadrant.

3. Individuals should create their own SWOT items first and then place them on a common wall chart for group analysis. This works well when the group is small. If the group is large, then form teams of two, three or four to first discuss among themselves ideas for all four quadrants and place on the wall chart randomly.

4. Ask for volunteers, preferably one person from each of the sub-groups, to create clusters of like type of ideas. Circle the clusters with a marker and give it a meaningful title. These titles become the themes.

5. Identify next steps; which may be to prioritize the themes and then create strategies or projects for further action. (Reference Tool #25, Prioritization of Options.)

AFTER ACTION REVIEW (AAR) (TOOL #2)

An After Action Review (AAR) is a structured approach to managing knowledge and continuous improvement of any activity, project, work session, or to build a culture of accountability. This approach permits the participants of an activity to discover for themselves what happened and why. It can also be used to solicit ideas on how a particular activity could have been performed better. It should be conducted after some significant activity or when an event in an organization has concluded.

The idea is to capture the learning immediately after the activity while the ideas are fresh in the minds of the participants as to what went well and what could be improved in the future. AAR's are not critiques because they do not determine success or failure. They are professional discussions of activities and events with the intent of capturing knowledge and sharing it for future improvement.

The AAR, as an informal technique, may have existed from time immemorial and been used by battlefield commanders to learn from the mistakes made during the action and to plan their tactics for the next action, based on the learning. The US Army formally developed this technique during the early eighties as a lesson learned system. Over time these have morphed into an efficient and effective process for correcting mistakes in future endeavors from the lesson learned and for sustaining success. This technique is generally conducted in a group session, but it can be used in interview settings as well.

There are two types of AARs: informal and formal. *Informal* reviews are typically done after meetings, work sessions, or training sessions. These can be facilitated by one of the team members—who needs to be neutral in conducting this short session. They are done on the spot, immediately after the close of the event.

Formal reviews are a planned activity where relevant and key stakeholders are invited to a facilitated session that may be designed and conducted by a neutral and independent facilitator. They are done for large initiatives such as the launch of a product or service, the building of a structure, the rolling out of new strategies that may involve people, and for processes and technology. This type of session may be held over one or two days, or even longer. The sessions are conducted under the sponsorship of the senior executive responsible for the overall program or activity of focus.

INFORMAL AFTER ACTION REVIEW

The following template is worded in a manner that facts can be expressed honestly without offending anyone or pointing fingers at anyone. To apply this technique the facilitator prompts the participants to address these key questions: What was planned? What actually occurred (facts not judgments)? What went well and why? What can be improved and how?

The method for this review includes the following process.

1. Identify and gain agreement on the topic for After Action Review assessment. Two approaches can be used:

   a. Using a flip chart, solicit items for *I Liked* or *I Wish* in a random order—without judgment or debate:

I Liked	I Wish
Example of a training workshop: *The content of the topic*	Example of a training workshop: *There were more visuals in the material*
Example of a group session: *The agenda design*	Example of a group session: *The facilitator had allowed more time for exercises*

   b. Using a wall-chart, ask participants write their items on sticky notes and place them on the chart. Have volunteers cluster the ideas to create topic themes.

2. Frame (explain the context) the definition of an After Action Review for the participants and conduct the assessment.

3. Identify next steps for how the learning will be documented and communicated to all relevant stakeholders and further used for improvements.

Note: an alternate template can be used instead that is similar to the one mentioned here, but with different wording. *What Worked Well (WWW)* and *Even Better If (EBI)*. It is simply a matter of the facilitator's preference.

FORMAL AFTER ACTION REVIEW

The method for this review includes the following process.

Plan the session:

- Establish the AAR objective.
- Identify and engage a facilitator.
- Review the plan of the activity and its outcomes.
- Identify the participants (stakeholders and those who have direct involvement).
- Select training and orientation aids for the participants.
- Select a facilitation-friendly AAR facility.
- Draft an AAR Plan/Agenda.

The facilitator prepares the plan:

- Develops a detailed agenda in collaboration with the sponsor/manager.
- Prepares communications for the manager to send invites to the potential participants.
- Gathers supplies needed for the session and follows up on other logistics, such as food.

Conduct the session:

- Review the objectives of initiative or activity being discussed.
- Facilitate the discussion and capture information in an organized manner.
- Agree on the documentation and dissemination of the session outputs.

Following is an example and a template for planning and conducting a formal AAR.

Table 12.1 – Template for Planning and Conducting a Formal AAR

#	Approach	What	How
	Pre-Workshop Preparation	This may include interviews and/or sending pre-work to key stakeholders.	Tools: Information Gathering Template
1	What were we trying to do?	Create common understanding of what the objective of the program/imitative was.	Presentation from management and key stakeholders – giving facts
2	What actually happened?	Create common understanding of what the result of the program/initiative was (individual contribution).	Presentation of facts by all involved in the program/initiative
3	What did I like?	Individual contribution to the topic—both facts and opinion: "I Liked…"	Data generated needs to be clustered into themes, e.g., projects, teams, logistics. May identify "defining moments."
4	What would I do differently?	Individual contribution to the topic—both facts and opinion: "I Wish…"	Data generated needs to be clustered into themes e.g., projects, teams, logistics. May identify "defining moments".
5	What lessons have we learned and what do we recommend?	Groups take each of the themes and identifying lessons learned and recommendations for each lesson (all participants).	Groups provide specific and tangible recommendations for action. Tools: Lessons and Recommendation Template.
6	How will we evaluate the lessons and recommendation?	Brainstorm approach.	Define guiding principles and actions.
7	Prioritize Recommendations	Develop criteria for prioritization and brainstorm.	Recommendations will be documented as a first pass on priorities.
8	Recommendation Actions	Draft specific initiatives to be taken. Determine documentation, storage and dissemination of AAR outputs—for sharing knowledge.	Identify Key Stakeholders, Business Area Ownership, and Dependencies. Tools: Initiative Planning Template.
9	Key Stakeholder Communication	Develop summary message and recommendation; Develop communication plan.	Next step action. Tools: Communication Summary Template.
10	Wrap-up and Close Session		

BANNERS AND CHARTS (TOOL# 3)

There are five types of possible banners and charts that can be used in workshops:

1. Education and transfer of knowledge
2. Facilitation for solutions (for all types described in Mahal Facilitation Framework)
3. Inspirational and motivational
4. Marketing of products and services
5. Promotion of concepts, ideas, organizational proposals, and others.

In this tool, I am sharing ideas for items 1, 2 and 3 from the list above. While presentations can be made on tools such as PowerPoint and Video, they are momentary in nature and pass on as time goes on. Banners and charts can stay in workshop facilities for longer time periods. The participants continually see the visuals, which teach concepts, inspire ideas, and help raise provocative questions for deeper insights.

Charts made of paper that are around three feet by four feet in size can be printed on special commercial printers or obtained from print shops. But paper charts like these are typically disposed of and may not be reusable in their original condition. Banners made of a variety of stronger and durable materials can be reused over and over and are also portable. These hardier banners must be made by specialty suppliers. I have had a lot of success in getting reusable banners in a fabric that is durable yet very light to carry. It can be folded for travel, does not crease, and looks new even after years of use. My banners are made of "Poly Knit" material. The specialty suppliers simply take a PowerPoint slide and create the banner from it. The banners can have grommets put on all four corners for hanging on walls. Because the material is light, these can be placed on walls with either pushpins or artist tape that does not damage wall paint or wall paper.

The following examples are sample posters from my own facilitation kit as well as training in Business Process Management. The banner in Figure 12.3 is used for business process improvement workshops (Source: ASM Group, Inc.).

Figure 12.3 – Business Process Structure

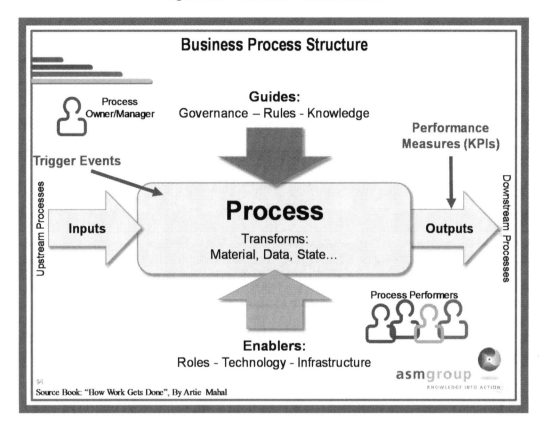

RICH PICTURE – (TOOL #4)

This is a valuable team exercise with several benefits and objectives including: using as an icebreaker for session participants, creating a future vision for an organizational unit or product or service, identifying stakeholders, identifying process work flow for mapping, and sparking creativity. All types of visuals, including pictures and graphics, are an effective way of framing concepts and communicating ideas in a group setting. For just about any topic of analysis, participants can be asked to draw a picture on a flip chart for what they believe to be the representation of the details around a topic.

Figure 12.4 – Rich Picture Diagram

For example, if a vision is to be created for a product or a service, the team members can create a "visual story" or a map of how the product/service would be used in the marketplace. Similarly, a vision can be outlined for a department or a process—regardless of the industry. The participants are encouraged to use many colored markers as color promotes right-brain thinking—the creative side of the brain.

I use this technique for opening just about any work session where solutions and strategies are to be developed. It is also a natural icebreaker as the participants coalesce around a common topic of interest and demonstrate creativity while having fun and promoting team collaboration.

PROCESS

1. Identify the scope of what the group is charged to do: solving a problem, understanding how work is done or should be done, creating a future vision, or another activity.

2. Form a small group of four to five participants into teams and provide them with the following instructions:

   a) Draw a picture on a flip chart using multiple colored markers.

   b) Use icons, symbols etc., but *no* text in any language is to be used. (This avoids people trying to wordsmith, which inhibits the flow of creative thinking and consumes time.)

   c) The total time allowed is nine minutes. For a larger team there could be multiple sub-teams doing this exercise separately. (Note that using an odd number stays in participants' memories longer than using an even number such as ten minutes.)

3. Have the teams present their pictures to the entire group or a have them take a "gallery walk" where each team moves around and observes the other teams' pictures.

4. Agree on the next step of documenting the pictures, which becomes a deliverable of the session and may be further used to identify stakeholders, ways of working, and even areas of improvement and priority.

PICTURE SIMULATION (TOOL #5)

This is a visual story telling exercise conducted by individuals or teams to express their feelings or insights about the topic of focus.

PROCESS

1. Establish the purpose of the Picture Simulation exercise. Obtain/prepare a deck of about thirty or more picture cards that are five inches by seven inches or, preferably, six inches by eight inches. The pictures need to be of a large variety of images, scenes, objects, etc. and pictures can be sourced from various websites or you may create a set of your own photographs.

2. Form a small group of two or three participants.

   a) In training workshops ask the participants to look through the deck of pictures and identify one picture each that reflects the experience of receiving training. If a participant chooses the butterfly picture example in Figure 12.5, it could reflect: "As the butterfly morphs out of the larva, I feel that the knowledge I have gained is helping me to transform my skills to a higher level of competency."

Figure 12.5 – Picture Simulation Cards

Butterfly   Bee on a flower

b) In a business solutions workshop, ask the participants to identify a picture that represents their value proposition to the business (assuming the group is composed of Information Technology analysts and their users—in this example). If the bee on the flower is chosen, it may reflect: "As the bees draw nectar from the flower center surrounded by the petals, we provide a network of data sources providing quality data in the central hub for the users to obtain good quality information, when they want it."

3. After the individuals and the teams have shared their pictures and the messages, the trainer or facilitator can summarize the overall theme based on the topic of discussion.

GRAPHIC TEMPLATES (TOOL #6)

Drawn by an artist and then digitized, graphic templates can be created as standard editable templates for ease of use. (Such templates can also be purchased. See the Resources Chapter.) These editable templates can be used for preparing work sessions and for documenting and presenting outputs. The graphic visual with colors promotes engagement of the participants and the interest of those who receive the information.

Figure 12.6 – Editable Graphics Template Example

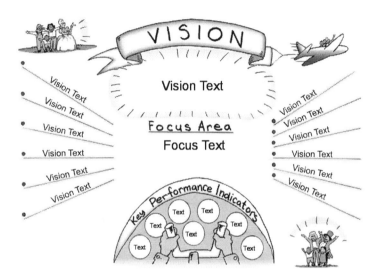

COMMUNICATION GUIDELINE (TOOL #7)

A facilitator must communicate with clients, workshop participants, management, and other stakeholders. A basic set of communication guidelines are essential to use as a checklist when sending written communication or when the workshop outputs are disseminated.

Approach:

- What is the business objective (what should this communication accomplish)?
- What is the communication goal—to inform, educate, get buy-in, or motivate to action?
- What is the key message or messages this communication should convey?
- What deadlines are involved in this communication?

- Is this part of any larger communication effort that should be considered?

Audience:

- Who are the audience and the stakeholders for this communication?
- Will separate communication to any of the stakeholders be needed?
- What is the audience's preferred method of communication?
- What action should this communication prompt the audience to take?

Application:

- Are there any legal or regulatory considerations to this communication?
- Is the length of this communication appropriate? Will it fit in an e-mail? Will it require attachments?
- Will all members of the audience have access to the vehicles being used (e.g., e-mail, internet)?
- Will face-to-face communication be needed for meetings or training?
- For webinars, teleconferences, or remote facilitation, have the time zones for all participants been considered?
- Who is responsible for creating the communication?
- Who is responsible for disseminating communication to various stakeholders?
- What's the internal approval process?

DATA MODEL (TOOL #8)

Data may be defined as facts needed to execute process and to understand work done. These facts are input to a process and then, through its execution, are consumed or transformed into information. Data only becomes information when it is transformed through some process to achieve specific outputs. Process and data are co-dependent—one without the other has little value. If process is the "body," data is the "nervous system" that flows through it. For example, if you order a book online, you provide data facts as input on a website, which in turn triggers the order fulfillment process of the supplier.

Similar to process modeling, data modeling has its own discipline, modeling conventions, and terminology. Data models help identify data needs and business rules for getting work done, and thus support the execution and governance of processes. There are three types of data models: Conceptual Data Models, Logical Data Models, and Physical Data Models. Each of these depicts data facts in a structure known as an Entity Relationship Diagram or ER Diagram, as shown in Figure 12.7. This is a visual model of how a customer places an order for a product.

Figure 12.7 – Conceptual Data Model

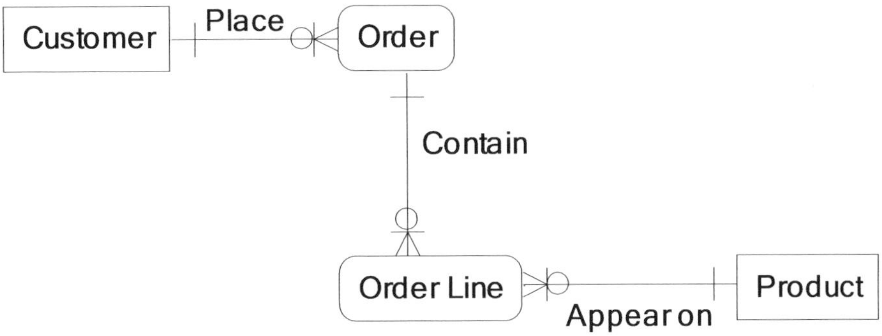

Data requirements for a business need are represented in a format known as metadata, or data about data, that is the basis for defining data models and structures. The basic components of a data model are:

- *Entity* is a set of data about a person, place, concept, thing or event needed by the business to perform their functions and execute processes. For example, Customer, Product, and Employee.
- *Attribute* is a basic data element which belongs to, and describes, an entity. For example, Customer Name, Product Number, and Employee Name.
- *Relationship* shows an association between two entities and the number of each involved. For example, one Customer places many Orders, and one Order is for one Customer.

Using this as a communication tool, business requirements that include business rules and functional requirements are identified for an application. Progressive versions of data models are developed from the beginning of a business need to the creation of databases and applications. Conceptual models facilitate business context and support policies, logical models facilitate data and business rules support, and physical data models provide the data store structures to support business functions and application systems.

PROCESS

1. Intent: Agree on the scope of the data requirements needed. It can be for a department, process, project, and so on, to gather information with the purpose of understanding user needs for a computer application, as an example. Facilitate a session with business users and process and data analysts as appropriate.

2. Framing: Explain the concepts of data entities and data models, and how they are used as input for an automated business application. Give a simple example of "customer places an order for a product." Explain that first the data entities will be identified and then data models will be created (conceptual data models to start with).

3. For the scoped area, brainstorm and identify fundamental data entities. Have volunteers write one data entity per Sticky note and place it on a wall chart. Remind the participants that data entities are named as singular nouns—Customer, not Customers. Examples of data entities can be: Customer, Product and Order.

4. Have a few volunteers come up to the wall chart and collectively create a conceptual data model (See Figure 12.7). This will generate meaningful discussion and debate about the data entity definitions, entity relationships, business rules and data attributes, and others. Document all this information, which is called metadata.

5. Identify next steps for how the data requirements will be documented, validated, used, and communicated.

DOTOCRACY (TOOL #9)

While there are numerous ways to prioritize information gathering in brainstorming exercises, the use of "Dots" or "Sticky Dots" in a group work session is very effective. It is efficient, promotes equal participation in decision making, and the result of the group opinions is visible to all. Thus the term "Dotocracy" is used; a play on the word Democracy. The formal name of the "Dots" is Removable Color Coded Labels. Typically these labels are made of round paper and come in the colors red, yellow, green, and blue etc. Each of these "Dots" is about 0.75 inches in diameter or 1.9 centimeters.

Figure 12.8 – Dots (Removable Color-Coded Labels)

Note: In decision making, Gary Rush points out three insights that should to be kept in mind: *Contention produces change; Compromise can be lose-lose; and Consensus is win-win.*

PROCESS

1. Brainstorm and gather information on the topic of focus. Establish the purpose of prioritization (e.g., to gain agreement on the top three items or clusters to work on).

2. Prioritization Exercise: Perform a simple "Dots" exercise by giving each of the participants a set number of dots for voting on the items of their preference. Typically each participant is given a set number of dots (odd number) depending on the volume of data generated for priority and the number of participants. For example: if there are ten participants and the quantity of data for options is small, give each person eleven dots for voting. For larger quantities of data, reduce the number of allocated dots appropriately. The rule is that participants may put all their dots on any one item or spread them across many items. In this exercise, the

color of the dots does not matter. This type of voting can be done on each item or on clusters/themes.

3. Quality Review: In this approach, the dots are used based on an agreed legend by the group. For example if a review is being done to determine the health of a process such as *Recruit and Hire Employees Process*, the legend for the use of dots to determine the status of process attributes can be: red—broken or does not work well; yellow—works so/so, sometime it works and sometime it does not; and green—works well, the process is okay. After going through this exercise, if there are many red dots, the group may wish to further prioritize items to be fixed based on time or money constraints. A blue dot can be used to signify a high priority consideration on the red dotted items.

Note:

a) If the "Dots" are not available, colored markers can be used instead.
b) Multiple dots on the same items are acceptable, signifying a stronger preference.
c) This tool provides many possibilities. Improvise.

MANAGING CHALLENGING PARTICIPANTS AND SITUATIONS (TOOL #10)

A facilitator must develop good listening skills and also learn to read the body language of the participants. Just as the light house scans the horizon all around with the light beacon, so should be the facilitator continuously be aware of the level of engagement of the participants, be able to infer the meaning of the various behaviors, and decide if an intervention is needed.

For example, if in a training workshop a participant seems to be uncomfortable with the topic of study, it is best to ask the group if they are comfortable with what was just covered. This gives the participant (or participants) an opportunity to speak up and express what they are feeling. The same is true for any type of workshop. Some principles should be adhered to:

a) Never embarrass someone or put anyone on the spot by giving undue attention, regardless of their behavior.

b) Always maintain a professional composure and be matter of fact in dealing with the situation.

c) Always deal with the issue at hand as a good leader would—diplomatically and not alienating anyone. Prior to your intervention, first determine whether the problem is a bad situation or a difficult and challenging participant. Some behaviors may be due to a genuine organizational urgency or a personal matter of the participant, such as child care, elder care, or health issues in the family.

d) Be aware of cross-cultural considerations. Reference Chapter 9, Cross-Cultural Facilitation.

For managing group dynamics, the concept of "Make the rounds, before you make the rounds" is critical, meaning that you must understand the personalities of all the stakeholders while planning the session engagement and designing the agenda.

The following Group Dynamics Guide (Table 12.2) outlines common people issues and strategies to deal with them in a workshop setting. These are by no means all the possible behaviors that can be present. But with practice, you will become good at mastering all situations—whatever they may be. Remember the Facilitator's Mantra: "Keep calm and carry on." This mantra is your best friend at all times.

Table 12.2 – Group Dynamics Guide

Behavior	Some Attributes	Strategy
Dominating Participants	• Backseat Driver has a habit of telling others what to do. • Broken Record repeats the same things over. • Loudmouth tries to show her importance. • Know It All has been in the organization a long time and shows off his knowledge. • Interpreter interprets what others say.	• Have session norms agreed to in the beginning and remind those to the group as needed. • Maintain structured discussion on the topic in scope. • Remain focused on the objectives and timeframes. • Encourage equal participation. • Ask the participant to write her issue on a sticky notes and place it on the parking-lot chart and address its later. • A one to one off line discussion may be necessary—in private.

Behavior	Some Attributes	Strategy
The Skeptic	• Late Comer / Early Leaver: (Someone who wants to show his importance and may be of higher rank; or there may be a valid reason. • Attacker challenges every point without valid basis.	• Make sure the schedule is communicated and accepted. • Establish session norms/ground rule penalties for interruptions. • Communicate value of all participants' opinions and contribution. • Sometimes a one to one off line discussion may reveal that there is some business constraint or a personal issue which the participant is trying to deal with. This needs empathy and a different strategy to address the situation. Note: This type of behavior is common when there is an organizational change underway and the employees may be concerned about their job security or business change.
Making it Personal	• Head Shaker repeatedly disagrees in a negative way. • Doubting Thomas has a negative view about things being addressed "this will never work…" • Dropout chooses to drop out of participating in important topic.	• Encourage feedback on the approach. • Enlist suggestions for change in the approach underway. • Try to clarify the reason for the course of discussion. • Do your homework on understanding the personalities of the participants "*make the rounds.*" • Ask the participant to come up to the flip chart and write their issue in their own hand.
The Sidebar	• Whisperer • Gossiper • Busy Bee	• Move physically toward gossiping individuals while carrying on with the topic and take a check point: "are you all comfortable with what we are covering" while looking directly and naturally at them in a bit of a raised voice. But do not let them feel that you have put them on the spot. • Ask for their input regarding the topic at hand. • Move on—don't embarrass them and find another way to engage them in a discussion. • Ask one of those participants to volunteer and write the topic points being discussed on the flip chart or on a sticky note. • Remind everyone of the one conversation rule that you established at the beginning, as the session norm.

Behavior	Some Attributes	Strategy
Disengaged	• Not participating actively • Blank look (Seems to not understand what is going on) • Disinterested	• Without undue focus, try to engage this participant proactively in some session activity such as writing on the flip chart. • Take a checkpoint on the progress being made in the session and that if everyone is comfortable with the activities. • A one to one off line discussion may be necessary—in private. Note: This type of behavior may be because of professional or person issues the individual might be going through at that time or s/he has been told by the superiors to be in the session without understanding the purpose and value to the individual.

BODY LANGUAGE (TOOL #11)

Body language is the unconscious and conscious transmission and interpretation of feelings, attitudes, and moods, through body posture; movement; physical state; position; and relationship to other bodies, objects and surroundings; facial expression; and eye movement. The transmission and interpretation of body language can be quite different from the spoken word.

Body language, technically known as kinesics (pronounced ki-nee-siks), is not an exact science. Signals and gestures from individuals may be expressions of certain emotions. Since the publication of Charles Darwin's *The Expression of the Emotions in Man and Animals* in 1872, many theories and detailed studies have been conducted on this topic by experts in human behavior and science. Body language goes both ways:

- Your own body language reveals your feelings and meanings to others.
- Other people's body language reveals their feelings and meanings to you.

The sending and receiving of body language signals happens on conscious and unconscious levels. In this context, my purpose of introducing the subject of body language is to ensure that facilitators are fully aware of the need to observe the expressions and body language of participants to nurture their engagement in sessions. Remember that facilitators must be like a lighthouse beacon—scanning the audience to have a pulse on the session dynamics at all times, observing emotions and gestures for clues that intervention is needed.

PROFESSOR ALBERT MEHRABIAN'S COMMUNICATIONS MODEL

Professor Albert Mehrabian has pioneered the understanding of communications since the 1960s. He devotes his time to researching, writing, and consulting on body language and nonverbal communications.

The value of Mehrabian's theory relates to communications where emotional content is significant, and the need to understand it properly is great. This is often applicable in management and business, where motivation and attitude have a crucial effect on outcomes. Here is one representation of Dr. Mehrabian's findings than is typically cited or applied:

- Seven percent of messages pertaining to feelings and attitudes are in the words that are spoken.
- Thirty-eight percent of messages pertaining to feelings and attitudes are paralinguistic (the way that the words are said).
- Fifty-five percent of messages pertaining to feelings and attitudes are in facial expressions.

Refer to Dr. Albert Mehrabian's key book, *Silent Messages*, which contains much information about nonverbal communications (body language). (Reference: www.kaaj.com/psych.)

In this book, the Body Language concept is being introduced for awareness only. The student of facilitation is recommended to study the art and science of recognizing signals the body sends through the eyes, mouth, head, arms, hands, handshake, legs, and so forth. There is plenty of literature, and tools such as body language cards, available elsewhere.

While minor variations and differences have been found among obscure and isolated tribes-people, the following basic human emotions are generally used, recognized, and part of humankind's genetic character. It is generally accepted that certain basic facial expressions of human emotion are recognized around the world, and that the use and recognition of these expressions is genetically inherited rather than socially conditioned or learned. These basic facial expressions are shown in Figure 12.9.

Figure 12.9 – Facial Expressions of Human Emotion

| Happiness | Sadness | Fear |
| Disgust | Surprise | Anger |

LOTUS BLOSSOM (TOOL#12)

The Lotus Blossom concept developed by Yasuo Matsumura of Japan, is a technique of ideation for new ideas, problem solving and exploring options for implementing existing solutions. Using Matsumura's Lotus Blossom concept, you take one of the emerging themes, create another core and expand upon it. See Figure 12.10. This approach provides many possibilities that can be prioritized based on the ideation criteria and within the limits of given constraints. This method works well in smaller groups for one given problem area at a time. General brainstorming guidelines apply in this method.

Figure 12.10 – Lotus Blossom Ideation

Lotus Blossom Ideation Template

6	3	7	6	3	7	6	3	7
2	F	4	2	C	4	2	G	4
5	1	8	5	1	8	5	1	8
6	3	7	F	C	G	6	3	7
2	B	4	B	Main Idea	D	2	D	4
5	1	8	E	A	H	5	1	8
6	3	7	6	3	7	6	3	7
2	E	4	2	A	4	2	H	4
5	1	8	5	1	8	5	1	8

Concept Developed by Yasuo Matsumura of Clover Management Research, Chiba City, Japan

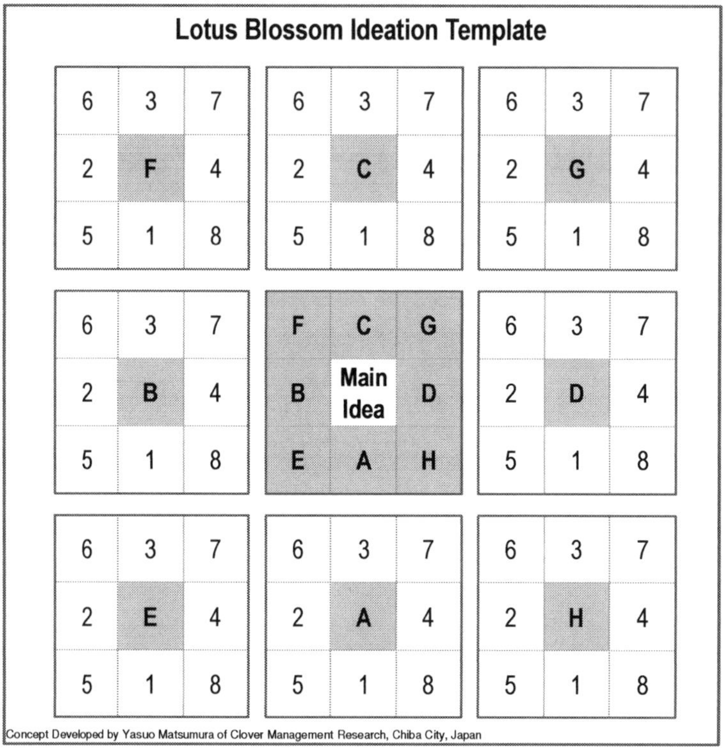

PROCESS

1. Establish the purpose for using a Lotus Blossom and identify a topic of interest. Create a template on computer or use a wall chart where participants can interactively collaborate in brainstorming. This technique works well for about six to eight participants per one template. For larger groups, have separate Lotus Blossom templates.

2. Explain the concept to the participants and have them use sticky notes for ideation. Starting with the core, the participants would continue to generate items until they have exhausted all ideas or they believe they have enough to move on to the next step.

3. Prioritize ideas, solutions, options, and other results by marking with colored markers or applying colored dots. Identify next steps for action.

For example, a group of people intend to hold a planning workshop for their non-profit organization and are looking for a suitable location. Therefore, "Find Location for Conducting a Workshop" is the central issue/challenge for the ideation exercise. Once they have identified ideas as shown in Figure 12.11, they may choose Day Rental as one of the options to be the central theme and conduct ideation around the eight "leaves" of the lotus template. The team would do the same for all the ideas on the other leaves. This continues until the team decides that they have enough ideas and can wrap up this part of the exercise.

Figure 12.11 – Lotus Blossom Example

Park—Open Area	Municipal Building	Hotel
Church Hall	**Find Location for Conducting a Workshop**	**Day Rental**
Virtual Session	Home of a Volunteer	Town Library

BIOMIMICRY (TOOL #13)

The design discipline of biomimicry seeks sustainable solutions by emulating nature's time-tested patterns and strategies, such as a solar cell inspired by a leaf. The core idea is that nature, imaginative by necessity, has already solved many of the problems we are grappling with: energy, food production, climate control, non-toxic chemistry, transportation, packaging, and a whole lot more.

Biologist Janine Benyus coined the term biomimicry in 1997. Through her consulting firm, Biomimicry 3.8, she works with major corporations to use nature in helping create smarter products and services. In an August 2014

Reader's Digest article *Spiderwebs and Other Inspirations* by Andy Simmons, Janine tells this story about using nature to solve problems: *A company called Arnold Glas was concerned about all the birds killed when flying into windows. The company's scientists wondered how nature solved this kind of problem. The answer, Benyus says, is spiders. "Spiders build webs for bugs," she explains. "But birds obviously would destroy the webs, so spiders weave in strands of silk that reflect UV light. Birds can see it, but bugs and humans can't." So, the company includes UV-reflection material in its Ornilux glass. "Now it sells bird-safe windows," says Benyus.* (See one education source: www.asknature.org.)

When facilitating for ideas for innovation in products, services, processes, and other innovations, participants need to be made aware of this emerging discipline of mimicking nature. While humans have been mimicking nature since the beginning of time (trying to fly like a bird), this discipline is now taking a formal approach in its own right.

BRAINSTORMING (TOOL #14)

Brainstorming is described in detail in Chapter 6. Many of the tools being defined in this section have an applied brainstorming component.

The general purpose of brainstorming is to generate ideas and discover insights about a specific topic around problem solving, strategy development, ideation, and other issues. Typically, participants come up with their own ideas, which are collectively harvested for the whole group by a facilitator. The disparate ideas go through affinity analysis, where "like things fall together" and are grouped into clusters and given titles as themes for further use. This data and their themes provide insights into the subject matter and become input to actions for implementing solutions. The generic process below may be modified for those variations.

PROCESS

1. Topic: Identify the topic of interest and the scope the group is charged to deliver. Based on this purpose select one of the various

brainstorming options and conduct the workshop. Describe the rules of brainstorming to the group.

2. Ideas: If the group is small—from five to ten people—each of the participants is asked to generate individual ideas. Note: Alex F. Osborn, the father of brainstorming, emphasized that individuals must take five minutes to think about their ideas before listing them. For larger groups—ten to twelve people—form small subgroups of three or four participants, have them generate individual ideas, list them, and then collectively create sticky notes—one idea per sticky-note—and place them on a wall chart.

3. Analysis: Determine what information is to be harvested from the "raw" data in the previous step; and why. In some cases the entities are identified for analysis as in the case of data entities for creating data models. In other cases affinity analysis is done to cluster "like types of items" into useable themes. For clustering, ask for volunteers to identify like items and create logical clusters relevant to the topic of interest on a wall chart. With a marker, have them circle the clusters and give them titles, which are considered themes. Have the volunteers report out the themes for a common understanding by the group.

4. Priority: All the themes may not be equally important. To assess the opinions of the participants as to their preference, have the group vote using "sticky dots" ("dotocracy," as in democracy). This may provide the basis for consensus and prioritization for actions.

5. Action: Identify the next possible action the group would like to take. It may be to create an action plan of the themes, whereby each theme can be an initiative or a project and then timeframes can be identified for each of the themes.

6. Next Step: Upon conclusion, agree on who will document the output and deliverables and who will communicate the outcome to relevant stakeholders.

INFORMATION IDENTIFICATION GUIDE (TOOL #15)

In the context of facilitation, a facilitator has to study the nature and scope of the topic at hand and prepare to engage in the design of the work session including formulating questions for interviews.

Table 12.3 is a useful tool for identifying common organizational objects in an effective and efficient manner. When you identify an information type as shown in the first column, it corresponds to the organizational object of interest shown in the second column. This is more of a craft than science. With practice it becomes second nature to analyze any information in this manner. Once the objects are identified, they serve multiple methodologies for analysis and critical thinking in an organization.

Table 12.3 – Information Identification Guide

Information Type Examples	Potential Object for Analysis	Meaning and Usage
Activity or Work	Process	A process to "Do Something"—a series of steps to accomplish something. Expressed as verb and noun combination. Example: Recruit and Hire an Employee.
Activity or Action with Options	Decision	This is usually described as an "Activity" but with Two or More Mutually Exclusive Options. Example: Reject Application.
Activity Based on a Particular Need or Criteria	Event	An activity that is based on a particular criteria of time or an event. In process analysis this is usually an "Event Trigger" Example: Hiring fair at a university for recruitment process.
Business Application	System	A collection of tasks or activities to accomplish something of value. This is considered an "Enabler." Example: Employee Payroll System.
Equipment or Facility	Infrastructure	Buildings, roads, facilities, or equipment that has multiple uses is usually considered an "Enabler" to activities or processes. Examples: Truck, HR Interview Room.
Location/Physical Area	Geography	Physical locations or geographic regions may be considered "Infrastructure" as well as "Data Entities."

Information Type Examples	Potential Object for Analysis	Meaning and Usage
Mechanism / Platform	Technology	A Technique or Automation of an activity or a series of activities. This may be an "Enabler" to one or more business applications.
Organization, Division, Department Name	Organization and/or Organizational Unit (Sometimes can be a Stakeholder as well)	An "Entity" engaged in some work of interest. Example: Human Resource Department.
Person Name	Stakeholder	Those who have "Vested Interest" in the scope and/or outcome of an activity. Example: Job Applicant.
Person Title	Role	Someone who is "Doing" something. This may be considered an "Enabler" of an activity or a process. Example: CEO.
Policies, Regulations	Constraints / Rules	These may be "Guides" of a business process i.e., the "Controls" on an activity. Example: Managers must be proficient in organizational leadership competencies.
Singular Noun / Datum	Data Entity	Person, place, thing, or event about which an "Organization has Will and Means to Store Information." It is expressed as singular noun. Example: Employee (Not Employees), Organization (Not Organizations).
Skills	Competency	Knowledge, skills, abilities and experience to perform a specific role or roles. The competencies may be "Effectiveness" (leadership/managerial/behavioral) or "Functional" (technical/specialized/role specific). Example: Manage Vision and Purpose (Effectiveness), Project Management (Functional).

Example: The NewAge Food Company is a fictitious organization. The first paragraph provides a brief overview of their business. The second paragraph has been analyzed to identify organizational objects—shown in parenthesis and italics. This is what an analyst or a facilitator might do to get a deeper understanding of the organization in terms of its purpose and supporting structure.

THE NEWAGE FOODS COMPANY

The NewAge Foods Company makes foods containing antioxidants and other supplements consistent with popular trends in the market place. The business is a family-owned operation based on the East Coast of the United States. The company primarily focuses on ready-to-eat snacks which are sold through various channels that include grocery, drugs, theaters, health stores, vending outlets, and the like. In addition to the mass production of snacks such as cookies and energy bars, the company produces specialized snacks such as cookies for diabetics—which they sell through their mail-order part of the business.

The *NewAge Foods Company* (Organization and Data Entity) *makes foods* (Process) containing antioxidants and other *supplements* (Data Entity) consistent with popular *trends* (Event) in the market place. The business is a *family-owned* (Stakeholders) *operation* (Organizational Unit and Data Entity) based on the *East Coast of the United States* (Geography/Data Entity). The company primarily focuses on *ready-to-eat snacks* (Product Data Entity) which are *sold through* (Process) various *channels* (Data Entity) that include grocery, drugs, theaters, health stores, vending *outlets* (Data Entity), and the like. In addition to the *mass production* (Process and Infrastructure) of snacks such as cookies and energy bars, the company produces (value proposition) specialized snacks such as cookies for *diabetics* (Customers/Stakeholders)—which they sell through their *mail-order* (Process/Technology) part of the business model.

VOICE IN THE ROOM (TOOL #16)

Participants in a session must be given the opportunity to say something personal in the very beginning. If not, they may hold back and not participate fully because their presence is not "recognized." There are thousands of ways this type of introduction can be done. Here are simple yet effective examples for using this concept, which also serve as icebreakers.

A) Ask the participants to tell the "story" of their name. Every person's name generally has a very interesting origin. Ask them the meaning of their name, who chose it, why was it chosen, what the middle name stands for, and what their last name represents. I generally have the participants stand in a circle and speak. For example my name is Arjit Singh Mahal. In the Punjabi language, Arjit is a combined word made up of "Ar" and "Jit." "Ar" means enemy and "jit" means to win. So, the first name means "the one who wins over the enemy." (Enemy, in this case, means a constraint, challenge, or simply something negative.) The middle name "Singh" means Lion. Every Sikh has this as the middle name to represent courage. And the last name "Mahal" is a clan name of the Jat tribes, which migrated into India from Central Asia around the time of Alexander's invasion of India. So, you can see that a name tells a very interesting history.

B)   The Thumball™ by Answers in Motion, LLC, is available from various suppliers outlined in the Resources Chapter. They come in several options to suit different types of communication and interactions. For example there are balls for introduction icebreakers, group quizzes, exercises, and more. To use this technique, have the participants stand in a circle away from their chairs. Explain the exercise: "When you catch the ball, give your name, department name, expectations from the session, and a story about the item where your left or right thumb touches the ball. Have the participants throw the ball to other participants randomly.

Figure 12.12 – Thumball™

Premade   **Customize for your own purpose**

C)   Use a Specialized Ball for learning and knowledge consolidation. I have the ball shown in Figure 12.13, which has elements of Business Process Management around each of the panels. For example one panel has the term "Process," and another the term "Business Change." Ask participants to describe, in their own words, what the term means where one of their thumbs touches while catching the ball. This special ball is used in training sessions as well as facilitation sessions where a business process improvement is being facilitated. These balls can be customized to fit your needs or you can purchase a blank one, allowing you to create your own learning and engagement tool for any professional practice or learning situation.

Figure 12.13 – Process Learning Ball

D)   Custom learning and engagement ball for your client. A blank Thumball™, shown in Figure 12.12, can be used to create a unique tool for a specific client. For example one of my clients is an international food manufacturing organization with products ranging from chocolate snacks to pet food and coffee and tea. I have organizational-specific trivia labeled on each of the panels. In afternoons after lunch, when the participants tend to be a bit lethargic, I have them stand in a circle and do the exercise as described in step (B).

E)   Personal Shield. From ancient times, nobles and families of note wore their family crest and coat of arms as a mark of unique status in society. These crests, in addition to being used in their mansions, stationary, etc., were engraved on the shields when they went into battle. This concept can be used for introductions of participants in workshops—particularly when they are meeting other team members for the first time, for example global team members meeting to develop solutions and strategies. It can serve as both an icebreaker and a team building exercise.

Figure 12.14 – Introduction Shield Template

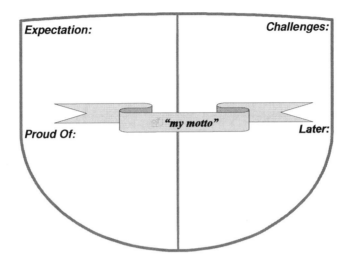

PROCESS

1. Pre-Workshop: Send the template of the shield (as a PowerPoint file) to the participants ahead of the session so that they may create their shields and submit them to the facilitator prior to the session. The facilitator loads them onto the computer in preparation of the opening of the session. (Note: The shield exercise can be done in the workshop for team building exercise as well.)

2. Instructions: "Develop your own shield using the template provided. Depict your own uniqueness, both professionally and personally. Use symbols, icons, figures, or another method to represent yourself—but don't use any words. In the banner in the middle, create your motto—who you are and what you stand for.

3. Presentation: At the opening of the session, participants present their shields. Here's my shield—used in a global workshop in the role of a facilitator.

Figure 12.15 – Introduction Shield of Artie Mahal—Example

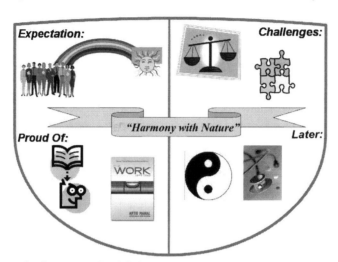

My explanation of what my shield depicts:

Expectation	As a facilitator I manage the process in a way that participants achieve the expected outcome "at the end of the rainbow."
Challenges	The balance of time and ensuring that all pieces of the puzzle fit to ensure a superior outcome from the session.
Proud of	Extensive reading on all topics. And writing my first book.
Later	Quest for spirituality. Managing better health.
My Motto	Harmony with Nature.

LAUGHING THERAPY (TOOL #17)

Laughter is the universal language of humor, fun, celebration, and enjoyment. In some cultures, individuals and groups use laughter on regular basis to relive stress and generate positive energy for their health and wellbeing. This is a good tool for facilitators to use in workshops as often as possible for icebreakers and, occasionally, to make a point on a topic. Humorous jokes and stories are encouraged for better engagement of participants in workshops.

There are hundreds of ways to generate laughter. Clown Noses come in various sizes and colors and are generally made of foam. I always use one technique of laughter therapy at the close of workshops to celebrate the successful end: "Clown Nose Laughter."

Have participants stand in a circle and give each one a "nose." Demonstrate how to put it on by first putting a "nose" on yourself. Have them touch their ears with their thumbs, wiggle their other fingers, face other participants and say, "Tee Hee, Tee Hee, Tee Hee," and laugh loudly. See Figure 12.16. This generates a lot of laughter. (Technique created by Dr. Annette Goodheart 1935-2011, laughter therapist, lecturer and author of the book *Laughter Therapy: How to Laugh About Everything in Your Life That Isn't Really Funny*.)

Figure 12.16 – Laughter Therapy

Note: Always distribute new and fresh clown noses. When the participants finish the exercise, they take them home. (Never reuse them in other workshops, for hygienic reasons.)

PERSONAL LIBRARY OF FACILITATION RESOURCES (TOOL #18)

Your personal library may include the following resources:

- Frameworks, methods, techniques, and tools on all four types of the facilitation groupings defined in the *Mahal Facilitation Framework*.
- Ready-to-use templates in support of facilitation methods and techniques.
- Engagers and energizers library and tools.
- Reference books on various methods and tools from a variety of professional experts relevant to facilitation and the subject areas of your interest in education, training and consulting.
- An active network with other professionals to share ideas and learn a variety of approaches.

- Subscriptions to professional journals, saving articles future reference.
- Helpful hints and tips for improving your facilitation capability and improving the facilitation process.
- Stories, metaphors and anecdotes to be used to inspire and motivate participants.
- Case studies for training workshops.
- Videos for teaching aids and a catalogue of relevant websites.
- Learning Aids or "Thinkertoys." Research and use learning tools and "toys" for engagement and energy.
- A collection of posters and banners to use in facilitation. Some of these can be the methodologies of the topic being facilitated. Those can be displayed on walls for visual and common understanding.

LISTENING LADDER (TOOL #19)

Epictetus, the Greek sage and philosopher (AD55-135) stated: *Nature gave us one tongue and two ears so that we could hear twice as much as we speak.* The idea that we should be good listeners has a profound meaning for anyone in the role of a facilitator. The facilitator must be a good listener throughout the facilitation process. The following technique can be easily mastered with practice.

Table 12.4 – The Listening Ladder

Look	At the person speaking to you. Make eye contact to express that you are interested in what the other person has to say.
Ask	Questions. Ask follow-up open ended questions to comprehend the meaning of what is being said by the speaker.
Don't	Interrupt or be interrupted. Ensure that the interruption is only for clarification of what has been said.
Don't	Change the subject. You will get an indication to change the topic when the speaker is finished with one thought. Look for cues to transition to another topic.
Empathize	With the speaker. Demonstrate this by a gesture such as "nodding your head" so that the speaker gets the message that you are interested in what is being said.
Respond	Verbally and nonverbally. Through body language such as nodding your head, eye/eyebrow movements, acknowledge that you are just as engaged in the conversation as the speaker is. You can do this without interrupting the speaker by saying, "...I see..." or "...I understand..."

Here is an exercise to demonstrate the value of good listening in team building or work sessions.

PROCESS

1. Team Formation. Ask participants to pair up in sub-teams.

2. Instruction: Have Person One tell a story about any topic to Person Two. Person One is the speaker and Person Two is the listener. Instruct Person Two to not pay any attention to what Person One says. Instruct Person One to begin telling the story—for one minute only.

3. Debrief: After Step #2 is complete, ask Person One how he/she felt. The usual response is, "Person Two was disengaged and not interested in what I had to say. It was uncomfortable to go on telling my story."

4. The Listening Ladder. Now explain the concept of Listening Ladder as an awareness and skill building tool. Have the sub-teams repeat the exercise in Step #2 but this time, Person Two is asked to apply Listening Ladder principles in the conversation with Person One.

5. Debrief: Ask Person One and Person Two how they both felt in this exchange. The typical response is that Person One is satisfied that she was able to convey her story well and Person Two expresses that he was fully engaged and interested in what Person One had to say.

PRESENTATION SKILLS (TOOL #20)

The subject of presentations can be lengthy and make for a very large chapter. In this section my objective is to provide some basic presentation concepts and techniques that a facilitator should be aware of and use effectively.

Material Organization. Based on the topic to be covered, organize your material using the Four W's: *What* is the topic of focus? *Why* am I giving this presentation? *Who* is the audience? And *What* is in it for them? It may help to think about the outcome you expect from the presentation and then work through the four W's.

Delivery Framework. There is an old saying about presentations: *Tell them what you are going to tell them; tell them; and then tell them what you told them*. This is a basic three-part framework. First, know your subject well and succinctly describe your topic to the audience to get them interested in what is about to be delivered to them. "Wet their appetite" using an attention grabber. Then deliver the topic in an engaging way so that it is not a lecture but, rather, a productive dialogue. (Remember that more of them and less of you is better.) Upon completion of the topic, summarize what you have presented highlighting the key takeaways. Create a memorable close.

Timing. Winston Churchill once said: "I must apologize for making a rather long speech this morning. I didn't have time to prepare a short one!" Presentations can drag on if not properly planned and rehearsed for time. The rule of thumb is to prepare your presentation then cut it by fifty percent. It is probable that unforeseen factors could cut into your allotted time. The shorter the better.

Questions. John Townsend of The Master Trainer Institute of France, has this very practical approach to handling questions and interruptions. Many audience questions are not necessarily questions but, rather, requests for clarification or attempts to gain the spotlight. Facilitators must answer succinctly as follows.

Reflect	Back to the questioner what you thought was the question: "If I understand correctly, you're asking..."
	Depending on how the questioner reformulates the question, answer it or Deflect it.
Deflect	*Group*: "How does the rest of the group feel?" or "Has anyone else had a similar problem?"
	Reflect: (to one participant—perhaps a subject matter expert) "John you're an expert on this...what do you think?"
	Reverse: (back to the questioner) "You've probably done something like this before. What's your view?"

Flip Charting. Today, it is common not to have flip charts available in conference rooms. The notion is that facilitators have laptops to make their presentations using an overhead projector. I believe that while use of automation enhances productivity, it may not be as impactful as the presenter writing some key messages on a flip chart (or a wall chart) while presenting through a computer. There is a place for being "high tech" and there is a place for being "high touch." Both are needed. A smart presenter—particularly in the role of facilitation—has flip charts available in order to create a visual impact when needed.

Here are some considerations. Prepare key charts in advance, and give a title to each chart. Write big and bold and use bullets for emphasis on key items. Write in what is called "highway writing" as in signs on the highway, which are a combination of capital and lower case letters—making it easier for the eyes to read. Use multi-colored and water washable markers (multiple colors engage the right side of the brain, which promotes creative thinking). Speak loudly while writing as you will be facing away from the audience. (Another strategy is to ask a volunteer write on the flip chart.)

When I have to write rather fast, I tend to make spelling errors. The audience likes to point out errors promptly. I draw a round circle with a dot in the middle (representing an electric button/switch) on one of the flip charts and state, "I have a high-tech spell checker. At the end of the session when I press the button, all my misspellings are corrected." Or I tell them with humor that Mark Twain felt sorry for people who could spell only one way! Participants laugh at these and no one complains about misspellings thereafter. (Note: I am not condoning poor spelling skills, but giving you a tool for how to manage such situations.)

"Frame the flip charts." Put a frame around the flip chart using a thick bold marker. This enhances the messages on the flip chart.

Engagers and Energizers. Review the concepts, techniques and tools outlined in Chapter 5. Use them as appropriate along with Howard Gardner's Multiple Intelligences Framework—described in that same chapter—to engage the audience in a most effective manner.

Checklist. The solution to Murphy's Law of, "If something can go wrong—it will," is a checklist of supplies, preparing and practicing the delivery of material in advance, and ensuring that the equipment works and that the room is set up properly.

HELPFUL HINTS

- Learn about your audience: who they are and what matters most to them.
- Don't create "death by PowerPoint," meaning minimize slides and maximize engagement through dialogue, stories and interactive transfer of messages.
- Use voice with "color" showing emotion. Speak loudly to ensure everyone can hear you.
- Have high visibility marker colors on hand. "Bruise" colors (black, blue, purple, maroon, and brown) offer the best visibility. Avoid red markers to the extent possible (color blind people cannot differentiate red from certain other colors.)
- Check the facility, equipment, supplies, and arrangements beforehand.
- Before delivery: Practice, practice, practice!

BRAINWRITING (TOOL #21)

Brainwriting is a way to solve problems using intuition, states Michael Michalko in his book *Thinkertoys*. This exercise can be used in conjunction with brainstorming as preparation by individuals to contribute ideas to the group information gathering exercise.

PROCESS

1. Find a quiet space and get relaxed. Write down your particular challenge and concentrate on it for a few minutes—almost like focused meditation of the mind.

2. Write down relevant questions about your challenge: What is it that I am looking for? How does it help my interest in the cause? What are alternatives and options? Which option should I pick and why?

3. Write down as many responses as you can to the questions in Step #2. Your inner mind will provide you answers that you can rationalize and take action on as appropriate.

For example when I was in charge of the learning and development group of a large organization, my challenge was to roll out a set of new training modules for the managers—with just about no headcount available to hire trainers. I was told by the VP of human resources "Artie, read my lips, no head count increase is available." The brainwriting exercise helped me come up with a rather creative solution of outsourcing the delivery of training modules to an external training organization.

One module was about Organizational Culture and Values. External trainers would not be appropriate for such training delivery. Through this meditative exercise of brainwriting, it occurred to me that we could engage a couple of retirees from our organization who were well respected facilitators. The outsourced organization was asked to hire these retirees as contract trainers and deploy them to deliver this unique training in our organization. The VP thought it was a brilliant solution and it was implemented with success.

LATERAL THINKING (TOOL #22)

The term *Lateral Thinking* was coined in 1967 by Edward de Bono. According to de Bono, lateral thinking deliberately distances itself from standard perceptions of creativity as either "vertical" logic (the classic method for problem solving—working out the solution step by step from the given data) or "horizontal" imagination—having a thousand ideas but being unconcerned with the detailed implementation of them.

Critical thinking is primarily concerned with judging the true value of statements and seeking errors. Lateral thinking is more concerned with the movement value of statements and ideas. A person uses lateral thinking to move from one known idea to creating new ideas.

The use of a set of criteria is necessary in a variety of professional practices where a judgment or a decision has to be made based on a common understanding of a rule or a test. One approach is to use lateral thinking for identifying an initial set of criteria and then further refining it for some specific use. The example used here is of a community college that is attempting to improve their student enrollment process. The improvement team must identify criteria for evaluating the new design of the process—before they come up with ideas for changes.

PROCESS

1. Agree on the purpose. (In our example it is to determine criteria for the redesign of the student enrollment process.)

2. On a flip chart, draw a table with three columns as shown in Table 12.5.

Table 12.5 – Attributes, Stretch Thinking, Criteria

(Example: Empty Water Bottle)

Attributes	Stretch Thinking (brainstorm)	Criteria
Plastic	Not expensive, durable	Cost effective to manage the process
Empty	Paperless, multiple content, mass customization	Flexible Process
Label	Informative	Clear Documentation
Blue top	Branding	Brand the Project
Thin	Lean, Streamlined	Lean Process (no waste)
16 Oz.	Size, Capacity	Scalable to changing student demographics
Clear	Transparent	Transparent and easy to follow process
Recyclable	Reusable	Repeatable
Flexible	Adaptable	Adaptable to changing student needs
Container	End result, self-contained, location, infrastructure	End-to-end seamless process flow
Shape	Efficient	Efficient Process
Refillable	Reusable	Applicable in multiple locations of the college

3. Ask the group to pick any one object in the room. Ask one participant to point to the object he/she has chosen. (In our example it is an empty water bottle.)

4. Ask the group to randomly call out attributes or characteristics of the identified object and list them in the first column: *Attributes*.

5. Ask the group to stretch their thinking for each of the attributes in the left column in terms of how they might be used to standardize the

student enrollment process. Show one example to the group for clarity. Identify their responses in the second column: *Stretch Thinking.*

6. For the third column, *Criteria*, have the group discuss and determine which of these items would be meaningful to them for evaluating the redesign of the process in question and change the wording to suit the applicability.

7. Identify next steps for how these criteria will be used and presented to key stakeholders for gaining their agreement.

PROCESS SCOPE DIAGRAM (TOOL #23)

A Scope Diagram can be used for a variety of objectives in organizations. For instance scoping an organizational unit such as a department; ways of working for a team; project scope; business process scope; developing products, services, or strategies; and so on. The template is called the *Burlton Diagram*, named after Roger Burlton who modified the earlier concept developed for process analysis in the US Government. I further improvised the concept by classifying the process *Guides* into three types: Governance, Rules and Knowledge. The template is commonly referred to by the acronym IGOE: Inputs, Guides, Outputs and Enablers.

Inputs are transformed into Outputs. Guides are the rules and knowledge needed to manage the scope. Enablers are roles people play; technology such as systems; and infrastructure such as facilities, hardware, communications, etc. The Inputs come from particular sources and the Outputs go to designated destinations. You can also conduct a "health check" of the scoped area of analysis for improvements.

PROCESS

1. Agree on the topic (a business process in this case) to be analyzed for improvement.

2. Create an IGOE template on a large chart as in Figure 12.17, and have the participants identify Outputs, Inputs, Guides and Enablers. (Using

the principle of "begin with end in mind," identify outputs first.) Also identify Trigger Events that kickoff the execution of a process.

Figure 12.17 – Process Scope Diagram Template (IGOE)

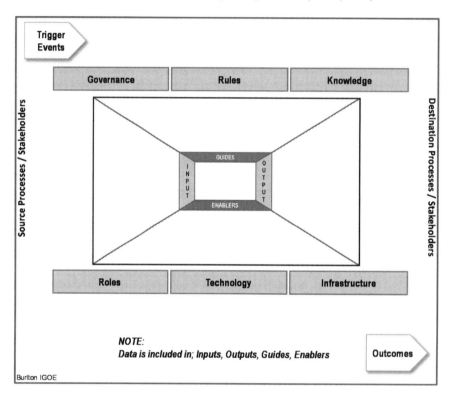

3. Identify process and stakeholder touch points on outputs side and input side.

4. Conduct process "health check" around all items that constitute a process. Establish a legend for marking items. Red = broken/not working well. Yellow = so/so. Green = okay. (Colored dots can also be used for this purpose.)

5. Prioritize and identify areas for improvement.

Here is an example of the Process Scope Diagram for the Recruit and Hire Employee Process.

Figure 12.18 – Recruit and Hire Employees Process Scope Diagram

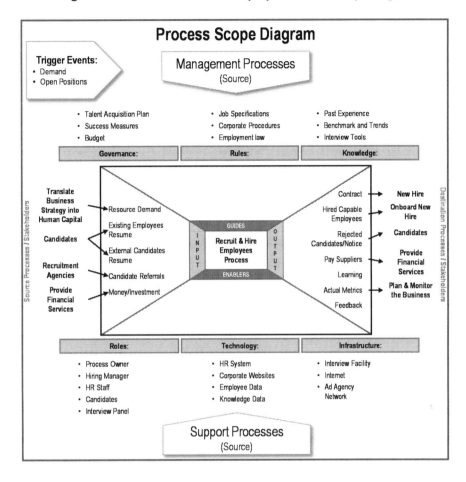

PROCESS MAP (TOOL #24)

The diagrams that represent a process flow are called Process Models or, simply, Process Maps. These are typically developed after the Process Scope Diagram has been created. (See Tool #23, Process Scope Diagram.)

Industry standards exist on how process models/maps should be documented that include BPMN (Business Process Modeling Notation), otherwise known as "swimlanes," and are outside of the scope of this book.

A simple yet effective way of developing a process map using another tool is documented in this chapter, See Tool #4, Creative Visualization: Rich Picture exercise. A Rich Picture is a visual chart created by a group of participants who have vested interest in the performance of the process.

PROCESS

1. Rich Picture. Reference the steps in Tool #4, Creative Visualization, to create a Rich Picture of the business process-in-focus. See Figure 12.19. This Rich Picture is developed by a group for the *Recruit and Hire Employees Process*.

2. Process Activities. On a flip chart, identify each of the activities from beginning to end as the process flows. In the left column identify what is going on and in the right column give it a name in the verb-noun convention of naming processes. See Table 12.6.

3. Process Map. Document a process map flow, from left to right showing the beginning and end of the process. See Figure 12.20.

Figure 12.19 – Rich Picture

Table 12.6 – Flip Chart Information

Vacancy (manager's unhappy face)	Identify Need
Money available to create a job request on computer system (Bag of Dollars)	Secure Budget
Decision to be made to regarding internal or external recruiting (Decision Boxes)	Determine Candidate Sourcing
Post job (Computer System)	Post Job
Candidates apply for job (several candidates)	Receive Application
Interview on phone to screen candidates	Screen Candidates
Interview and select (panel interview)	Interview and Select
Make offer and formally hire as employee (job offer and deployment)	Make Job Offer and Hire

Figure 12.20 – Business Process Map/Model

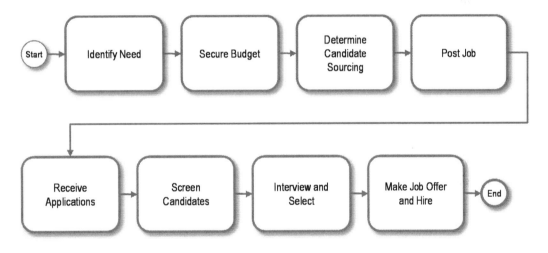

PRIORITY MATRIX (TOOL #25)

A Priority Matrix helps classify information based on perceived value of the level of effort required to implement ideas or solutions. A Priority Matrix is also called a Payoff Matrix.

PROCESS

1. Purpose. Establish the purpose and scope of brainstorming and prioritization. Make a template on a chart as shown in Figure 12.21.

2. Brainstorm. Conduct brainstorming for ideas using sticky notes (one idea/concept per sticky note). Have participants discuss and gain agreement, and place the sticky notes on one of the four quadrants as appropriate, based on impact and effort needed to implement.

3. Clustering. Conduct affinity analysis by clustering like items. Create title themes for these clusters based on the subject matter.

4. Prioritization. Give a set number of colored dots to participants and vote on the clusters. The top three or five clusters, as established by the greatest number of dots, become the candidates for next action.

Figure 12.21 – Priority Matrix

	Difficult to Implement	Easy to Implement
High Impact On Organization	2	1
Low Impact On Organization	4	3

APPRECIATIVE INQUIRY AND KIPLING'S "FRAMEWORK" (TOOL #26)

Asking the right questions about a topic of interest by anyone is very important. For a facilitator, the art of developing questions is a critical skill. At the time of engagement of an assignment, asking the right questions establishes a productive relationship with the client to gain a clear understanding of expectations.

To solicit the right information from the stakeholder interviews, specific and comprehensive questions need be developed. During sessions, facilitators continually ask questions of the participants to engage them in promoting appropriate discussions and assisting in the decision making process. And occasionally, groups need to formulate questions to address the support of new products and services being planned. The following tools are practical for developing questions by an individual or in a group setting.

APPRECIATIVE INQUIRY

Appreciative Inquiry (AI) is an organization development tool that promotes asking questions in a positive way, such as, "What worked well in the past?" and "What might be possible in the future?" rather than focusing on "What is wrong?" It is philosophical approach of thinking of what is good and can be made better instead of focusing on problems alone.

Developed and extended since the mid-eighties primarily by students and faculty of the Department of Organizational Behavior at Case Western Reserve University, AI revolutionized the field of organization development and was a precursor to the rise of positive organization studies and the strengths-based movement in American management. In the original 1987 article on AI by David Cooperrider and Suresh Srivastva, they argued that the overuse of problem-solving reduced the ability of managers and researchers to come up with new theories and models of organizing. More details on this topic are widely available elsewhere. Here I want to show you a practical application of how you may create questions using the AI technique.

Sue Annis Hammond, in *The Thin Book of Appreciative Inquiry,* has identified eight assumptions that simplify the understanding of AI's application:

1. In every society, organization or group, something works.

2. What we focus on becomes our reality.

3. Reality is created in the moment, and there are multiple realties.

4. The act of asking questions of an organization or group influences the group in some way.

5. People have more confidence and comfort to journey to the future (the unknown) when they carry forward parts of the past (the known).

6. If we carry parts of the past forward, they should be what is best about the past.

7. It is important to value differences.

8. The language we use creates our reality.

Sample Questions using Appreciative Inquiry

-   Describe a time when you felt the department's employees collaborated among each other really well—as a team.
-   Describe a time when you were proud to be a member of that team. Why were you proud?
-   What do you value most about being a team member of that department? Why?

Questions framed in this way provide profound insights of what has been good and can be even better.

KIPLING'S "FRAMEWORK"

I have found that for formulating questions for *any* purpose, Rudyard Kipling's poem *The Elephant's Child* in his story provides me with a practical framework—one that works every time. Born in Bombay, India (now Mumbai), Joseph Rudyard Kipling is considered one of the greatest English writers and was the recipient of the Nobel Prize for literature in 1907.

Rudyard Kipling's Story: *The Elephant's Child*
(Partial poem from the story)

I KEEP six honest serving-men
(They taught me all I knew);
Their names are <u>What</u> and <u>Why</u> and <u>When</u>
And <u>How</u> and <u>Where</u> and <u>Who</u>.
I send them over land and sea,
I send them east and west;
But after they have worked for me,
I give them all a rest...

The six words What, Why, When, How, Where, and Who are the basis of thinking through formulation of questions. As a facilitator, whether you are preparing for an interview with the clients or stakeholders, or conducting a work session and must engage the participants in a meaningful dialogue, Kipling's "six serving-men" are your friends indeed.

I have also used this framework of six words when I am asked to how to write a strategy or a position paper. The concept is simple yet powerful when you are starting to write on a blank piece of paper.

QUESTIONS BRAINSTORMING (TOOL #27)

This process involves brainstorming the questions, rather than trying to come up with immediate answers and short-term solutions. Theoretically, this technique should not inhibit participation as there is no need to provide solutions. Through brainstorming, questions are identified, clustered into themes, and then become input to the feasibility of an organization's plan.

PROCESS
1. Establish the precise purpose for developing questions and the expected outcomes. For example: What questions need to be addressed for the launch of a new service that makes snacks available through vending machines? The team is made of cross-functional subject matter experts.

2. Hold a general brainstorming session about what aspects of this idea the group should be thinking about. For example, the result is a set of ideas that include cost, return on investment, technology, locations, and competition.

3. Sub-Teams. Agree on and create sub-teams based on the topics that need to be addressed and for which the questions must be created. For example: finance, technology, location, marketing, and so on. Introduce aids in framing questions (such as Kipling's "six serving-men").

4. Questions Brainstorming. Each sub-team brainstorms only the questions to be addressed (not solutions). Each team clusters their items into relevant themes and reports out to the entire group. For

example, the Technology Sub-Team's themes may include space, utilities, maintenance, security, consumer interface, and others.

5. Agree on next steps for conducting a feasibility study of all aspects of this initiative.

6. Agree on project lead and membership and next steps.

Note: This tool was inspired by *Q-Storming™ for Innovation: An Inquiry Method for Generating Breakthroughs*, by Andrea Zintz, Ph.D. Senior Vice President. Based on QuestionThinking™—a method developed by Marilee Adams, Ph.D.

RELAXATION RESPONSE—MEDITATION (TOOL #28)

Osho (Rajnish), one of the Indian philosophers known for teaching meditation (among other aspects of life), described mediation this way: "Remember one thing: meditation means awareness. Whatsoever you do with awareness is meditation. Action is not the question, but the quality that you bring to your action. Walking can be a meditation if you walk alertly. Sitting can be a meditation if you sit alertly. Listening to the birds can be a meditation if you listen with awareness. Just listening to the inner noise of your mind can be a meditation if you remain alert and watchful."

For participants in work sessions to relax, they need to be aware and watchful of what is happening by being alert and in the moment. It is all in the mind.

Dr. Herbert Benson is a Mind/Body Professor of Medicine at Harvard Medical School, and Director Emeritus of the Benson-Henry Institute (BHI) at Massachusetts General Hospital. He is a pioneer in mind/body medicine, one of the first Western physicians to bring spirituality and healing into medicine. His work serves as a bridge between medicine and religion, East and West, mind and body, and belief and science. In his research, the mind and body are one system, in which meditation can play a significant role in reducing stress responses. Per Dr. Benson, the relaxation response is a physical state of deep rest that changes the physical and emotional responses to stress and is the opposite of the fight or flight response.

Dr. Benson amalgamates Eastern and Western methods of meditation into the concept of Relaxation Response and proposes a Tibetan "two step process." First, you evoke the Relaxation Response and reap its healthy rewards. Then, when your mind is quiet and when focusing has opened a door in your mind, visualize an outcome that is meaningful to you.

Disclaimer: The author of this book does not have qualifications and expertise in medicine or spiritual sciences. The reader needs to practice this technique to be comfortable using this tool.

PROCESS

Permission. Ask the participants if everyone is comfortable with the idea of you showing and using the meditation technique of relaxation. If they are not, then it is better to use another tool for relaxation.

1. Pick a focus word, short phrase, or prayer that is firmly rooted in your belief system.

2. Sit quietly in a comfortable position.

3. Close your eyes.

4. Relax your muscles, progressing from your feet to your calves, thighs, abdomen, shoulders, head, and neck.

5. Breathe slowly and naturally, and as you do, say your focus word, sound, phrase, or prayer silently to yourself as you exhale.

6. Assume a passive attitude. Don't worry about how well you're doing. When other thoughts come to mind, simply say to yourself, "Oh well," and gently return to your repetition.

7. Continue for ten to twenty minutes.

8. Do not stand immediately. Continue sitting quietly for a minute or so, allowing other thoughts to return. Then open your eyes and sit for another minute before rising.

9. Practice the technique once or twice daily. The best times to meditate are before breakfast and before dinner.

RACI (Tool #29)

RACI (Responsible, Accountable, Consulted, and Informed) responsibility charting is a technique used for establishing roles and responsibilities of cross-functional work teams. In addition to a common agreement on who does what when, this technique helps bring into the open any issues that need to be resolved regarding responsibility and accountability. While there can be many roles for a function or a process representing R, C, and I, there can be only one A—the accountable person. The objective of RACI Charting is to:

- Identify and clarify individual roles in a functional area, project, or process.
- Define roles: who is accountable, who is responsible, who is to be consulted, and who is to be informed.
- Align team members' work activities to eliminate redundancy, remove any ambiguity in decision points, and promote cooperation.

RACI Charting use includes: organization and team design, project management, process management, and communication plans.

WHY IS RACI NEEDED?
Consider the tale of four people: Everybody, Somebody, Anybody, And Nobody.

There was an important job to be done and everybody was asked to do it. Everybody was sure somebody would do it. Anybody could have done it, but nobody did it. Somebody got angry about that, because it was everybody's job. Everybody thought that anybody could do it but nobody realized that everybody wouldn't do it. It ended up that everybody blamed somebody when nobody did what anybody could have done.

~ (Author unknown)

If this story sounds familiar in real life scenarios, then it is clear that RACI can help establish accountability among team members to ensure cooperation and collaboration for success.

Table 12.7 – RACI Guide

Responsible (The Doer)	The one who is responsible for activities The "Responsibly" is defined by "A" the accountable one Responsibility can be shared by others
Accountable (The Buck Stops Here)	There is only one "A" role in one scoped area for charting The "A" Accountable role has Yes/No Veto authority
Consulted (Keep in the Loop)	The role to be consulted before final decision Provides special or subject matter expertise Has two-way communication
Informed (FYI—For Your Information)	Informed as and when needed—particularly after a decision is made One-way communication

Figure 12.22 contains a RACI template (general) for organizational units, functions, and projects.

Figure 12.22 – RACI Template (General)

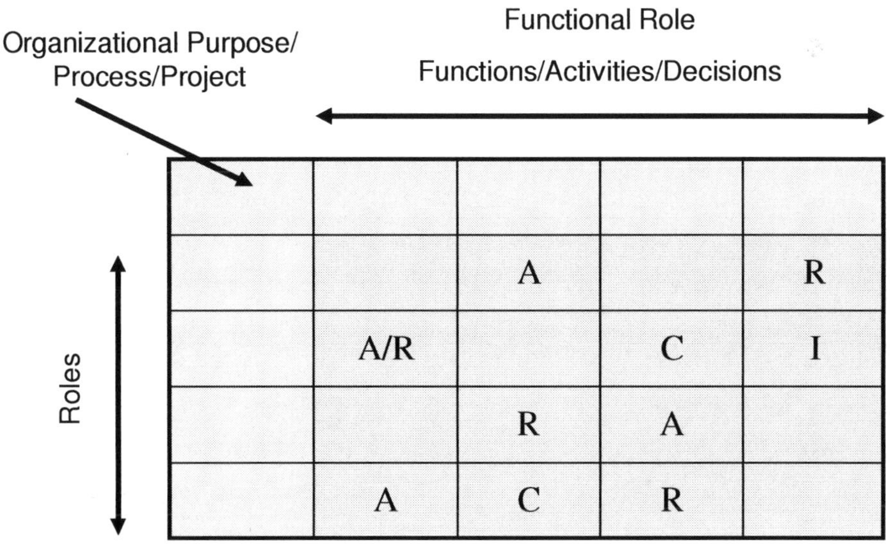

Figure 12.23 contains a RACI Template for a sales process.

Figure 12.23 – RACI Template (For a Specific Business Process)

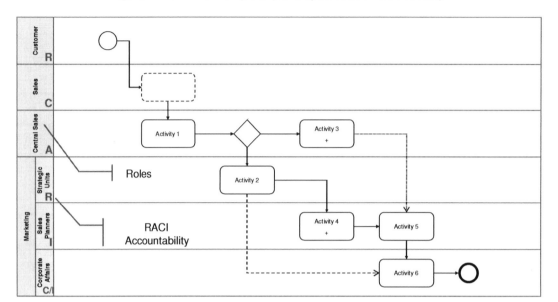

ISHIKAWA (A.K.A. "FISHBONE") (TOOL #30)

Ishikawa diagrams (also called fishbone diagrams or cause-and-effect diagrams) were first used in the twenties (and later popularized by Kaoru Ishikawa in the sixties) and show the causes of a specific event. The Ishikawa diagram is used for discovering root causes of problems in a variety of situations. The topic may include products or services or any other area in an organization where improvement is needed. The causes are grouped into some logical themes for further analysis and actions.

The diagram template has the main topic identified on one end as the "head of a fish" and like the skeleton of a fish there are side "bones" or areas to identify issues and cluster them into themes. The participants make the template, identifying one topic or problem area of focus. Then they brainstorm causes of the problem around each "bone" and cluster the causes into logical themes relevant to the topic. The themes can also be identified first if the topic of focus is very familiar to the participants.

In the example in Figure 12.24, after the barnstorming is done, the team decides to identify some Quick Win actions to fix the problem in an agreed timeframe.

Figure 12.24 – Root Cause Analysis Example

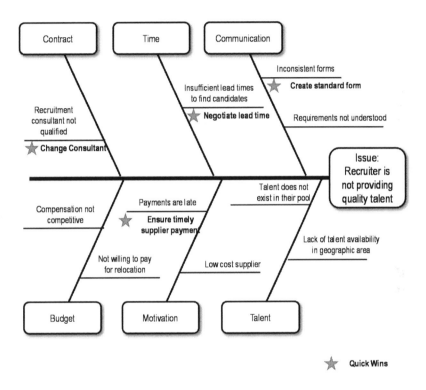

Problem Root Cause Analysis: Recruiter is not providing quality talent

STORIES AND SUCH (TOOL #31)

"Tell me a fact and I'll learn.

Tell me a truth and I'll believe. But tell me a story and it will live in my heart forever."

~ Indian Proverb

From the beginning of human history, messages of all aspects of life have been transferred to others through stories. Early humans passed down these stories through verbal communication, petroglyphs, hieroglyphs, and later through writing as the written word was invented. Now these messages are communicated through multi-media mechanisms such as films, digital equipment, music, and other devices.

Whether you're facilitating for a religious institution, a non-profit/for-profit organization, or any group in society, stories are powerful tools for communicating ideas and messages. Storytelling is extremely effective for opening sessions, framing topics of focus, and inspiring and engaging participants. Stories can range from commercial, historical, spiritual, and geographical in nature to nearly any genre you can think of. So, what do we mean by *story*?

In his book, *Story*, Robert McKee states, "A story is not only what you have to say but how you say it...we shape the telling to fit the substance." In facilitation, finding a story that is relevant to the topic is a matter of awareness and research. The ability to deliver stories with impact is an art form that facilitators should develop and practice. A facilitator, both for transfer of knowledge and for work sessions needs to be ready to use stories on a variety of subjects, and must be a good story teller.

Webster's Ninth Collegiate Dictionary defines a story to be "An account of incidents and events; a statement regarding the facts pertinent to a situation in question..." For our purpose here, a facilitator's library of stories is referred to as "Stories" (in quotes). "Stories" include anecdotes, figurative language, humor, poetry, fables, and all story subjects including commerce, wellbeing, history, geography, science, people, places, and so on. Note that it is important to ensure that certain principles govern the "Stories" in terms of content—in the context of facilitation.

PRINCIPLES FOR "STORIES"
- They must be honorable in content and delivered respectably and artfully.

- Stay away from topics that include religion, politics, sex, alternative life styles, ethnicity, and any other aspect that might offend the participants or society in general.
- When using war stories for making a point, first ask permission of the audience before you deliver it (many people find talk about wars to be offensive).
- There should be a deliberate purpose/message in the story that is relevant to the topic at hand unless it is a "filler," an icebreaker, or a humorous way to frame a topic or to make the transition between activities interesting.
- Authenticate the material for its credibility in terms of source and meaning.
- In cross-cultural situations, be aware of any sensitivity to story topics.

FIGURATIVE LANGUAGE—WHAT'S WHAT

Here are examples of figurative language that you should be aware of when developing "Stories" for presentations or workshops.

- **Analogy:** Similarity in some respects between things otherwise unlike; partial resemblance. An explanation of something by comparing it point by point with something similar. Example: Like a ship sailing a stormy sea.
- **Anecdote**: A short account of an incident or event of an interesting or amusing nature, often biographical. (Source: The FreeDictionary)
- **Simile:** A figure of speech in which two dissimilar things are compared using "like" or "as." Example: His heart is as big as a whale.
- **Metaphor:** A figure of speech containing an implied comparison, in which a word or phrase ordinarily and primarily associated with one thing is applied to another. Example: All the world is a stage. *Mixed Metaphors*—Using two or more inconsistent metaphors in a single expression. Example: The storm of protest was nipped in the bud.
- **Hyperbole:** Exaggeration for effect and not meant to be taken literally. Example: His speech lasted about three weeks.
- **Paraprosdokian**: Is a figure of speech in which the latter part of a sentence or phrase is surprising or unexpected in a way that causes the reader or listener to reframe or reinterpret the first part. It is

frequently used for humorous or dramatic effect, sometimes producing an anticlimax. Examples: "Money can't buy happiness, but it sure makes misery easier to live with." "War does not determine who is right—only who is left." "I used to be indecisive. Now I'm not so sure."

SOME THOUGHTS ON HUMOR

Humor in presentations and work sessions helps balance the seriousness of the material and creates a new perspective for conveying the message you're trying to get across. Humor promotes fun in a session and helps gain the attention of the audience in an engaging manner. Ron Culberson, a humorist, classifies the use of humor in three areas: Verbal Humor, Visual Humor and Experiential Humor (Reference: ronculberson.com):

- **Verbal Humor:** Use personal funny stories, funny quotations, or humor experienced by others. Use jokes if they are unique and not generally accessible to others.
- **Visual Humor:** Use fun props as visual aids. Use creative and funny slides including cartoons. Have video clips available that are relevant to the topic at hand.
- **Experiential Humor:** Invite the audience to participate in a funny quiz or questions. Have funny props that sub-groups can use as a humorous exercise.

When incorporated in workshops, these humor types may be considered yet another effective engager. Humor can be created around the subject-of-focus using organizational tribal knowledge—as an example. The quotes are succinct and easy to memorize.

PLANNING TEMPLATE FOR "STORIES"

This template can be used as a guide to develop ideas for "Stories." Invite the audience to participate in a funny quiz or questions. Use funny props.

A library and a catalogue of "Stories" are essential for facilitators. This material should be easily accessible based on the type of engagement you are asked to support.

Table 12.8 – "Stories" Planning Template

Topic?	
Who is the audience?	
The message I want to convey is?	
Why and how would this message benefit the audience?	
What "Stories" can I use (verbal, visual, or experiential)?	
Prepare the material: Writing, slides, videos, etc.	
Rehearse the material delivery.	

EXAMPLES OF "STORIES"

Aesop's Fables: Aesop's Fables is a collection of short-stories with a moral credited to Aesop, a slave and story-teller believed to have lived in ancient Greece between 620 and 560 BCE. Of diverse origins, the stories associated with Aesop's name have descended to modern times through a number of sources. They continue to be reinterpreted in different verbal registers and in popular as well as artistic mediums.

The Miser and His Gold

Once upon a time there was a Miser who used to hide his gold at the foot of a tree in his garden; but every week he used to go and dig it up and gloat over his gains. A robber, who had noticed this, went and dug up the gold and decamped with it. When the Miser next came to gloat over his treasures, he found nothing but the empty hole. He tore his hair, and raised such an outcry that all the neighbors came around him, and he told them how he used to come and visit his gold.

"Did you ever take any of it out?" asked one of them.

"Nay," said he, "I only came to look at it."

"Then come again and look at the hole," said a neighbor; "it will do you just as much good."

Moral: Wealth unused might as well not exist.

Mullah Nasrudin is a folk hero of medieval origin who has jokes and anecdotes with a message. Middle East and Central Asia claim him as their own. His role changes. Sometimes he is a sage, sometimes a fool; he is a courtier, beggar, physician, judge and teacher. Whether his anecdotes are studied for their hidden wisdom, or enjoyed for their pungent humor, they are an enduring part of the world's cultural heritage.

High Cost of Learning

Mullah Nasrudin decided that he could benefit by learning something new. He went to see a master musician. "How much do you charge to teach lute-playing?"

"Three silver pieces for the first month; after that, one silver piece a month."

"Excellent!" said Nasrudin. "I shall begin with the second month."

Message: The development of skills and competency is accomplished through planning, learning, and application. Clearly there are no short cuts.

SAMPLE QUOTATIONS FOR VARIOUS OCCASIONS

Behavior:

"I've learned that people will forget what you said, people will forget what you did, but people will never forget how you made them feel."
~ Maya Angelou, American Author, Poet, Actress, and Singer

Call to Action:

"Talk does not cook rice."
~ Chinese proverb (found in a fortune cookie)

Conflict:

"He who is hard pressed will regard the greatest daring as the greatest wisdom."
~ Carl Philipp Gottfried von Clausewitz, German General and Military Theorist

Development:

"Reading maketh a full man, writing an exact man, and conversation a ready man."
~ Francis Bacon, English Philosopher and Statesman

Humor:

> *After all is said and done, more is said than done.*
> *~ Aesop, Greek storyteller*

Intelligence:

> *"The true sign of intelligence is not knowledge but imagination."*
> *~ Albert Einstein, German-born Theoretical Physicist*

Leadership:

> *"If your actions inspire others to dream more, learn more, do more*
> *and become more, you are a leader."*
> *~ John Quincy Adams, American Statesman and Sixth President*

Life:

> *"We make a living by what we get; we make a life by what we give."*
> *~ Winston Churchill, British Prime Minister*

Productivity:

> *"Nothing is less productive than to make more efficient*
> *what should not be done at all."*
> *~ Peter Drucker, American Management Consultant*

PERSONAL STORIES

Stories and anecdotes from your personal experiences make very interesting engagers and fillers in workshops. I maintain a library of these experiences in my toolkit. Here are some examples of my personal experiences at home which I narrate occasionally as fillers in my workshops.

My Instruction Manual

My wife tells me regularly:

- Don't walk quickly; you are raising dust from the carpet.
- Every time I open the refrigerator, I see your finger marks on it. Can't you just touch the handle?
- If there is something wrong in the house somewhere, I can count on it being your handiwork.
- You are too loud, use your "inside voice."

My Retirement Vision

When I was in a corporate job, I had this vision of retiring early, becoming a part-time consultant and working out my home-office. One of the perks would be to get a cup of coffee, go into my home-office in my pajamas, and log into my computer.

- Around lunchtime, I called to my wife from downstairs and asked her to make me a sandwich for lunch. She replied, "Come over to the steps." When I did so, she told me, "At this time I'm watching a soap opera on the kitchen TV. You are on your own; make your sandwich. But if you come upstairs to eat, keep your mouth shut!"

- Again around 3:00 p.m., I called to my wife and asked her to make me a cup of tea that I could take downstairs in my office. I heard her say, "This time I'm watching another soap opera. Get a coffee machine for your office."

So, the message was clear: become a consultant and get out of the house to do work. I became a full-time facilitator.

Stories such as these depict human drama that everyone can relate to. When you tell honorable and appropriate stories about your own self and at your own expense, they promote good humor and offend no one.

STRATEGY DEVELOPMENT AND VALUE PROPOSITION (TOOL #32)

In the book, *The Discipline of Market Leaders*, authors Michael Treacy and Fred Wiersema identify three dimensions that every organization must be competent in: Customer Intimacy, Product Leadership and Operation Excellence. They further propose that to be successful, organizations must be good in all dimensions but can excel and be known for only one.

Inspired by the approach of three dimensions, I created a Value Proposition Model (shown in Figure 12.25). I added the term "service" along with the "product" dimension and have successfully used this model as a technique to develop value propositions and their supporting strategies. I have found that this model works equally well for value proposition/strategies development at all levels of organizational units, including business units, divisions, and departments.

Figure 12.25 – Value Proposition Model

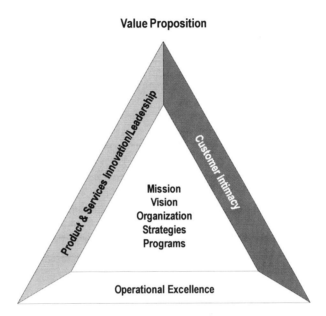

PROCESS

Understand the purpose and scope of the organizational unit for which the value proposition and strategies are to be developed. Explain this technique to the sponsor and the participants of the workshop. Develop a Running Order Agenda based on the following steps:

1. Customer Intimacy: This dimension is about understanding the customers and their expectations for delivery of products and services. (Note that stakeholders includes customers.) Through brainstorming, identify a list of customers/stakeholders of the organization-in-focus. Use large- to medium-size sticky notes in this and the remainder of the steps.

2. Expected Value: Have the participants develop expectations of each of the stakeholder types by asking a question such as: "What value do the stakeholders expect when their organization delivers products and services at their best?" Cluster these ideas into themes.

3. Products and Service Leadership: Have the participants brainstorm and identify products and services that deliver the expected value to

stakeholders/customers as represented in the themes identified in step 2. Cluster the products/service into themes.

4. Operational Excellence: This dimension includes processes, organizations/people roles, technology, infrastructure, and other factors peculiar to the organization of focus. Have the participants brainstorm in each of these categories to determine items that ensure that through the operations of the organizational unit, products and services are delivered at the expected or promised value proposition.

5. Mission, Vision, Strategies and Programs: As shown in the middle of the "triangle" in Figure 12.22, first, the Mission statement can be developed by looking at the themes of all three of the dimensions (Mission is the purpose of being or existence). Second, a Vision statement can be developed (Vision is the desired future state). Based on the purpose of the workshop, now the Strategies can be identified around all three dimensions. The strategies would align the value proposition, delivery of product and service, and the needed operational enablers. The Programs to execute the identified strategies can be further developed by using Program/Project Management techniques.

Note: At the conclusion of this exercise, an optional discussion can be held on what one dimension the organization is known for or would want to be known for. Sticky-dots can be used to have the participants vote for their personal view. The result of this exercise could be very important for shaping the strategies in support of the value proposition.

SIX THINKING HATS (TOOL #33)

(This tool was created by Edward de Bono in his book *Six Thinking Hats*.)

This technique opens up the opportunity for creativity within information gathering and decision making. The technique also helps persistently pessimistic people to be positive and creative. Six Thinking Hats is a good technique for looking at the effects of a decision from a number of different points of view.

Many successful people think from a very rational, positive viewpoint. This is part of the reason that they are successful. Often, though, they fail to look at a problem from an emotional, intuitive, creative, or negative viewpoint. This can mean that they underestimate resistance to plans, fail to make creative leaps, and do not make essential contingency plans.

Similarly, pessimists may be excessively defensive, and more emotional people may fail to look at decisions calmly and rationally.

If you look at a problem using the Six Thinking Hats technique, you will solve it using all approaches. Your decisions and plans will mix ambition, skill in execution, public sensitivity, creativity, and good contingency planning.

You can use Six Thinking Hats in meetings or on your own. In meetings it has the benefit of blocking confrontations that happen when people with different thinking styles discuss the same problem. Each "thinking hat" is a different style of thinking. They are explained in Table 12.9.

Table 12.9 – Six Thinking Hats

 White Hat	With this thinking hat, you focus on the data available. Look at the information you have, and see what you can learn from it. Look for gaps in your knowledge, and either try to fill them or take account of them. This is where you analyze past trends, and try to extrapolate from historical data.
 Yellow Hat	The yellow hat helps you to think positively. It is the optimistic viewpoint that helps you to see all the benefits of the decision and the value in it. Yellow Hat thinking helps you to keep going when everything looks gloomy and difficult.
 Green Hat	The Green Hat stands for creativity. This is where you can develop creative solutions to a problem. It is a freewheeling way of thinking, in which there is little criticism of ideas. A whole range of creativity tools can help you here.

Red Hat	'Wearing' the red hat, you look at problems using intuition, gut reaction, and emotion. Also try to think how other people will react emotionally. Try to understand the responses of people who do not fully know your reasoning.
Black Hat	Using black hat thinking, look at all the bad points of the decision. Look at it cautiously and defensively. Try to see why it might not work. This is important because it highlights the weak points in a plan. It allows you to eliminate them, alter them, or prepare contingency plans to counter them. Black Hat thinking helps to make your plans 'tougher' and more resilient. It can also help you to spot fatal flaws and risks before you embark on a course of action. Black Hat thinking is one of the real benefits of this technique, as many successful people get so used to thinking positively that often they cannot see problems in advance. This leaves them under-prepared for difficulties.
Blue Hat	The Blue Hat stands for process control. This is the hat worn by people chairing meetings. When running into difficulties because ideas are running dry, they may direct activity into Green Hat thinking. When contingency plans are needed, they will ask for Black Hat thinking, etc.

PROCESS

Buy a set of Six Thinking Hats cards. In your meetings and workshops, depending upon the topic at hand, pick up one of the cards and announce that you are about to gather information on the issue/challenged and raise the colored card that is relevant to the specific intent. Then proceed to capture the ideas generated on a flip chart (or have someone volunteer for this). Similarly use other hat cards as appropriate.

VISUAL DICTIONARY (TOOL #34)

Visuals are very effective tools for the mind to make meetings, facilitation, and training interesting and engaging. While everyone is not a professional artist, there is an artist in everyone. We all have the ability to draw simple icons and images on flip charts, presentations, and charts that are relevant to the topic at hand.

Figure 12.26 – Visual Dictionary (Simple Icons/Stick Figures/Images for Drawing)

Happy	Stick Person	Star Person	Male
Female	Checklist	Bullets	Title
List	Flipchart	Target/Goal	Report
Time (Clock)	Time (Hourglass)	Money	Conflict

VOICE CARE: TIPS ON CARING FOR YOUR VOICE (TOOL #35)

By: Carol Weiss Riches

As an opera singer and voice teacher for over forty years, I have learned some things about voice care that might be helpful to those who find themselves with tired or strained voices. Talking for long, uninterrupted periods can be very fatiguing to one's vocal cords, so the "trick" is to try to rest them at various intervals. Of course, this is easy to say but how do you do this when you're giving an all-day seminar? My suggestion is to leave the lecture area during your breaks and use that time as your rest period. If you have a group lunch, use part of that time, too (all of it if possible) or perhaps go to your quiet hotel room. The "key" is to not talk and rest your voice.

I hate to say it, but alcohol is not helpful either. We all know that a small amount can help with a mild case of the jitters but it can swell the vocal cords, and that's not good. I have found the most beneficial drink to keep the throat open is warm herbal tea with honey. Take a thermos with you to sip during your sessions. I like Lemon Zinger by Celestial Seasonings, and it also helps with phlegm. As you might guess, ice water should be avoided—it can tighten up your throat.

Standing out in very cold weather and having long conversations with colleagues is not helpful to your voice. I've always required high school cheerleaders to begin voice studies after football season as it is an exercise in futility to begin sooner. The combination of yelling and the cold just shreds their voices. Opera singers are often joked about because they wrap their faces and necks in warm scarves and wear hats in the cold. But, our livelihood is to make beautiful sounds and when you're sick and/or hoarse you can't do your job!

Being nervous or even "keyed-up" can lead to dry mouth, not very pleasant, but there are over-the-counter artificial saliva sprays available—Oasis Moisturizing Mouth Spray and Stoppers 4 Dry Mouth Spray—that can temporarily solve the problem. I've always kept a small bottle in my costume pocket and voilà—no more lips sticking to my teeth!

A very helpful vocal cord protection gargle can come from your own kitchen cabinets. My students and friends alike "swear" by it. Start with ¼ teaspoon each of baking soda, Karo syrup and salt. Mix these ingredients with 6 oz. of warm water and gargle for three minutes. Then have nothing to eat or drink for ten minutes.

Continual abuse of one's voice can lead to damage to the vocal cords, including nodes (bumps) and, in extreme cases, (as with some rock singers) bleeding vocal cords. I've worked with a few voice students recommended by their throat doctor to work on changing their singing technique to alleviate their developing nodes. Teaching them to breathe properly helped a great deal. Proper breathing supports the voice and relieves quite a bit of stress that can be put on the cords. Working with a vocal teacher or coach can also be beneficial. The National Association of Teachers of Singing (NATS) has a website (www.nats.org) that can guide you to speech coaches, and so on, in your area.

Resources

There are tens of thousands of resources available for facilitators to learn and draw from. These include reading materials, audio/visual materials, training and facilitation materials, professional forums, consulting firms, and websites. As references, I am providing in this book a set of resources that I have experience with and/or know about from my facilitation practice. Collect your own resources and maintain a library for reference and to inspire your thinking.

BOOKS

77 Tips for Planning and Leading Exceptional Virtual Meetings. By Nancy Settle-Murphy.

A Short Guide to Facilitating Risk. By Penny Pullan, Ruth Murray-Webster.

Beyond Words: A guide to drawing out ideas. By Milly R. Sonneman.

Consulting Fee: A Guide for Independent Consultants. By Andrea Coutu.

Creative Thinkering: Putting Your Imagination to Work. By Michael Michalko.

Effective Learning. By Alan Mumford.

Frames of Mind. By Howard Gardner.

Graphics for Presenters: Getting Your Ideas Across. By Lynn Kearny.

How Work Gets Done: Business Process Management, Basics and Beyond. By Artie Mahal.

Ingenius: A Crash Course On Creativity. By Tina Seelig.

Laugh And Learn: 95 Ways to Use Humor for More Effective Teaching and Training. By Doni Tamblyn.

Mulla Nasrudin: The Exploits of the Incomparable (and others in this series). By Idries Shah.

Panchtantra: India's Greatest Fable Literature. By Vishnu Sharma.

Presenting and Training With Magic. By Ed Rose.

Rapid Problem Solving with Sticky Notes. By David Straker.

Six Thinking Hats. By Dr. Edward DeBono.

Tales for Trainers: Using Stories and Metaphors to Facilitate Learning. By Margaret Parkin.

The Adult Learner. By Malcolm S. Knowles, Elwood F. Holton, & Richard A. Swanson.

Think And Grow Rich. By Napolean Hill.

Thinkertoys: A Handbook of Creative-Thinking Techniques. By Michael Michalko.

Training For Dummies. By Elaine Biech.

Visual Meetings: How Graphics, Sticky Notes & Idea Mapping Can Transform Group Productivity. By David Sibbet.

GENERAL REFERENCE SOURCES

Aesop's Fables: http://www.taleswithmorals.com/.

Businessballs.com: Methodologies, Techniques, Tools and Templates.

Business Terms Dictionary: http://www.businessdictionary.com/.

Consulting Journal Blog: http://consultantjournal.com/blog/setting-consulting-fee-rates (Andrea Coutu).

Encyclopedia and Dictionary: http://encyclopedia.thefreedictionary.com.

Humor: HumorPalooz, Newsletter by Ron Culberson. http://www.ronculberson.com.

Intellimins: Learning-On-the-Go. Actionable Business Solutions. https://www.intellimins.com/.

Mindtools, Methods and Techniques: http://www.mindtools.com/pages/article/newTED_07.htm.

Quotations: http://www.brainyquote.com/.

PROFESSIONAL FORUMS

Australia and New Zealand
Institute for Learning Professionals: http://ilpworldwide.org/.

Europe
International Association of Facilitators (IAF Europe): http://www.iaf-europe-mena.org.

The British Institute of Learning and Development http://www.thebild.org.

The International Federation of Training and Development: http://www.cipd.co.uk.

North America
American Society of Training and Development: http://www.astd.org/.

Institute of Management Consultants: http://www.imcusa.org/.

International Association of Facilitators: http://www.iaf-world.org.

Organizational Development Network: http://www.odnetwork.org/.

FACILITATION AND TRAINING SUPPLIES
Note: Only sample product offerings are documented under the supplier names.

Australia and New Zealand
Neuland: www.neuland.com. Workshop facilitation supplies: planning cards, refillable markers.

Training Games & Learning Resources, Springwood, NSW: http://www.traininggames.com.au. Products include games, books, card packs and Thumball™.

Europe
Neuland: http://www.neuland.com. Workshop Facilitation supplies: planning cards, refillable markers.

The Training Shop UK: http://www.thetrainingshop.co.uk. Training toys and props. http://www.pinpoint-facilitation.com (UK partners with Neuland).

India
Whappi Workplaces Pvt. Ltd. Pune: http://www.happiatwork.com. Build happier workplaces and through re-imagining engagement, energize minds and celebrate work. Products include Thumball™.

North America
Answers In Motion, LLC: http://www.thumball.com. Thumball™ and ThirstyTalk™ products. Manufacture and distribute products that promote learning and improved communication among people of all ages. From schools, to rehab centers, homes to office trainings.

Clown Noses: http://www.Justclownnoses.com: multi-color clown noses for "laughing therapy" and team celebrations.

Homer Miller Company: http://www.homermiller.com. Large multi-color sticky notes "Idea-Catchers."

http://Istockphotos.com: Supplier of photographs for purchase for Simulation Exercises.

Neuland: http://www.neuland.com. Workshop Facilitation supplies: planning cards, refillable markers.

OfficeOxygen: http://www.officeoxygen.com. Workplace tools aimed at engaging office team work, effective meetings, stress reduction and fun in workplace. Products include Thumball™.

The Grove Consultants International: http://www.grove.com/site/index.htm. Visual/Graphics Facilitation supplies include: paper rolls, cutting knives, artist tapes, large sticky-notes, and ready to use editable graphic templates.

The Thiagi Group: http://www.thiagi.com. For motivation and effectiveness, Thiagi Group develop games, simulations and performance-based experiential activities for training and products.

Trainers Warehouse: http://www.trainerswarehouse.com. Supplies include: learning and facilitation aids and "toys," Thumball™, music, books, games, teamwork materials, luggage, reward and recognition Items.

Videos from movie clips: http://www.wingclips.com.

South America
Neuland: http://www.neuland.com. Workshop Facilitation supplies: planning cards, refillable markers.

United Arab Emirates
10 Degrees North, Dubai: http://www.10degreesnorth.com. Developing people and managing change. Products include Thumball™ and Board Games.

Notes

Introduction
Gary Rush, one of the thought leaders in facilitation provides historic perspective. MGR Consulting eNewsletter: April 2012 article *Future of Facilitators*.

Chapter 1: Facilitation Framework
What is Organization? And Organizational Structure. From the book *How Work Gets Done: Business Process Management, Basics and Beyond* by Artie Mahal. Published by Technics Publications, LLC. www.technicspub.com.

Programs. The definitions are provided by Earnest Baker. Reference PMBOK Guide, 5th Edition Glossary.

Competency Framework. Reference *A Way to Enhance Learning from Experienced*, by Peter Honey.

70/20/10 Learning Framework. Was developed by Morgan McCall, Robert W. Eichinger and Michael M. Lombardo at the Center for Creative Leadership and is specifically mentioned in *The Career Architect Development Planner, 3rd edition,* by Michael M. Lombardo and Robert W. Eichinger.

A Learning Organization. Reference *Effective Learning* by Alan Mumford.

Cooperating and Collaboration: High Performance Collaboration Framework. For High Performing Teams has been developed by Carlos Valdes-Dapena, a Consultant at Mars University, Mars, Incorporated.

Strategy. Definition by Anne Pauker Kreitzberg, Co-Founder and Principal, Cognetics Interactive and Center for Agile Thinking.

Business Process Manifesto. Roger Burlton, BPTrends Associates. www.bptends.com.
Business Process Architecture. Process Renewal Group.

Chapter 2: Value Proposition
Career-Steps Framework. Inspired by *Leadership Pipeline*, by Robert W. Eichinger and Michael M. Lombardo.

Chapter 3: Facilitation Process
During Session Process. Inspired by Gary Austin and Justine Marchant, of circleindigo, Enabling Through Facilitation, www.circleindigo.com.

Chapter 4: Facilitation Leadership

Leadership. Think and Grow Rich (1937) by Napoleon Hill. Napoleon Hill foundation http://www.naphill.org/.

Value and Ethics. The Statement of Values and Code of Ethics was adopted by International Association of Facilitators (IAF) Association Coordinating Team (ACT) June 2004. The Ethics and Values Think Tank (EVTT).

Skills and Competencies. International Association of Facilitators (IAF) Core Facilitator Competencies.

Chapter 5: Engagers and Energizers

Adult Learning Theory. Source literature by Dr. Malcolm Shepard Knowles. http://www.eadulteducation.org/adult-learning/malcolm-knowles-and-the-six-assumptions-underlying-andragogy/.

Dr. Knowles--the six assumptions, cited in Merriam, Caffarella, & Baumgartner, 2007.

Additional Reference. The Clinical Educator's Resource Guide, August 31, 2010 by Shirley Caruso. http://www.qotfc.edu.au/resource/?page=65375.

Multiple Intelligences. Frames of Mind: the Theory of Multiple Intelligences, by Dr. Howard Gardner of the Harvard Graduate School of Education.

Chapter 6: Tools

Brainstorming. http://en.wikipedia.org/wiki/Brainstorming.

Chapter 8: Virtual Facilitation

Chapter Written by: Angela Gallogl, VP of USA Operations, Advanced Team Concepts. www.atctraining.com.

Article Source References: Cheryl Kartes, CTF and ToP Mentor Trainer [Sourced from: http://www.top-network.org/gifts-challenges-of-virtual-meetings], Technology of Participation (TOP) Network, www.top-network.org. Nancy Settle-Murphy, *77 Tips for Exceptional Virtual Meetings*, Guided Insights, 2009, www.guidedinsights.com. Clark, Ruth Colvin & Mayer, Richard E., e-Learning and the Science of Instruction, Second Edition, San Francisco, Pfeiffer, 2008, Print.

Chapter 9: Cross-Cultural Facilitation

Chapter Written by: Catherine Mercer Bing. Managing Director, ITAP Americas, Inc., www.itapintl.com.

Source References: 1) Cross-Cultural Consumer Behavior: A Review of Research Findings. Journal of International Consumer Marketing, 23:181–192, 2011. ©2011 Marieke de Mooij and Geert Hofstede). 2) Quote of Professor Roy Y.J. Chua-Blanding, Michael, Cultural Disharmony

Undermines Workplace Creativity, Harvard Business School Working Knowledge Magazine, 09 Dec 2013.

The Platinum Rule: Do Unto Others as They'd Like Done Unto Them. By Tony Alessandra and Michael J. O'Connor.

Chapter 10: Visual Facilitation
Figure 10.3 and Visual Facilitation Methodology by Artists Kevin Woodson and Michael Stark of Visual Ink Creative. www.vicreative.com. Same source for: Figure 10.4: and Figure 10.5.

Chapter 11: Self-Development
Development Plan. Inspired by the learning and development approach proposed by Robert W. Eichinger and Michael M. Lombardo.

Chapter 12: Tools Library
Tool #3: Banners and Charts. Business Process Structure (Figure 12.3): From the book *How Work Gets Done, Business Process Management, Basics and Beyond* by Artie Mahal. Published by Technics Publications, LLC. www.technicspub.com.

Tool #6: Figure 12.7: Editable Graphic Template. By Kevin Woodson, Visual Ink Creative.

Tool #8: Conceptual Data Model, Figure 12.8. From the book *How Work Gets Done, Business Process Management, Basics and Beyond* by Artie Mahal. Published by Technics Publications, LLC. www.technicspub.com.

Tool #11: Body Language. BuisnessBalls.com. http://www.businessballs.com/body-language.htm#body-language-introduction.

Reference: Dr. Albert Mehrabian's key book is *Silent Messages*, which contains much information about nonverbal communication (body language). www.kaaj.com/psych.

Tool #12: Lotus Blossom Ideation, Figure 12.11. Source: *Thinkertoys, Second Edition, A Handbook of Creative-Thinking Techniques* by Michael Michalko. *Note:* Lotus Blossom technique was developed by Yasuo Matsumura of Clover Management Research in Chiba City, Japan.

Tool #16: Thumball ™ by Answers in Motion, LLC. www.anssersinmotion.com.

Tool #17: Laughing Exercise. This technique created by Dr. Annette Goodheart 1935-2011; Laughter therapist, lecturer and author of the book, *Laughter Therapy: How to Laugh About Everything in Your Life That Isn't Really Funny.*

Tool #19: Listening Ladder: Source: Vice Arecchi in Intellimins.com.

Tool #21: Brainwriting. By Michael Michalko in his book *Thinkertoys.*

Tool #22: Lateral Thinking: Source: Dr. Edward de Bono. For more information see the website: http://edwdebono.com/.

Tool #23: Process Scope Diagram Template (IGOE), Figure 12.18. Process modeling template is also referred to as the Burlton Model. Source Book: *How Work Gets Done: Business Process Management, Basics and Beyond* by Artie Mahal. Same source for: Figure 12.19 and Figure 12.21.

Tool #26: Appreciative Inquiry. Source: *The Thin Book of Appreciative Inquiry* by Sue Annis Hammond. Six Serving Men: in Poem *Elephant*, by Rudyard Kipling.

Tool #27: Questions Brainstorming: Reference Q-Storming™ for Innovation: An Inquiry Method for Generating Breakthroughs, Andrea Zintz, Ph.D. Senior Vice President. Based on QuestionThinking™—a method developed by Marilee Adams, Ph.D.

Tool #28: Relaxation Response: Dr. Herbert Benson is a Mind Body Professor of Medicine at Harvard Medical School and Director Emeritus of the Benson-Henry Institute (BHI) at Massachusetts General Hospital. See: Resources: www.mindbody.harvard.edu.

Tool#29: RACI. http://en.wikipedia.org/wiki/Responsibility_assignment_matrix.

Tool #30: Figure 12.25 *is f*rom the book *How Work Gets Done: Business Process Management, Basics and Beyond* by Artie Mahal.

Tool #31: *Storytelling.* Three areas of humor classification: Verbal Humor, Visual Humor and Experiential Humor. (Reference: www.ronculberson.com).

Tool #32: Strategy Development. Value Proposition concept in Chapter 10 is referenced from *The Discipline of Market Leaders*, by Michale Treacy and Fred Wiersema. The diagram is created by Arjit Mahal. Figure 12.26 is from the book *How Work Gets Done: Business Process Management, Basics and Beyond* by Artie Mahal.

Tool #33: Six Thinking Hats. Source: Dr. Edward de Bono. For more information see the website: http://edwdebono.com/.

Tool#35: *Voice Care.* Carol Weiss Riches, member, National Association of Teachers of Singing (NATS).

Index

Bold page numbers indicate definitions

Made in the USA
Middletown, DE
24 March 2018